新闻报道
汉译英精选

黑黟 ◎ 主编
吴 越 ◎ 副主编

上海财经大学出版社
SHANGHAI UNIVERSITY OF FINANCE & ECONOMICS PRESS

上海学术·经济学出版中心

图书在版编目(CIP)数据

新闻报道汉译英精选 / 黑黟主编. -- 上海：上海财经大学出版社, 2025.5. -- ISBN 978-7-5642-4633-4

Ⅰ.G212

中国国家版本馆 CIP 数据核字第 20250V9N12 号

□ 责任编辑　徐　超
□ 封面设计　贺加贝

新闻报道汉译英精选

黑　黟　主　编
吴　越　副主编

上海财经大学出版社出版发行
(上海市中山北一路369号　邮编200083)
网　　址:http://www.sufep.com
电子邮箱:webmaster@sufep.com
全国新华书店经销
上海叶大印务发展有限公司印刷装订
2025年5月第1版　2025年5月第1次印刷

710mm×1000mm　1/16　24.25印张(插页:2)　314千字
定价:98.00元

前　言

在全球化的时代背景下,跨文化交流日益频繁,新闻报道作为信息传播的重要载体,其准确外译对于促进国际相互了解、文化交流和信息共享起着至关重要的作用。

随着中国在国际舞台上的影响力不断提升,越来越多的国内外人士渴望了解中国的发展动态、科技创新、文化特色等信息。新闻报道的汉译英工作不仅是语言的转换,更是文化的传递和价值观的交流。在这样的背景下,《新闻报道汉译英精选》一书应运而生,以满足提高新闻报道汉译英质量这一迫切需求。

本书内容涵盖了政策、医学、航空、核能、海洋、宇航、交通、环境、娱乐、出版、材料、生物、农业、基因、通信、物理、资本、教育、新能源、计算机、共享经济及人工智能等二十余个领域的最新、最具代表性的新闻报道汉译英实例。这些实例既反映了国内外时事热点的最新动态,也展现了我国科技进步、社会变迁、文化交流的多元面貌。

本书具有以下两大显著特点:

首先,专业性强。书中的翻译实例均经过精心挑选和严格审核,以确保译文的准确性和专业性。在翻译过程中,译者运用了恰当的翻译策略与技巧,为读者提供了高质量的学习范本。

其次,领域广泛。涵盖二十余个不同领域的新闻报道,能够满足不同读者的阅读需求,无论是对特定领域感兴趣的专业人士,还是希望拓宽知识面的普通读者,都能从中找到有价值的内容。

本书适用对象范围广泛。对于新闻工作者而言,是提升翻译质量、丰富表达手段的得力助手;对于翻译专业师生来说,是一本不可多得的教材和学习资料,有助于系统学习新闻翻译的方法和技巧;对于广大英语爱好者而论,则是拓宽国际视野、了解中国和世界的重要窗口。

我们衷心希望《新闻报道汉译英精选》一书能够成为广大读者提升新闻翻译水平、拓宽国际视野的有益工具，为促进跨文化交流和信息共享贡献一份力量。

目　录

1. 政策篇 ·· 1
2. 医学篇 ·· 17
3. 航空篇 ·· 69
4. 核能篇 ·· 75
5. 海洋篇 ·· 83
6. 宇航篇 ·· 97
7. 交通篇 ·· 113
8. 环境篇 ·· 139
9. 娱乐篇 ·· 147
10. 出版篇 ·· 157
11. 材料篇 ·· 161
12. 生物篇 ·· 179
13. 农业篇 ·· 201
14. 基因篇 ·· 209
15. 通信篇 ·· 221
16. 物理篇 ·· 249
17. 资本篇 ·· 303
18. 教育篇 ·· 327
19. 新能源篇 ·· 335
20. 计算机篇 ·· 343
21. 共享经济篇 ·· 351
22. 人工智能篇 ·· 359

1

政策篇

放"大招"整治无人机"黑飞"

从 6 月 1 日起,我国将正式对质量在 250 克以上的民用无人机实施实名登记注册。为保证机场及周边飞行安全,加强对无人机的管理,民航局将于 5 月 18 日发布首批 155 个机场保护范围数据,后续还将不断补充完善。

来源:《解放日报》

China's big actions to deal with unregistered drones

Since June 1st, China will formally require civilian drones weighing over 250g in China to be registered with real names. To ensure flight safety around airports and the surrounding areas and to improve drone management, Civil Aviation Administration of China will release the first list of clearance scope data of 155 airports, with follow-up data to be added later.

Source: *Jiefang Daily*

中匈签署资助双方科研合作项目备忘录

近日,中华人民共和国科学技术部与匈牙利国家研发与创新署正式签署《关于联合资助中匈科研合作项目的谅解备忘录》。在随后举行的会谈中,双方就深化中匈科技创新合作事宜深入交换意见,并达成广泛共识。根据备忘录,双方将在共同实施联合研发合作项目基础上,推动建立联合研发中心、科技成果商业孵化中心等合作平台。

来源:《科技日报》

China and Hungary sign *MOU on Joint Funding to R&D Projects*

Recently, the Ministry of Science and Technology of China signed *the Memorandum of Understanding on Joint Funding to Research and Develop-*

ment Projects* with the National Research, Development and Innovation Office of Hungary. In the subsequent meeting, the two sides exchanged opinions on deepening Sino-Hungary sci-tech innovation cooperation and reached extensive consensus. According to the MOU, the two sides will promote the building of cooperation platforms such as joint R&D center and business incubation center for sci-tech achievements, based on jointly implementing joint R&D projects.

Source: *Science and Technology Daily*

《国家技术转移体系建设方案》发布

国务院9月26日印发《国家技术转移体系建设方案》,明确提出了加快建设和完善国家技术转移体系的总体思路、发展目标、重点任务和保障措施,部署构建符合科技创新规律、技术转移规律和产业发展规律的国家技术转移体系,全面提升科技供给与转移扩散能力。

以往,国有技术类无形资产在进行科技成果转化时程序复杂,还要向有关部门报备。新的《国家技术转移体系建设方案》提出,根据科技成果转化特点,优化相关资产评估管理流程,探索通过公示等方式简化备案程序。

来源:看看新闻网

National Program for Development of Technology Transfer System issued

The State Council issued the *National Program for Development of Technology Transfer System* on September 26. The program specifies that it is necessary to quicken the pace of working out an overall plan, development goals, key tasks and safeguards for the national technology transfer system, build such a system that is in line with the laws of scientific and technological innovation, technology transfer and industry development, and fully increase the capability for technology supply, transfer and diffusion.

State-owned intangible technological assets used to be reported to competent departments for commercialization, which was a complex process. The revised program states that it is essential to optimize the assets assessment management procedure according to the characteristics of commercialization of scientific and technological achievements, and make attempts to simplify the filing procedures through public notification, etc.

Source: kankanews.com

2035年我国制造业基本完成智能化转型

"未来20年,我国智能制造将实现两个阶段性目标:2025年,数字化网络化制造在制造业全面普及,新一代智能制造开始推广应用;2035年,制造业基本完成智能化转型,新一代人工智能技术得到普遍应用。"中国工程院《中国智能制造发展战略研究》课题组在9月28日举行的智能制造学术报告会上,提出了我国智能制造的战略目标。

来源:科学网

China's to initially complete intelligent transformation of manufacturing industry

"In the next 20 years, China will strive to realize two goals of intelligent manufacturing: firstly, by 2025, adopting digital and networked way of manufacturing across the industry, with the new generation of intelligent manufacturing technologies starting to be promoted and applied in the industry; secondly, by 2035, preliminarily completing the intelligent transformation of the industry, with the new generation of intelligent manufacturing technologies reaching universal application", said the research group of the "Strategic Research on the Development of Intelligent Manufacturing in China" project of Chinese Academy of Engineering (CAE), at the symposium on intelligent manufacturing held on September 28, which proposed the strategic goals for China's intelligent manufacturing.

Source: ScienceNet. cn

《上海服务国家"一带一路"建设发挥桥头堡作用行动方案》出炉

10月11日下午,上海市政府新闻办举行新闻发布会,《上海服务国家"一带一路"建设发挥桥头堡作用行动方案》正式发布。

《上海服务国家"一带一路"建设发挥桥头堡作用行动方案》共8个部分,明确了上海在服务国家"一带一路"建设中发挥桥头堡作用的功能定位、实施路径,尤其是聚焦六大专项行动,提出了60项实实在在的行动举措。作为重点内容之一,科技创新合作专项行动主要围绕全面对接国家"一带一路"科技创新行动计划,加强与科技创新中心联动,利用优势科技资源,依托功能性平台和项目,促进科技联合攻关和成果转化。

来源:看看新闻网

Action Plan for Shanghai to Play the Role of a Bridgehead in Serving the National B & R Initiative published

In the afternoon of October 11, Shanghai Municipal Government Information Office held a press conference for the official publishing of *Action Plan for Shanghai to Play the Role of a Bridgehead in Serving the National B&R Initiative*.

The *Action Plan* is composed of eight chapters, stating clearly the functions and roadmaps and, in particular, six special operations for Shanghai so that it could play the role of a bridgehead in serving the national Belt and Road Initiative, laying out 60 practical actions and measures. As one key part, special operation on scientific innovation and cooperation is centered on serving the national B&R scientific innovation action plan to strengthen the interaction with efforts of developing Shanghai into a scientific and technological innovation center, make use of superior science and technology resources and leverage functional platform and projects to promote scientific and technological breakthroughs and transformations through cooperation.

Source: kankanews.com

中国制造 2025 添百亿元资金，25 项任务入围

获悉，我国将根据《中国制造 2025》总体规划，继续以专项资金等方式支持中国制造 2025 重点项目发展。近期工信部已确立了制造业创新能力建设、产业链协同能力提升、产业共性服务平台、新材料首批次应用保险 4 个方面共 25 项重点任务，并正在协同相关部委和组织进行项目遴选工作。

来源：《经济参考报》

With 25 tasks, Made in China 2025 plan adds 10 billion of funds

China is reported to continue to allocate special funds to support the major projects in the newly released *Made in China* 2025 plan. China's Ministry of Industry and Information Technology (MIIT) has confirmed 25 key tasks in four areas, including developing innovation capability in manufacturing, improving industry chains collaboration, building common service platforms for industries, and providing insurance for trial application of new materials. Meanwhile, the MIIT is collaborating with related government departments and organizations on prioritizing the tasks.

Source: *Economic Information Daily*

中国机器人标准化白皮书发布

日前,记者从中科院沈阳自动化所获悉,在由国标委主办、国家机器人标准化总体组承办的《国家机器人标准体系建设指南》培训班上,《中国机器人标准化白皮书(2017)》(下称《白皮书》)正式发布。专家认为,《白皮书》对我国机器人标准化战略和规划提供了有益的参考和指导,为我国机器人标准立项和研制提供了科学依据,对推动我国机器人自主创新能力和促进机器人产业健康发展提供了有效支撑。

来源:科学网

China published the *Robot Standardization White Paper*

According to information obtained recently from Shenyang Institute of Automation Chinese Academy of Sciences, China officially published the "*China Robot Standardization White Paper* (2017)" (hereafter the "*White Paper*") during the training course on Guidance for Building National Standard Robotics System hosted by Standardization Administration of the PRC and organized by General Group for National Robot Standardization. The White Paper provides useful reference and guidance for the strategy and planning for China's robot standardization and a scientific basis for setting up projects for standards and carrying standard-related research, helping effectively improve China's capabilities of independent innovation for robots, as well as drive the healthy development of the robot industry.

Source: ScienceNet. cn

国务院办公厅印发《关于创建"中国制造2025"国家级示范区的通知》

国务院办公厅日前印发《关于创建"中国制造2025"国家级示范区的通知》,

对"中国制造2025"国家级示范区创建工作进行全面部署。

《通知》明确,直辖市市辖区和副省级市、地级市均可申请创建示范区,距离相近、产业关联度高的城市可联合申请创建示范区。申请城市(群)应具备主导产业特色鲜明、产业配套体系相对完善,产业创新支撑能力强、协同创新体系较为完善,微观政策支撑体系比较灵活、市场发展环境好等条件。

来源:新华社

General Office of the State Council issued *Notice on the Establishment of "Made in China 2025" National Demonstration Zones*

The General Office of the State Council recently issued the *Notice on the Establishment of "Made in China 2025" National Demonstration Zones*, making full plans for the establishment of such zones.

The Notice clarifies that the districts of municipalities directly under the jurisdiction of the Central Government, sub-provincial cities, and prefecture-level cities can apply to establish demonstration zones. Cities at a close distance and with a great industrial relevance can jointly apply to establish such zones. Cities or city groups that apply to establish the zones should meet the following conditions: distinctive leading industries, a relatively complete industrial supporting system, great industrial innovation capacity, a perfect collaborative innovation system, a flexible micro-policy support system, and a favorable market development environment.

Source: Xinhua News Agency

国内首个氢能领域团体标准发布

国内首个氢燃料电池氢气品质团体标准《质子交换膜燃料电池汽车用燃料氢气》日前正式对外发布,旨在规定FCV(燃料电池汽车)用氢气的品质,规范其测试方法,在保证燃料电池的性能与耐久性的同时,降低其使用成本。

来源:techWeb

China releases its first group standard for hydrogen energy

Fuel Specification for Proton Exchange Membrane Fuel Cell Vehicles—Hydrogen, China's first group standard for the hydrogen quality of hydrogen fuel cells, has been officially released in a bid to stipulate the hydrogen quality of fuel cell vehicles (FCV), standardize its testing methods, and reduce the cost while ensuring the performance and endurance of fuel cells.

Source:techWeb

上海发布智能网联汽车道路测试管理办法,自动驾驶渐行渐近

3月1日,记者从上海市经信委获悉,上海经信委、公安局、交通委联合印发的《上海市智能网联汽车道路测试管理办法(试行)》明确了智能网联汽车道路测试申请条件、测试申请及审核、测试管理、事故处理、违规操作责任等方面的要求。

来源:中国证券网

Shanghai released regulations on road testing of intelligent connected vehicles: self-driving is approaching

On March 1, according to Shanghai Economic and Information Commission (SHEITC), SHEITC, Shanghai Public Security Bureau, and Shanghai Municipal Commission of Transport jointly issued the "*Regulations on Road Testing Intelligent Connected Vehicles（for trial implementation）*", which specifies application criteria, test application and approval, test management, accident settlement, non-compliance penalties for road tests of connected vehicles.

Source: cnstock. com

上海办理护照等出入境证件"只跑一次"

5月1日起,全国实行办理护照等出入境证件"只跑一次",确保申请人到出入境接待窗口一次即可完成申办护照等出入境证件的全部手续。

据上海公安出入境管理局介绍,近年来上海不断优化办证流程、简化办证手续,先行先试"一门式服务"、自助填表、多证同办"跑一次"等出入境证件办理便民举措。此次新政出台,上海也将同步落实"只跑一次"制度,进一步完善便民服务举措。

来源:东方网

Applications for exit and entry documents can be processed at one time in Shanghai

Starting from May 1, the applications for exit and entry documents including passports can be processed at one time throughout the country, and the applicants will find it easier to complete all the procedures for applying for related documents at the reception windows.

According to Government Affairs of Exit-Entry Administration Bureau of Shanghai Public Security Bureau, Shanghai has always been improving and streamlining the procedures for processing the applications in recent years, as evidenced by such measures as launching one-stop services, facilitating self-service completion of application forms, and processing applications for more than one document at one time. Shanghai will implement the new policy of processing all exit and entry documents at one time, so as to further improve the services for the public.

Source: eastday. com

科技部：将严查严重违背科研诚信要求行为，建立终身追究制

据中国之声《全国新闻联播》报道，中办、国办近日印发《关于进一步加强科研诚信建设的若干意见》。科技部近日表示，《意见》将严肃查处严重违背科研诚信要求的行为，做到"一处失信，处处受限"。《意见》要求加强对科研活动全流程诚信管理。现在所有申报国家科技计划项目的负责人，第一轮评审到最后一轮评审，都要到严重失信行为数据库中进行审核。一旦发现过去有发生严重失信行为的记录，取消后续资格。

来源：央广网

MOST: Scientific research integrity problems to be severely investigated and punished, a lifelong accountability system to be established

The General Office of the CPC Central Committee and the General Office of the State Council have recently issued a document titled the *Opinions on Further Building Up Scientific Research Integrity*, according to a report by Xinwen Lianbo, a daily news program on China National Radio. The Ministry of Science and Technology said that violations of the *Opinions* will be severely investigated and punished, so that "if one breaks his promise, he/she will be strictly limited everywhere". The *Opinions* requires that integrity management of scientific research activities should be strengthened. Officials in charge of applying for national science and technology projects should go through the database of serious faithless acts all the way from the first round of review to the last one. Those who are found to have such acts will be disqualified.

Source: cnr. cn

上海出台 55 条惠台措施，为台胞创业、就业提供同等待遇

近日，上海市政府台办举行新闻发布会，上海市《关于促进沪台经济文化交流合作的实施办法》(《实施办法》)从即日起正式发布实施，这是中国大陆首个省级层面推出的惠台政策措施。上海市台办表示，这是为了深入贯彻党的十九大精神和习近平总书记关于深化两岸经济文化交流合作的重要思想，结合上海实际，研究出台便利台湾同胞在本市学习、创业、就业、生活的重大政策举措。这将为台湾同胞更好融入上海城市发展，进一步深化沪台经济文化交流合作，创造更好条件。

来源：央视网

Shanghai government introduces 55 favorable measures to provide equivalent treatment for Taiwan compatriots in entrepreneurship and employment

Recently, Shanghai Municipal Government Taiwan Office held a press conference and released *The Measures for Promoting Economic and Cultural Exchange and Cooperation between Shanghai and Taiwan* (hereinafter referred to as "the Measures"), which has taken effect on the same day, and is the first policies and measures favorable to Taiwan introduced at provincial level in mainland China. Shanghai Municipal Government Taiwan Office says that the Measures which will benefit Taiwan compatriots for study, business startup, employment and living are introduced to implement the spirit of the 19th National Congress of the Communist Party of China and General Secretary Xi Jinping's thought of deepening the economic and cultural exchange and cooperation between the mainland and Taiwan based on the actual conditions of Shanghai. It will create better conditions for Taiwan compatriots to involve them in the development of Shanghai and deepen the economic and cultural exchange and cooperation.

Source: cctv. com

7月1日起科技人员职务科技成果转化奖金享个税优惠

近日,财政部、税务总局、科技部联合发布通知,为进一步支持国家大众创业、万众创新战略的实施,促进科技成果转化,7月1日起科技人员取得职务科技成果转化现金奖励,个人所得税可享优惠。通知明确,依法批准设立的非营利性研究开发机构和高等学校(以下简称非营利性科研机构和高校)根据《中华人民共和国促进科技成果转化法》规定,从职务科技成果转化收入中给予科技人员的现金奖励,可减按50%计入科技人员当月"工资、薪金所得",依法缴纳个人所得税。

来源:财政部税政司

Scientists and engineers who promote transformation of sci-tech achievements will be eligible for personal income tax benefits of their cash bonus from July 1

Recently, the Ministry of Finance, the State Administration of Taxation, and the Ministry of Science and Technology jointly issued a notice that: to further implement the strategy of mass entrepreneurship and innovation and promote the transformation of scientific and technological achievements, scientists and engineers will be eligible for personal income tax benefits of their cash bonus from July 1. In accordance with the Law of the People's Republic of China on the Transformation of Scientific and Technological Achievements, non-profitable research institutes and institutions of higher learning should give some earnings from transformation of scientific and technological achievements to related scientists and engineers as a cash bonus, and half of this sum of money will be included into their income from wages and salaries, and the personal income tax shall be deducted according to law.

Source: Department of Taxation under the Ministry of Finance

上海发布"技能提升计划" 技能人才待遇明显提高

日前,上海发布《技能提升三年计划》,明确到 2021 年,劳动者整体技能素质明显提升、技能人才待遇明显提高,基本建成具有国际竞争力的技能人才高地。在技能人才的培养、评价、使用、激励、保障等方面,《技能提升计划》着力破除体制机制障碍,畅通 9 条路径。其中既包括深化职业技能证书与学历证书的双证融通试点,又包括通过居住证、居转户、直接落户等政策健全梯度化技能人才引进机制,还包括加大表彰奖励力度等。

来源:看看新闻网

Shanghai releases "skill improvement program" to notably improve treatment of skilled talent

Shanghai has recently released the "*Three-year Skill Improvement Program*", which clearly states that, by 2021, the city will primarily build itself into an internationally competitive hub of skilled talent, with notable improvement in worker's overall skills and treatment. In terms of skilled talent's cultivation, assessment, use, incentive and support, *the Skill Improvement Program* focuses on removing institutional obstacles, and clearing 9 pathways, including the pilot of integration of professional skill certificate and academic certificate, the improvement of graded introduction mechanism for skilled talent through policies regarding residence permit, conversion from residence permit to hukou status, direct grant of hukou status, as well as providing more incentives for talent, etc.

Source:kankanews.com

2

医学篇

寨卡病毒可用于对付脑肿瘤

寨卡病毒虽然恶名远扬,但它或许能帮助一种癌症患者。英国癌症研究会近日宣布,将测试用寨卡病毒来对付胶质母细胞瘤,以便开发治疗这种脑肿瘤的新方法。

胶质母细胞瘤是一种恶性脑瘤,现有治疗方法的效果有限。原因包括在脑部血管与脑组织之间有个"血—脑"屏障,一些药物无法穿过这个屏障;还因为药物剂量不能使用过多,否则容易误伤健康的组织。

来源:新华社

Zika Virus may treat brain tumors

The Zika virus, though being notorious, may help to treat a certain type of cancer patient. Cancer Research UK recently announced that they were to test Zika Virus on glioblastoma, in order to pioneer a new method to treat the brain tumor.

Glioblastoma is a vile brain tumor, yet current treatment for it has rather limited effect. One reason is that some drugs could not pass the blood-brain barrier between brain vessels and brain tissues; Another reason is that an overdose of drugs tends to hurt healthy tissues.

Source: Xinhua News Agency

观测人体内部的"哈勃望远镜"亮相

在近日举行的中国国际医疗器械博览会上,由上海联影医疗科技有限公司与美国顶尖分子影像科研团队"探索者"联盟携手打造的"史上最强PET-CT"——世界首台全景动态扫描 PET-CT uExplorer 探索者,全球首度亮相。

PET-CT 又称为正电子发射断层显像,相比于常见的 CT、磁共振等医学扫描设备,它能更早更清晰地发现肿瘤。

来源:《科技日报》

"Hubble Telescope" for observation of human body unveiled

At the recently held China International Medical Equipment Fair, "the most sophisticated PET-CT in history"—the world's first panoramic dynamic scanning PET-CT uExplorer—was first unveiled to the world. It was jointly developed by Shanghai United Imaging Healthcare Co., Ltd. and the US top molecular imaging research team Explorer Consortium.

PET-CT is also known as Positron Emission Computed Tomography. Compared with common CT, magnetic resonance and other medical scanning devices, it can find the tumor much earlier and more clearly.

Source: *Science and Technology Daily*

美儿科学会建议 1 岁以下儿童不喝果汁

美国儿科学会 5 月 22 日发布儿童果汁饮用指南,指出果汁对 1 岁以下儿童弊多利少,家长不应该给他们喝果汁。

此前,美国儿科学会一直建议不要给 6 个月以下的婴儿喝果汁。但鉴于越来越多的证据显示饮用果汁可能会引发儿童肥胖和龋齿,该组织决定把不喝果汁的年龄建议从 6 个月提高至 1 岁。

来源:科学网

No fruit juice for kids under 1, pediatricians advise

Fruit juice does more harm than good to children under 1 year old, and parents should not give them juice, according to new guidelines from the American Academy of Pediatrics, published on May 22.

The group had previously advised parents to wait to offer juice until a child reached 6 months old but decided to make the change based on rising rates of obesity and concerns about tooth cavities.

Source: ScienceNet. cn

科学家找到暴食症开关

为什么有些人明明吃了很多,却还想进食;而有些人滴水未进,却完全没有食欲?原来,大脑中有一个控制"开关"。《科学》杂志5月25日载文称,研究人员在小鼠大脑发现了一群特异性神经元,当其被激活时会立即触发小鼠暴食样进食行为;长时间反复刺激这些神经元会令小鼠体重暴增。

来源:《科技日报》

Scientists found the switch for bulimia

Why do some people have the impulse to eat more when they are already full and some have no appetite at all even when they haven't eat for a long time? It turns out that there is a "switch" in human brain to control this. Academic journal *Science* published an article on May 25, announcing that researchers found a group of specific neurons which would trigger mice's bulimia when stimulated; repeated stimulation of this group of neuron over time will lead to sudden weight-gaining for mice.

Source: *Science and Technology Daily*

巧克力与心律失常风险降低有关

根据对丹麦人的一项最新研究发现,每个月吃一到三次巧克力的人比每月吃巧克力不到一次的人，诊断出心房颤动的几率低10%左右。"作为健康饮食的一部分，适量摄取巧克力是一种健康的零食选择。"该研究领衔作者、哈佛大学陈曾熙公共卫生学院及波士顿贝斯以色列女执事医疗中心的伊丽沙·莫斯托夫斯基（Elizabeth Mostofsky）说。

来源：科学网

Chocolate intake relates to less risk of irregular heart rhythm

According to a new study of Danish people, those who eat chocolate one to three times a month are 10% less likely to be diagnosed with irregular heart rhythm than those who eat less than once a month. "As a part of healthy diet, proper amount of chocolate is a good choice for snack", said the lead author Elizabeth Mostofsky, who works in Harvard T. H. Chan School of Public Health and Beth Israel Deaconess Medical Center.

Source：ScienceNet. cn

基因突变如何导致不育，上海科学家首次发现致病机理

中科院生化与细胞所刘默芳研究组与上海市计划生育科学研究所施惠娟研究组合作研究，经过6年的努力，在国际上首次发现人类Piwi基因突变可导致男性不育，并深入揭示了其致病机理，为相关男性不育症的早期分子诊断及精准医疗提供了理论依据。近日，国际著名学术期刊《细胞》在线发表了该项研究成果。

——来源：新华社

Shanghai scientists discovered the relationship between male infertility and genetic mutation

After 6 years' study, the research team from the Chinese Academy of

Sciences' Institute of Biochemistry and Cell Biology, which is led by Liu Mofang, and the research team from the Shanghai Institute of Planned Parenthood Research, which is led by Shi Huijuan, have discovered that the mutation of Piwi would cause male infertility and have revealed its pathogenic mechanism for the first time. Their study has laid theoretical foundation for early molecular diagnosis and has made treatment possible for the disease. Recently, the discovery has been published on *Cell*, a famous international biological journal.

Source: Xinhua News Agency

新抗体有助于增加骨量减少体脂

英国《自然》杂志5月底在线发表的一篇医学研究论文报告称,美国科学家新发现了一种抗体,在更年期模型小鼠身上进行的试验表明,其有助于增加骨量,减少体脂。该抗体有潜力用于应对人类涉及内脏脂肪的疾病,并能推动治疗骨质疏松症和肥胖等疾病相关药物的研发。

来源:中国科技网

New antibody conducive to boosting bone mass and reducing body fat

The British magazine, *Nature*, has published a medical research paper online at the end of May, which holds that American scientists have discovered a new antibody. The antibody, tested on mice model of menopause, may help to increase bone mass and reduce body fat. It not only shows promise as treatment for visceral adiposity, but also aids the R&D of drugs to help treat both osteoporosis and weight gain.

Source: stdaily. com

研究人员用转基因猪探究糖尿病及并发症

日本研究人员日前利用转基因技术在猪身上再现了糖尿病及视网膜病和肾衰竭等并发症。在大型哺乳动物身上再现这些疾病,将有助于研究引起并发症的机制及相应的治疗方法。

来源:新华社

Researchers use transgenic pigs to study diabetes and its complications

Japanese researchers have applied transgenic technology on pigs to let them get diabetes and its complications, including retinopathy and renal failure. The reproduce of these diseases on large mammals will help researchers study pathogenesis of the complications and find out corresponding treatments.

Source:**Xinhua News Agency**

上海硅酸盐所提出"纳米催化医学"肿瘤治疗新策略

近日,中国科学院上海硅酸盐研究所研究员施剑林、陈雨带领的科研团队提出了"纳米催化医学"的新型肿瘤治疗策略,利用多元化、高选择性和高特异性的催化反应实现安全、无毒药物在肿瘤区域微环境刺激下原位转化为有毒物质,从而达到选择性杀死肿瘤细胞而不对正常组织产生毒副作用的目的。最新的一项将纳米催化医学策略成功应用于肿瘤治疗的工作发表在《自然·通讯》上。

来源:上海科技

SICCAS discovers a tumor-selective catalytic nanomedicine for tumor treatment

Recently, a research team led by Shi Jianlin and Chen Yu of Shanghai Institute of Ceramics of Chinese Academy of Sciences (SICCAS) has discovered a catalytic nanomedicine for cancer therapy. In detail, it delivers safe and non-toxic catalytic nanomedicine to tumor sites where a series of highly-selective and high specialty catalytic reaction will take place under the influence of the tumor microenvironment, so as to transform the non-toxic drugs into toxic substances in situ. The goal is to kill the tumor cells and cause no harm to the healthy tissues. The latest study on catalytic nanomedicine for tumor treatment has been published on *Nature Communications*.

Source: stcsm. gov. cn

新型摄像头可"透视"人体,辅助医疗检测

医疗上检查身体内部情况通常使用昂贵的扫描设备,例如 X 光。近日,科学家已研发出一款新型摄像头,能够透视人体内部,与内窥镜等医疗用具协同使用,运用于人体内部检查中。新型摄像头可以检测光子,它易感光,能够捕捉到穿透组织的微弱光线。它同样也能记录光穿过身体的时间,这意味着这款摄像头能够探测到内窥镜的具体位置。

来源:环球网

New camera can "see through" human body, helping medical test

In medical sector, doctors usually have to rely on expensive scans, such as X-rays, to trace internal progress. However, scientists have developed a camera that can see through human body. The device can cooperate with medical devices such as endoscope during internal examinations. The new camera can detect photons and is so sensitive that it can catch tiny traces of light passing through tissue. It can also record the time taken for light to pass through the body, which means the device is able to work out exactly where the endoscope is.

Source: huanqiu. com

"吃甜食心情好"或有另说

"吃甜食会让人心情变好"似乎是人们口耳相传的一条"真理"。然而已经有多项研究表明,糖分摄入水平越高,抑郁症患病可能性越大。

英国《自然》旗下《科学报告》杂志 7 月 30 日刊登的一篇研究报告称,饮食中大量来自甜食或饮料的糖类可能会导致常见心理疾病(比如焦虑症和抑郁症)产生的可能性增加,这揭示了糖类与人类心理健康之间的关联。

来源:《科技日报》

Desserts make us feel good? It may not be true

That desserts make us feel good seems a "truth", which everyone is familiar with. But researches show that higher sugar intake is linked to higher odds of the occurrence of depression.

A study published by the Scientific Reports of the Nature on July 30 suggests excessive sugar intake from sweet food and beverages will cause higher incidence of common mental diseases, including anxieties and depression, which unveils the correlation between sugar consumption and human mental health.

Source: *Science and Technology Daily*

中科院生化与细胞所发现哺乳动物心脏发育新机制

中科院生化与细胞生物学研究所周斌研究组发现哺乳动物心脏发育过程中心肌致密化的细胞和分子新机制。相关成果日前在线发表于《自然·通讯》。

研究表明,心肌致密化不全不能仅归因于心肌小梁本身过度化的缺陷,胚胎期致密心肌层的扩增及其参与心肌混合区的形成,对发育形成正常的心室壁起着至关重要的作用,这项研究为进一步探索心肌致密化不全的发病机制提供了重要信息。

来源:科学网

Institute of Biochemistry and Cell Biology, CAS found the new mammalian heart development mechanisms

A research team led by Zhou Bin from Institute of Biochemistry and Cell Biology of SIBS, CAS found new mechanisms of cells and molecules of compacting myocardium during mammalian heart development. Related results were published on the website of *Nature Communications*.

The research shows that noncompaction of ventricular myocardium is not only due to excessive trabeculations. The expansion of compact myocardium during embryonic period and forming of hybrid myocardial zone participated by compact myocardium plays an important role in normal ventricular wall development. The research provides some crucial information for further researchers in pathogenesis of noncompaction of ventricular myocardium.

Source: ScienceNet.com

阿尔茨海默病患者"丢失"的记忆有可能找回

记忆障碍是阿尔茨海默病(又称早老性痴呆症)的主要症状之一,美国科学家通过动物实验发现，患者的记忆信息可能并没有真的丢失，只是大脑读取记忆的能力出了问题。

英国《新科学家》杂志日前报道说，美国哥伦比亚大学研究人员利用激光刺激神经元，使患有阿尔茨海默病的实验鼠恢复了特定记忆。如果相关发现也适用于人脑，将有可能开发出帮助人们找回记忆的治疗手段。

来源：新华社

Patients suffering from Alzheimer's disease might get their memory back

Memory loss is one of the major symptoms of Alzheimer's disease. However, American scientists have found through animal experiments that memories assumed to be lost in patients suffering with the disease may not be really gone. It's the brain's accessing ability that has gone wrong.

According to a recent article in the UK-based magazine New Scientist, researchers of Columbia University in the US have successfully recovered specific memories of lab rats with Alzheimer's disease by stimulating their neurons with laser. The finding, if found applicable to the human brain, might help to develop treatment to revive people's memories.

Source: Xinhua News Agency

新型滴鼻剂有望高效预防流脑

英国南安普敦大学近日发布的研究成果显示，一种新型滴鼻剂能够通过特殊细菌在鼻腔中形成强效保护作用，有效预防流行性脑脊髓膜炎（流脑）。

约10%成年人的鼻腔以及咽喉携带有脑膜炎奈瑟菌，多数携带这种致病菌的人不会出现任何症状。但在部分人中，这种细菌可能会进入血液，导致流脑，给患者大脑带来严重损害甚至死亡。

先前研究发现,一种名为乳糖奈瑟菌的细菌能够在人鼻腔中停留数月且不会带来副作用,同时能保护人体不受脑膜炎奈瑟菌感染。

来源:《中国科学报》

New nose drop expected to effectively prevent epidemic cerebrospinal meningitis

The University of Southampton in the UK has recently published research results showing that a new type of nose drop can have a strong protective effect through special bacteria in the nasal cavity and effectively prevent epidemic cerebrospinal meningitis.

About 10 percent of adults have meningitis neisseria in their nasal passages and throat, and most people who carry this pathogen do not have any symptoms. But in some people, the bacteria may enter the bloodstream, causing epidemic cerebrospinal meningitis and bringing severe damage to the brain and even death.

Previous studies have found that a bacterium called neisseria lactamica can stay in the human nasal cavity for several months without causing side effects while protecting the body from meningitis neisseria infection.

Source: *China Science Daily*

ARM 正开发可植入大脑的芯片 可帮病人康复

芯片设计巨头 ARM 正与美国研究人员展开合作,研发可植入人脑的芯片,使脑损伤、脊柱损伤患者能够重新支配自己的肢体。这款芯片将置于人的颅骨内,帮助那些患有脑损伤、脊柱损伤的人们。

来源:环球网

ARM is developing implantable chip for patients with brain or spinal injuries

Leading chip designer ARM is cooperating with American researchers to develop a chip that can be implanted in the skull of patients with brain or spinal injuries to help them re-control their body.

Source: huanqiu. com

澳科学家发现兴奋剂检测新蛋白标记物

澳大利亚麦考瑞大学的科学家们发现了兴奋剂检测的新方法,这将使测出运动员是否服用违禁药物变得更加容易。

人体生长激素(HGH)被认为是使用较多的违禁药物之一,但目前的检测手段和方法难以令人满意。麦考瑞大学阿拉姆吉尔汗博士领导的团队发现,新的蛋白质可以应用在兴奋剂检测中。阿拉姆吉尔汗在接受新华社记者电话采访时说,研究发现有8种蛋白质可以作为兴奋剂检测的生物标记物,有望在将来被世界各国的反兴奋剂机构使用。

来源:新华社

Australian scientists find new protein biomarkers for doping test

Scientists at University of Macquarie of Australia found a new method for drug test, which will make it easier to detect the intake of illicit drugs.

Human growth hormone (HGH) is considered to be one of the commonly used prohibited drugs taken by athletes, but the current detection approach is unsatisfactory. The research team led by Dr Alamgir Khan of Macquarie University found new protein marker that could be used in doping test. During a phone interview with the reporter from Xinhua News Agency,

Dr Alamgir Khan said 8 proteins have been identified that can be used as biomarkers in doping test with the potential to be adopted by anti-doping agencies worldwide.

Source: Xinhua News Agency

科学家替换帕金森病猴受损神经

8月31日《自然》发表的一项研究运用干细胞疗法,恢复了帕金森病猴的神经功能。这项临床前研究表明,植入人诱导多能干细胞(iPSC)源多巴胺能神经元可以改善患病猴子的运动,意味着这种方法有望在临床上用于治疗帕金森病人类患者。

来源:《中国科学报》

Scientists replace damaged nerves of Parkinsonian monkeys

On August 31, a *Nature* article stated the restoration of neurological function of Parkinsonian monkeys through stem cell therapy. This preclinical study says that implantation of human-induced pluripotent stem cells (iPSC) dopaminergic neurons can improve the movements of diseased monkeys, suggesting the likelihood of applying this approach to treat patients with Parkinson's disease.

Source: *China Science Daily*

中国有望成最大"移植器官仓库"

据世界卫生组织的数据显示,目前全球患者对器官的需求量已经大大超过供给量。仅中国每年就约有30万患者等待器官移植,而器官捐献者却还很少。

近年来,新型器官移植手术引起了全球的广泛关注,其中包括了疯狂又备受争议的人体头部移植。而同样备受关注是中国研究人员坚持试用转基因猪器官进行移植，并期望在未来两年内可以进行猪器官人体移植。

来源：环球网

China would become the largest "repository of transplants"

According to the data from World Health Organization (WHO), the global demand for transplants is much higher than supply. China alone has over 300,000 patients waiting for available transplants, yet organ donation is still rare.

In recent years, new types of transplantation surgeries have attracted attentions from around the globe, including the crazy and controversial head transplant. Chinese researchers' efforts are also arresting. They try to conduct transplantation with organs from transgenic pigs and hope to successfully transplant these organs to human body.

Source：huanqiu.com

张江企业生产心脏起搏器系列获 CFDA 批准

位于上海张江科技城的创领心律管理医疗器械（上海）有限公司生产的 RegaTM 心系列植入式心脏起搏器，近日正式获得国家食药监总局（CFDA）的批准，成为国内第一个具有国际先进品质的国产心脏起搏器，将惠及更多中国患者。

来源：人民网

CFDA approved pacemaker produced by company in Zhangjiang Hi-Tech Park

The RegaTM implanted pacemaker developed by Chuangling Cardiac

Rhythm Management Medical Equipment (Shanghai) Co., Ltd in Shanghai Zhangjiang Hi-Tech Park was approved recently by China Food and Drug Administration (CFDA), which became China's first international high-quality pacemaker product and is set to bring benefits to more patients in China.

Source: people. cn

香港中文大学研发出人工智能技术诊断肺癌及乳腺癌

9月6日,香港中文大学研究团队利用人工智能影像识别技术判读肺癌及乳腺癌的医学影像,准确率分别达91%及99%,识别过程只需30秒至10分钟。研究人员称,此项技术可大幅提升临床诊断效率,并降低误诊率。

来源:新华社

Chinese University of Hong Kong develops artificial intelligent systems for breast cancer diagnosing

On September 6, a research team of the Chinese University of Hong Kong developed an artificial intelligent image recognition technology to present the medical images of lung cancer and breast cancer, with accuracy of 91% and 99% respectively. The recognition only took 30 seconds to 10 minutes. Researchers said that the technology will increase the efficiency of clinical diagnosis and reduces misdiagnosis rate.

Source: Xinhua News Agency

科研人员提出纳米催化医学肿瘤治疗新策略

随着纳米科学与生物技术的发展,科学家们认识到肿瘤细胞的生态微环境与正常细胞有较大的差异,肿瘤微环境逐渐成为肿瘤选择性治疗的一个研究热点。中科院上海硅酸盐研究所施剑林研究员、陈雨研究员带领的科研团队提出了"纳米催化医学"的新型肿瘤治疗策略,利用多元化、高选择性和高特异性的催化反应实现安全、无毒药物在肿瘤区域微环境刺激下原位转化为有毒物质,从而达到选择性杀死肿瘤细胞而不对正常组织产生毒副作用的目的。

来源:科学网

Researchers put forward "nanocatalysis medicine" as a new strategy for tumor treatment

With the development of nanoscience and biotechnology, scientists have realized that the ecological environment of tumor cells is quite different from those of normal cells. Therefore, tumor microenvironment has gradually become a research focus of tumor selective therapy. A research team led by Shi Jianlin and Chenyu, researchers in Shanghai Institute of Ceramics, Chinese Academy of sciences put forward a new "nanocatalysis medicine" for tumor treatment, which leverages diversified, highly selective and highly specific catalytic reactions to transform safe, non-toxic drugs into toxic substances under the microenvironment of tumor area, so as to selectively kill the tumor cells without producing any side effects to the normal tissue.

Source: ScienceNet. cn

首都第一家专业预防医疗医院成立

9月8日,由腾湃健康产业集团投资成立的首都第一家专业预防医疗医院——北京腾湃国贸国际医学中心开业。这家特色医院汇聚中德顶级预防医疗专家,联合北京协和医院、天坛医院、安贞医院、阜外医院、中日友好医院等三甲医院权威专家组成实力专家团队,采用预防医学、环境医学、功能医学、分子医学、细胞免疫及生物医学技术,为亚健康与慢病高风险人群提供健康管理、慢病防控、环境健康及分子保健、抗衰老等优质预防医疗服务,将成为华北地区以预防医疗为基础的高端圈层交流平台。

来源:环球网

Beijing's first professional preventive medical hospital was established

On September 8th, Beijing's first professional preventive medical hospital invested by the TE-PEMIC Health Industry Group—Beijing TE-PEMIC Commerce and International Medical Center opened. This special hospital brings together the top-level preventive medical experts in China and Germany, as well as prestigious experts from the Peking Union Medical College Hospital, Tiantan Hospital, Anzhen Hospital, Fu Wai Hospital, Sino-Japanese Friendship Hospital and other 3A hospitals. With the help of preventive medicine, environmental medicine, functional medicine, molecular medicine, cellular immunity and biomedical technology, this team of experts offer the health management, chronic disease prevention and control, environmental health and molecular health care, anti-aging and other quality preventive medical services for people suffered with sub-health and chronic diseases. This medical center will become a preventive medicine-based platform for the high-end sphere in the North China.

Source:huanqiu.com

加拿大研发机械外骨骼装置 可助残疾儿童站立走路

近日,加拿大研发出一款全动力的机械外骨骼,可帮助残疾儿童站立行走,一次充电可用一整天。父母能使用装置上的平板进行跟踪以及参数调节,可从完全悬空到完全承重,以适应孩子不同时期的状况。此外,电力驱动的机械腿,能帮助协调孩子的膝盖和髋部,带动身体前进,这种体验近似于月球漫步。

来源:环球网

Canada developed an exoskeleton mechanical device helping disable children standing and walking

Recently, Canada developed a full-power exoskeleton mechanical device which can help disable children to stand and walk. The device can be used for a whole day once it is fully charged. Parents can use the pad connected to the device to track and adjust parameters, setting the device to a support state from a dangling state, so as to adapt to children's conditions in different periods. Besides, the mechanical legs powered by electric power can facilitate children to coordinate their legs and hips to move their bodies. Such experience is similar to walking on the moon.

Source: huanqiu. com

为砒霜安双"眼睛" 可变治疗慢性白血病良方

三氧化二砷俗称"砒霜"(ATO),自古被认为是"毒药之王"。然而,在湖南大学分子科学与生物医学实验室,砒霜经过叶酸和人血清白蛋白的孵化,就好像练就了"火眼金睛",可靶向作用于癌细胞,"毒药"亦可变成慢性白血病治疗的"良方"。日前,该成果发表在国际顶尖化学期刊《德国应用化学》上。

来源:人民网

White arsenic turned into cure for chronic leukemia

Arsenical trioxide (ATO), also known as white arsenic, has always been deemed as the king of poison. Yet researchers in Molecular Sciences and Biomedicine Laboratory of Hunan University incubate white arsenic with human serum albumin and folic acid to target cancer cell, turning the poison into medicine for chronic leukemia treatment. The research outcome is published on the top chemical journal *Angewandte Chemie*.

Source: people. com. cn

一种睡眠疗法可减轻抑郁和妄想症

研究发现，一种原本用于治疗失眠的疗法还能在治疗包括消极想法、焦虑、抑郁和精神错乱在内的一系列心理健康问题上派上用场。相关成果日前发表于《柳叶刀·精神病学》杂志。

通过对照试验，利用"睡好觉"疗法的人的睡眠比对照组好50%。同时，他们的幻觉症状减轻了30%，妄想症状减轻了25%，焦虑和抑郁症水平也比前者低20%。

来源：科学网

A sleep therapy can reduce depression and paranoia

A type of therapy originally designed for insomnia has been found to also help a range of mental health issues, including negative thoughts, anxiety, depression and psychosis. Related findings were published in *The Lancet Psychiatry*.

Overall, those using Sleepio slept 50 per cent better than the control group. Compared to this group, the Sleepio users also had a 30 per cent reduction in hallucinations, 25 per cent reduction in paranoia, and their anxiety and depression levels were 20 per cent lower.

Source: ScienceNet. cn

新技术用声波取外泌体诊断癌症

近日,美国一研究小组开发出一种运用声波从血液中快速提取细胞外泌体的新技术,能显著改进外泌体或胞外囊泡的提取过程。运用这一技术的微流体便携装置,有望成为血检新工具,使医生快速获得癌症等疾病的特征信息。细胞外泌体是活体细胞分泌的一种膜性囊泡,直径约30—150纳米,会携带蛋白质、RNA及其他一些重要的细胞分子,这些物质可以作为癌症、神经变性疾病和肾脏病等疾病的标志物,对病情诊断具有重要意义。

来源:《科技日报》

New technology uses sound waves to isolate exosomes for cancer diagnosis

An US research group has recently developed a new technology that enables fast sifting of exosomes, which has the potential to drastically improve the process of isolation of exosomes and other extracellular vesicles from blood. The portable microfluidic devices using this technology could become new tools for blood test, enabling doctors to rapidly acquire information regarding diseases like cancer. These vesicles, which are usually about 30 to 150 nanometers in diameter, can carry proteins, RNA, or other important cellular molecules. Such contents can serve as markers for disorders such as cancer, neurodegenerative disease, and kidney disease, among others, which are of great significance for disease diagnosis.

Source: *Science and Technology Daily*

新技术可在数分钟内完成眼部感染检测

近日,英国南安普敦大学一个团队成功研发了一种新型芯片,只要从被感染的眼部组织样本中提取其中的细菌,然后利用配备这一芯片的装置来分析,就可在数分钟内完成细菌性角膜炎的检测。这不但有助提高疾病诊断效率,也能减少抗生素的滥用。

来源:《中国科学报》

New technology can finish eye infection testing within several minutes

A team from University of Southampton has recently developed a new chip for rapid eye infection testing. Devices on-board with this chip can finish the testing of bacterial keratitis within several minutes by analyzing the bacterium extracted from infected eye tissue, helping increase diagnosis rate and decrease antibiotic misuse.

Source: *China Science Daily*

新抗体能抵御99%艾滋病病毒变种

据最新一期《科学》杂志报道,美国国家卫生研究院和制药商赛诺菲,利用基因工程技术联合开发的一种新抗体,可攻击99%的艾滋病病毒(HIV)株系,防止灵长类动物受到感染。该抗体已在猴子身上试验成功,人类临床试验将于明年启动。

来源:科学网

New antibody attacks 99% of HIV strains

According to the journal *Science*, scientists from the U.S. National Institutes of Health and the pharmaceutical company Sanofi collaborated to develop, through genetic engineering technology, an antibody that attacks 99% of HIV strains and could even prevent infection in primates. Experiments on monkeys have succeeded and those on human will start in 2018.

Source: ScienceNet. cn

研究称辛辣食品或有助减肥

美国亚利桑那州立大学最新研究成果显示,辣椒素类物质会增强人体新陈代谢,因此辛辣食品可能有助减肥。这项研究由来自中国的研究人员邓越等主导。邓越表示,该研究首次在辣椒素类物质与人体新陈代谢量之间建立直接而可信的关联,而辛辣食品可能有助减肥的原理"并不是这类食品会抑制人的食欲,而是能增加人体的消耗"。

来源:新华网

Spicy foods could help with weight loss

A new study from U. S. Arizona State University (ASU) showed the capsaicinoids, the active ingredient in chili peppers, could increase the metabolism, which may be conducive to weight loss. This study was held by the university's research team, led by Chinese scientists Deng Yue, etc. Deng said that the study validated the link between capsaicinoids and human metabolism for the first time ever, and the reason behind the possible weight loss induced by spicy food is "not that it reduces one's appetite, but that it increases the metabolism".

Source: xinhuanet. com

抑制癌症骨转移新药即将上市

9月25日,扬州大学化学化工学院宣布,由该院朱沛志教授研发的肝素双膦酸盐抗骨质疏松药物,可用于对骨质疏松症和骨折愈合的治疗,对肿瘤组织有极强的抑制作用。不久,该药物将面向市场。

据了解,骨转移是癌症常见的转移形式,乳腺癌、前列腺癌、肺癌、骨髓瘤等患者发生骨转移的可能性很高。骨转移最常见的症状是疼痛,此外还会造成骨折、脊髓压迫、肾衰等并发症,危及生命。

来源:《科技日报》

New drug capable of inhibiting cancer bone metastasis to be launched

On September 25, the College of Chemistry and Chemical Engineering of Yangzhou University announced that the new drug-"Heparin Bisphosphonates Anti-osteoporosis" developed by Professor Zhu Peizhi will be launched soon. The drug can be used for treatment of osteoporosis and bone fracture, boosting strong inhibitory effect on tumor tissues.

Bone metastasis is the most common form of cancer metastasis. Breast cancer, prostate cancer, lung cancer, myeloma, etc. all have high possibility for bone metastasis. The most commonly seen symptom of bone metastasis is pain. Besides it could also cause life-threatening complications such as bone fracture, spinal cord compression and renal failure.

Source: *Science and Technology Daily*

法国科学家:神经刺激"唤醒"昏迷15年植物人

日前,在胸腔植入迷走神经刺激器后,一名因车祸而处于植物人状态15年之久的35岁男子呈现出意识苏醒迹象,颠覆了学术界有关人持续昏迷超过12个月就无法唤醒的既有认识。负责研究的法国里昂马克·让纳罗认知科学研究所的安杰拉·西里古在新一期美国《当代生物学》杂志上说:"通过刺激迷走神经,我们发现能够增强(植物人)患者在这个世界的存在。"

来源:人民网

French scientists: nerve stimulation "aroused" a PVS patient unconscious for 15 years

A 35-year-old man who has been in persistent vegetative state (PVS) for 15 years due to a traffic accident has shown signals of consciousness, after a vagus nerve stimulator was transplanted into his chest. This challenges the current medical knowledge that people falling into coma for more than 12 months would no longer be awoken. Angela Sirigu, who led the work at the Institut des Sciences Cognitives Marc Jeannerod in Lyon, France, said in the latest *Current Biology* journal, "By stimulating the vagus nerve, we found that we could enhance the (vegetative) patients' presence in the world."

Source: people.cn

科学家取得新突破：或能逆转细胞老化

近日，科学家研发了一种可逆转细胞老化的技术。研究人员在寻找儿童早衰症的疗法时，意外取得了这项重大突破。专家认为，此次发现将改变我们对衰老的理解和治疗方法。该研究的首席调查员、休斯敦卫理公会研究所心血管科学分部主席约翰·库克博士(Dr John Cooke)称，两者有着天壤之别。

来源：新浪科技

New breakthrough by scientists may reverse cell aging

Recently, scientists have developed a reversible cell aging technology. A major breakthrough has been made unexpectedly as researchers looking for a cure for progeria. Experts believe the findings will change our understanding and treatment of aging. Dr John Cooke, the study's leading investigator and chairman of the Department of Cardiovascular Sciences at the Houston

Methodist Research Institute, said there was a world of difference between the two.

Source: tech. sina. com. cn

科学家发现治疗癌症新思路：提升人体 T 细胞战斗力

运动员为了提高耐力可能会去海拔高的地方训练。以色列科学家受这种训练方式的启发，让能杀死癌细胞的 T 细胞接受"缺氧训练"，提高它们的战斗力，给治疗癌症带来新思路。T 细胞是能杀死癌细胞的白细胞，魏茨曼科学研究所人员从老鼠身上提取 T 细胞，把它们一部分放在含氧量正常的环境中培养，把另一部分放在氧气浓度只有 1% 的环境中培养。之后把它们分别注入两组出现黑色素瘤的老鼠体内。在缺氧环境中培养的 T 细胞明显起到抑制肿瘤的作用。

来源：新华网

Scientists discovered a new way to treat cancer: improve human T cell fighting force

Athletes may go to high altitude training in order to improve stamina. Israeli scientists are inspired by this type of training and have new ideas for cancer treatment, which is said to allow T cells that kill cancer cells to undergo "hypoxia training" to improve the combat effectiveness. T cells are white blood cells that can kill cancer cells. Researchers from the Weizmann Institute of Science extracted T cells from mice, put part of them in a normal oxygen-conditioned environment, and put the other in an environment with only 1% oxygen concentration. And then they injected into two groups of mice with melanoma. T cells cultivated in hypoxia conditions clearly play a role in inhibiting tumorigenesis.

Source: xinhuanet. com

澳大利亚研究可能治疗青光眼的新方法

近日,根据澳大利亚一项最新研究,人体内天然存在的一种蛋白质能预防青光眼,但是这种蛋白质会因年龄增长和疾病等影响而减少,如果能找到让其持续存在的办法,有助开发出治疗青光眼的新方法。澳大利亚麦考里大学的维韦克·格普塔等人在英国学术刊物《科学报告》新一期上发表论文说,这种名为"神经源性丝氨酸蛋白酶抑制剂"的蛋白质对人类视网膜的健康至关重要,它可以调节视网膜中其他酶的活动状况,帮助预防青光眼。

来源:36氪

Australian studies may be used to treat glaucoma

According to a new study in Australia, a natural human protein can prevent glaucoma, but the number of the protein will decrease due to age increase, disease and other effects. If we can find a way to let it continue, then we can develop a new method for the treatment of glaucoma. Vivek Gupta of Macquarie University and other scientists published a paper in the UK academic journal *Science Report*, stating that the so-called "neurogenic serine protease inhibitors of protein" is essential to the health of human retina, which can regulate the activity of other enzymes in the retina to help prevent glaucoma.

Source:36kr

饮酒意愿与免疫系统有关

澳大利亚研究人员日前发现,大脑中的免疫系统与饮酒意愿有一定关联。阿德莱德大学一个研究团队在国际学术期刊《大脑、行为和免疫》上报告说,他们通过一种能阻断大脑免疫系统里某种特定反应的药物,"关闭"小鼠饮酒的动力。这表明大脑免疫系统和饮酒意愿之间存在关联。

来源:《中国科学报》

The brain's immune system holds key to thirst for alcohol

Australian researchers have found a link between the brain's immune system and the desire to drink alcohol.

A research team from the University of Adelaide published in the international academic journal *Brain, Behavior and Immunity* that they used a drug capable of blocking a specific reaction in the brain's immune system to "shut off" the motivation of mice to drink alcohol. This indicates that there is a link between the brain's immune system and the willingness to drink alcohol.

Source: *China Science Daily*

免疫细胞或治疗视网膜病变

澳大利亚莫纳什大学研究人员日前首次发现,眼部也存在免疫细胞。这一发现有望为早产儿视网膜病变、糖尿病视网膜病变等新生血管性视网膜病变提供新疗法。

莫纳什大学中央临床学院糖尿病系的研究人员发现,具有抗病功能的免疫细胞——调节性 T 细胞存在于人的视网膜中。研究人员之一、珍妮弗·威尔金森—贝尔卡教授说,眼睛和大脑一样有某种屏障,人们过去认为眼组织中不会有免疫细胞。她认为,这道屏障是有弱点的,可以让 T 细胞进入。

来源:《中国科学报》

Immune cells may hold key to retinopathy treatment

Scientists of Monash University in Australia have found for the first time the existence of immune cell in the eye. The findings hold potential for providing novel ways of treating retinopathy in prematurely born babies and the diabetic retinopathy.

Those scientists at the Central Clinical School's Department of Diabetes found that the regulatory T cells (Tregs)—disease-fighting white blood cells—are present in the retina. One of the researchers Professor Jennifer Wilkinson-Berka said that people thought there could not actually be Tregs in eye tissue because the eye, like the brain, has a barrier that stopped them from entering. But she believed "there might be a weakness in the barrier" that could allow the T cells to enter.

Source: *China Science Daily*

复旦发现抗 H7N9 禽流感强效全人源抗体

近日，复旦大学基础医学院医学分子病毒学教育部/卫生部重点实验室应天雷课题组，在 H7N9 禽流感药物研发方面取得重要进展，发现了可靶向 H7N9 禽流感病毒新表位的高活性抗病毒全人源抗体 m826。相关成果以《一种靶向 H7N9 流感血凝素 pH 敏感表位的强效全人源胚系单克隆抗体》为题，在线发表于《细胞》杂志子刊《细胞·宿主与微生物》上。

来源：上海科技

Fudan University discovers highly-effective and fully human H7N9 influenza antibody

Recently, a research team led by Ying Tianlei at the MOH/MOE Key Lab of Medical Molecular Virology School of Basic Medical Sciences of Fudan University made a significant progress in the R&D of drugs for H7N9 influenza, discovering an antiviral antibody m826 that targets new epitopes of the H7N9 avian influenza virus. Research findings have been published online in the journal *Cell Host & Microbe* with the title *A Potent Germline-like Human Monoclonal Antibody Targets a pH-Sensitive Epitope on H7N9 Influenza Hemagglutinin*.

Source: stcsm. gov. cn

源自人体细胞的肠道成功移植给大鼠

英国《自然·通讯》杂志近日发表了一项生物技术最新突破：美国科学家通过在特制支架上构建再生器官，成功向大鼠体内移植了源自人体细胞的、具有血管的肠移植物。这项成果意味着生物工程制造的功能性移植肠的未来前景光明。

来源：新华社

Intestinal tract derived from human cells is successfully transplanted to rats

A new study of a biotechnology breakthrough was published in the journal *Nature Communications*. Scientists of the United States regenerated an organ using a special stent and this organ with blood vessel derived from human cells was successfully transplanted to rats. This achievement means that there is a bright future for functional intestinal graft of organism manufacturing.

Source: Xinhua News Agency

新研究称人脑通过脑内淋巴管"排污"

通过扫描健康志愿者的大脑，美国科研人员日前发现，人脑通过淋巴管排泄代谢废物，这些淋巴管还可以充当大脑和免疫系统之间的运输管道。

意大利解剖学家曾在1816年报告在大脑表面发现淋巴管，但两个世纪后的研究人员并没有找到大脑中存在淋巴管的证据。因此医学界曾一度认为，大脑中是不存在淋巴系统的。

来源：新华社

New research suggests human brain drain some waste through lymphatic vessels

By scanning the brains of healthy volunteers, US researchers saw the first, long-sought evidence that our brains may drain some waste out through lymphatic vessels, the body's sewer system. The results further suggest the vessels could act as a pipeline between the brain and the immune system.

In 1816, an Italian anatomist reported finding lymphatic vessels on the surface of the brain. Until very recently, researchers in the modern era found no evidence of a lymphatic system in the brain. So, it was once thought in the medical world that the brain had no lymphatic system.

Source: Xinhua News Agency

我国在埃博拉病毒糖蛋白致病效应的研究中获进展

埃博拉病毒是目前已知的对人类最为致命的病毒之一，其致病机理尚不清楚。中国科学院武汉病毒研究所科研团队通过构建一系列腺病毒基因转移载体，系统地研究了埃博拉病毒包膜型糖蛋白在细胞以及小鼠模型中表达的致病效应。这意味着我国在埃博拉病毒糖蛋白致病效应及其实验模型的研究中取得的新进展。

来源：新华社

China made a progress in the research of pathogenic effect of Ebola virus glycoprotein

Ebola virus is one of the most fatal viruses to human in our current knowledge, whose pathogenic effect is still unclear. A research team from Wuhan Institute of Virology, Chinese Academy of Sciences systematically studied the pathogenic effect of Ebola virus glycoprotein expressed in cells and mouse models by building a series of adenovirus gene transfer vectors, which means China has made a new progress in the research of pathogenic effect and experimental models of Ebola virus glycoprotein.

Source: Xinhua News Agency

中国科学家发现肿瘤抑制因子新调控机制，为癌症靶向治疗提供新方向

中国科学家日前在肿瘤抑制因子调控机制研究领域取得新进展，首次发现一种转录因子的非剪切体对肿瘤抑制因子 p53 具有重要调控功能，为癌症靶向治疗提供了新的方向。相关研究成果已于北京时间 10 月 19 日在线发表在国际学术期刊《科学进展》上。

来源：新华网

New control mechanism of tumor suppressor discovered by Chinese scientists, pointing out a new way for targeted cancer therapy

Chinese scientists have recently achieved new progress in their research on the control mechanism of tumor suppressor. For the first time, they found a non-spliceosome of transcription factor that plays a key role in controlling the tumor suppressor p53, which points out a new way for targeted cancer therapy. The achievements have been published online in the international academic journal *Science Advances* on October 19 (Beijing Time).

Source: xinhuanet. com

我国首个重组埃博拉病毒病疫苗获新药注册批准

由我国独立研发、具有完全自主知识产权的创新性重组疫苗产品"重组埃博拉病毒病疫苗(腺病毒载体)"的新药注册申请近日获食药监总局批准。这是我国首个重组埃博拉病毒病疫苗获批注册。

来源：人民网

China approves its first Ebola vaccine

The China Food and Drug Administration (CFDA) recently approved the application for registration of an innovative recombinant vaccine product named recombinant Ebola virus disease vaccine (adenovirus vector), which was independently developed by China holding complete intellectual property rights. This is the first Ebola vaccine approved in China.

Source: people. cn

冬虫夏草抗癌性可能低于预期

虫草入药，在我国具有悠久的历史。67年前，虫草素的结构第一次被发现，这一成分后来被发现具有抗菌抗癌等生物活性，但其合成机理一直不为人们所知。日前，《细胞》子刊在线发表了中科院上海植物生理生态研究所王成树团队的最新研究成果。他们完整地解析了虫草素生物合成的分子机理，还首次发现蛹虫草能够合成具有抗癌活性的喷司他丁，这是虫草抗癌活性的首个证据。

与此同时，该研究还发现，人们所熟知的冬虫夏草其实并不能合成虫草素及喷司他丁。

来源：上海科技

The anti-cancer performance of cordyceps sinensis may be lower than expected

China has a long history in using cordyceps sinensis as a medicine. 67 years ago, the structure of cordycepin was found for the first time. Later, it was found to have bioactivities including antibacterial and anti-cancer activities. However, its synthesis mechanism was not known for a long time. Until recently, a new research result produced by the team led by Professor Wang Chengshu from Shanghai Institute of Plant Physiology and Ecology under Chinese Academy of Science (CAS) was published on the journal *Cell* online. The team analyzed the molecular mechanism of cordycepin biosynthesis and found out for the first time that cordyceps militaris could synthesize pentostatin with anti-cancer activity. Their finding is the first evidence suggesting that cordycepin has anti-cancer activity.

Meanwhile, the research revealed that the well-known cordyceps sinensis cannot synthesize cordycepin and pentostatin.

Source: stcsm. gov. cn

上海硅酸盐所等制备出 3D 打印仿生莲藕支架

近日，中国科学院上海硅酸盐研究所研究员吴成铁与常江带领的研究团队，在 3D 打印复杂结构生物陶瓷用于血管化大块骨缺损修复方面取得新进展。该研究团队受到自然界中莲藕内部平行多通道结构的启发，采用 3D 打印制备出仿生莲藕支架；并与上海交通大学附属第九人民医院蒋欣泉团队合作，进一步发现该类支架相对于传统 3D 打印支架，具有显著提高大块骨缺损的修复的能力。

来源：上海科技

Shanghai Institute of Ceramics developed a bionic lotus root stent using 3D printing technique

Recently, a research team headed by Wu Chengtie and Chang Jiang from Shanghai Institute of Ceramics of the Chinese Academy of Sciences made headway in applying the 3D printing technique using complex biological ceramics to repairing vascularized massive bone defects. Inspired by the unique structure of multiple parallel channels penetrating the lotus root, the team developed a bionic lotus root stent using the 3D printing technique. It also cooperated with a team headed by Jiang Xinquan from Shanghai Ninth People's Hospital of Shanghai Jiao Tong University in further finding that compared with traditional 3D printed stents, stents as such can significantly increase the ability to repair massive bone defects.

Source: stcsm. gov. cn

日本研发超级微型胶囊：可输送到人脑内部 药效或可放大 100 倍

近日，日本东京大学和东京医科齿科大学的科研小组使用氨基酸研发了一种直径仅有三万分之一毫米左右的超级微型胶囊。据报道，人脑除了成为营养源的葡萄糖等之外，血液中的物质几乎都无法进入其中，在治疗阿尔茨海默病等疾病方面，如何将药物输送到人脑内部一直是一个重大难题。而使用葡萄糖将这一胶囊的表面覆盖后，脑血管中的特定蛋白质与胶囊的葡萄糖相结合，从而可将胶囊输送到人脑内部。报道称，科研小组还注意到在空腹状态下特定蛋白质能积极地输送葡萄糖这一特点，并将胶囊用于空腹状态下的实验鼠时，成功地将胶囊输送到了鼠脑内部，其效果达到迄今为止药物的 100 倍左右。

来源：威锋网

Japan develops ultra small capsules that could be delivered to the brain with effects magnified by 100 times compared with usual capsules

Lately, research teams in Tokyo University and Tokyo Medical and Dental University has used amino acid to develop ultra small capsules with a diameter of about only one 30 000th millimeter. According to reports, other than glucose that serves as a source of nutrition, substances in the blood cannot enter human brain. Sending medicine inside the brain has always been a major issue in treating diseases like Alzheimer. Now, with glucose covering the surface of the capsule, specific proteins in brain veins can combine with the glucose in the capsules, thus delivering the medicine into the brain. Capsules have been successfully delivered into the brain of lab mice with an empty stomach, registering an effect that is about 100 times better than existed medicine.

Source: www. feng. com

新型人工氨基酸具有抗菌活性

英国《皇家学会开放科学》杂志近日刊登了一项人工氨基酸研究的最新成果:印度科学教育与研究院科学家合成出一种新型氨基酸,且这种氨基酸具有抗菌活性,能对抗包括革兰氏阳性菌、革兰氏阴性菌和霍乱弧菌等在内的多种细菌。

来源:《科技日报》

New artificial amino acid shows antibacterial activity

The *Royal Society Open Science* journal recently published the latest achievement regarding artificial amino acid: Scientists from the Indian Institutes of Science Education and Research developed a new type of amino acid that shows antibacterial activity. The amino acid can resist several types of bacteria, including Gram-positive bacteria, Gram-negative bacteria and Vibrio cholerae.

Source: *Science and Technology Daily*

癌症新认识：三分之二癌症主要源自 DNA 复制随机错误

近日，最新一项研究报告发表在《科学》杂志上，科学家基于数据证实了随机 DNA 复制错误对于癌症所起到的重要作用：28.9%癌症相关突变源于环境因素，5%源于遗传因素，66.1%源于 DNA 复制随机错误。科学家研究了全球69个国家17种类型癌症风险和正常干细胞分裂数量之间的关系，该数据揭示，无论环境怎样，癌症发病率和干细胞分裂之间具有较强的相关性。

来源：新浪科技

New understanding of cancer: 2/3 of cancers come from random DNA replication errors

According to a latest research report published in *Science*, scientists have recently proved based on data a key role played by random DNA replication in cancer: 28.9% of cancer-related mutations are caused by environmental factors; 5% are inherited; and the remaining 66.1% stem from random DNA replication errors. By studying the relations between 17 types of cancer risks in 69 countries and the total number of stem cell divisions, scientists discovered that there is a strong relativity between the incidence of cancer and stem cell division regardless environmental conditions.

Source: tech.sina.com.cn

全球超过 8 000 万人患有强迫症,相关人类基因变异已被找到

英国《自然·通讯》杂志近日在线发表的一篇遗传学论文报告称,科学家成功鉴别出与强迫症(OCD)相关的人类基因变异,找到了受这些变异影响的基因及神经通路。分离和表征这些基因,将帮助我们理解这种疾病背后的生物学原因,进而建立有效治疗方案。

来源:《科技日报》

Over 80 million OCD patients in the world: associated human genovariations identified

According to a paper on genetics published on the website of the English journal *Nature Communications*, scientists successfully identified human genovariations associated with OCD and hunted down genes and neural pathways affected by these variations. By identifying and expressing these genes, we will be able to understand the biological reasons of the disease and come up with effective therapeutic schedules.

Source: *Science and Technology Daily*

美国首次批准数字药丸:可助患者追踪药物摄入

美国监管机构日前批准了一款带有嵌入式传感器的数字药丸,可以追踪患者是否正确服用药物,标志着医疗保健和技术融合迈出了重要的一步。美国食品和药品监督管理局(FDA)表示,尽管数字药丸改善患者服药依从性的能力尚未得到证实,但追踪精神疾病药物的摄入可能对"某些患者"有用。患者服药依从性差是许多疾病领域的常见问题,特别是慢性病患者。

来源:环球网

US for the first time approves digital pills: helping track drug ingestion

US monitoring institutions recently approved a new kind of digital pill with inserted sensors, which can track whether patients correctly take drugs. This new product marks a key step in the integration of health care and technology. The US Food and Drug Administration (FDA) said, though the capability of digital pill to improve patients' drug compliance has not been proved, the tracking the ingestion of mental illness drugs may be helpful to "some patients". Bad drug compliance is a common issue among patients of a lot of illness, especially those with chronic diseases.

Source: huanqiu.com

哈医大参与世界首例人类头移植手术

备受争议的"头移植"手术又有了最新消息:英国《每日邮报》11月17日报道,意大利神经学家塞尔焦·卡纳韦罗当天在奥地利首都维也纳召开新闻发布会,宣布世界第一例人类头部移植手术已经在一具遗体上成功实施,而手术地点正是中国。卡纳韦罗说,中国哈尔滨医科大学的任晓平教授参与指导了这次手术。

来源:新华社

Harbin Medical University participated in world's first human head transplant surgery

The highly controversial "head transplant" surgery has new update. According to the report of the British newspaper *Daily Mail* on November 17, the Italian neurologist Professor Sergio Canavero announced at a press conference in Vienna that the world's first human head transplant had been successfully carried out on a corpse in China. And Professor Ren Xiaoping of China's Harbin Medical University participated in and directed the surgery.

Source: Xinhua News Agency

全球首例人体内基因编辑试验实施

美国《科学》杂志在线版近日报道了一项人类医疗史上的里程碑:科学家首次尝试在人体内直接进行基因编辑。他们向一名44岁的患者血液内注入了基因编辑工具,以永久性改变基因的方法来治愈严重遗传疾病。

来源:科学网

Scientists carried out world's first gene-editing trial inside of the human body

The online version of *Science* recently reported a milestone of human medical history: scientists for the first time have completed the editing of a gene inside of the human body. They infused a 44-year-old patient's blood with gene-editing tools in a bold attempt to permanently change his DNA to cure serious genetic diseases.

Source: ScienceNet. cn

早确诊早治疗,艾滋病患儿病死率可降低 76%

国际顶尖儿科杂志《美国医学会儿科杂志》近期在线发表了由中国疾病预防控制中心性病艾滋病预防控制中心治疗与关怀室副主任赵燕研究员完成的研究,结果显示,2011年到2015年期间,我国接受艾滋病抗病毒治疗的婴幼儿相较于未治疗的婴幼儿病死率减少76%。5年间,感染艾滋病病毒婴幼儿从诊断艾滋病病毒感染到启动抗病毒治疗,平均时间间隔从2011年的378天缩短到 2015 年的 45 天。

来源：人民网

Early diagnosis and treatment can reduce the fatality rate of HIV-infected babies by 76％

JAMA Pediatrics recently published the study of Researcher Zhao Yan, deputy director of the Treatment and Care office from National Center for AIDS/STD Control and Prevention, Chinese Center for Disease Control and Prevention. It is found out that from 2011 to 2015, infants in China who receive antiretroviral therapy (ART) are reported to have a fatality rate 76％ lower than those who do not. The average period from diagnosis to starting ART for HIV-affected infants was reduced from 378 days in 2011 to 45 days in 2015.

Source：people. cn

三种分子有助判断糖尿病风险

澳大利亚与美国科研人员的一项新研究发现，有三种分子可以用来检测实验鼠出现胰岛素抵抗的情况，从而判断其糖尿病患病风险。

科学家说，"C22:1 辅酶 A""乙酰肉碱"和"C16 神经酰胺"这三种与代谢有关的分子，是检测实验鼠胰岛素抵抗情况的最佳指标。将这三种分子结合起来考察，检测的准确率会更高。

来源：科学网

Three molecules help judge the risk of diabetes

A new study conducted by researchers from Australia and the US shows that three molecules can be used to detect insulin resistance in the body of lab rats so as to judge the risk of diabetes.

Scientists say C22:1 coenzyme A, acetylcarnitine, C16 ceramide are metabolism-related molecules. They are the best index to detect insulin resistance in lab rats. If these three molecules can be combined to use, the detecting accuracy will be improved.

Source: ScienceNet. cn

我国首批 CAR-T 细胞新药注册被受理,治疗肝癌和骨髓瘤

近日,我国首批 CAR-T 细胞抗癌新药注册被药品监管部门受理,标志着肿瘤免疫细胞疗法研发和管理进入一个新的阶段。这两个候选新药分别是科济生物医药(上海)有限公司申报的 CAR-GPC3T 细胞制剂、南京传奇生物科技有限公司申报的 LCAR-B38M 细胞制剂。前者治疗难治、复发的肝细胞癌,后者治疗多发性骨髓瘤,均于本月被受理,有望在政府部门监管下进入临床研究阶段。

来源:上海观察

China's first CAR-T cell anti-cancer drugs are accepted, to be used for treating liver cancers and myelomas

Recently, the registration of China's first CAR-T cell anti-cancer drugs have been accepted by competent drug regulatory authorities, marking a new stage in the development and management of tumor immune cell therapies. The two new candidate drugs are the CAR-GPC3T cell preparations applied by CARsgen Therapeutics and the LCAR-B38M cell preparations applied by Nanjing Legend Biotech, respectively. The former one treats obstinate and recurrent liver cancers, and the latter one treats multiple myelomas. The two drugs are expected to enter the clinical research stage under the supervision of competent government departments.

Source: Shanghai Observer

使用寿命更久，以色列用太空新材料置换人体关节

近日，以色列海法 Rambam 医疗中心发表声明称，医务人员成功地将由高分子聚合物构成的太空新材料 MP1 用于矫形外科手术中，代替人体关节，从而开创了关节替代新疗法。该新材料为以色列 M. M. A 技术初创公司的研究人员阿里扎·布赫曼（Aliza Buchman）与美国弗吉尼亚州的罗伯·布莱恩特合作研发，最初目的是帮助美国国家航空航天局在航天工业取代钢铁，但医学界很快认识到了其潜在价值。研发人员表示，高分子聚合物材料具有耐热性高、零磨损、强度高、重量轻的优点，这使其成为磨损关节的理想替代品。

来源：《科技日报》

Israel uses new aerospace material with longer service life to replace human joints

The Rambam Medical Center in Haifa of Israel recently announced that its medical staff had successfully utilized MP1, a new aerospace material composed of macro-molecular polymers, to replace human joints in orthopedic surgery, thus developing a new joint replacement therapy. The material, known as MP1, was developed by Aliza Buchman for the Israel start-up company M. M. A Tech, in collaboration with Rob Bryant of Virginia, US. It was intended to be used as a substitute for steel in the space industry for NASA, but the medical world also quickly realized its potential benefit. According to the developer, the advanced polymeric material has high heat resistance, zero wear, high strength and light weight, all of which make it ideal for replacing worn joints.

Source: *Science and Technology Daily*

我国甲肝疫苗获世卫组织预认证

据悉,北京科兴生物制品有限公司自主研发生产的国内首支甲型肝炎灭活疫苗——孩尔来福刚刚通过世界卫生组织(WHO)预认证。这意味着该产品可借助国际组织采购满足更多国家甲肝疫情防控的需要,同时也将加速该疫苗在世界各个国家和地区的准入。

来源:《科技日报》

China's hepatitis A vaccine gains WHO pre-qualification

It is reported that China's first hepatitis A inactivated vaccine Healive independently developed and produced by Sinovac Biotech Ltd has just passed WHO pre-qualification procedures. This means that the product can meet the needs of prevention and control of hepatitis A in more countries through procurement from international organizations and will also speed up the vaccine's access to all countries and regions in the world.

Source: *Science and Technology Daily*

美国首例CRISPR抗癌人体试验即将开展

据英国《自然》杂志网站、美国《麻省理工技术评论》网站近日消息称,美国宾夕法尼亚大学目前正在为CRISPR基因编辑技术抗癌的人类临床试验做最后阶段的准备,项目即将全面启动。这是美国使用CRISPR治疗癌症的首次尝试,标志着肿瘤治疗进入一个新时代,也打响了中美之间一场生物医学竞赛。

来源:《科技日报》

US first human CRISPR clinical trial to be conducted

According to the websites of the British journal *Nature* and the US journal *MIT Technology Review*, a research team from University of Pennsylvania is in the final steps of preparing for the first human CRISPR clinical trial. The team is now almost ready to begin their trial. This is the first trial in the US to combat cancers with CRISPR, marking a new era in cancer treatment, also sparking a biomedical competition between China and the US.

Source: *Science and Technology Daily*

浙大团队研究抑郁症获突破：找到快速抗抑郁靶点

浙江大学医学院和求是高等研究院胡海岚团队在抑郁症研究方面取得重大突破。近日，著名期刊《自然》杂志同期刊发该团队的两篇研究长文（Research Article）。文章揭示了快速抗抑郁分子的作用机制，推进了人类关于抑郁症发病机理的认知，并为研发新型抗抑郁药物提供了多个崭新的分子靶点。

来源：36氪

Zhejiang University makes breakthroughs in depression research: new rapid-acting antidepressant targets

The research team led by Hu Hailan from the School of Medicine and the Qiushi Academy for Advanced Studies at Zhejiang University has made major breakthroughs in depression research. Recently, the renowned *Nature* magazine published two research articles of the team in the same issue, unveiling the mechanism of rapid-acting antidepressant molecules, better informing us about the pathogenesis of depression, and providing multiple brand-new molecular targets for the R&D of new antidepressants.

Source: 36kr

中国科学家揭秘"激素引起肥胖"机理

记者近日从中国科学院上海生命科学研究院获悉,该院的郭非凡研究组发现了糖皮质激素通过大脑、引起肥胖的调控机制。相关论文新近在线发表于国际学术期刊《糖尿病》。

郭非凡研究员长期致力于寻找肥胖"脑管家"。此番寻找的是糖皮质激素的"肥胖结症"。糖皮质激素,是临床上使用最为广泛与有效的抗炎、抗休克药物和免疫抑制剂。这类药物虽然非常有效,但存在许多副作用,长期服用该药物的病人呈现肥胖症状,它的中枢调控机理此前不为人所知。

来源:中新网

Chinese scientists reveal the "hormone-induced obesity" mechanism

According to Shanghai Institutes for Biological Sciences, Chinese Academy of Sciences, a research team led by Guo Feifan found mechanism of glucocorticoid-induced fat mass gain through central nervous system. The results have been published online in *Diabetes*, an international journal.

Guo Feifan is committed to finding the reasons of obesity. This study aims to find the culprit of glucocorticoid-induced obesity. Glucocorticoids is widely used as an effective anti-inflammatory, anti-shock and immunosuppressive drugs in clinic settings. Although these drugs are very effective, they have many side effects. Long-term use of the drugs may lead to obesity while its implications on the central nervous system are poorly understood.

Source: chinanews.com

试管"迷你大脑"可用于研究脑褶皱

以色列魏兹曼科学院研究人员表示,他们找到了在试管中培育微型大脑的方法。这种微型大脑可以产生类似人脑的褶皱,研究它可为分析和医治小头症、癫痫和精神分裂症等疾病开辟新道路。

来源:中国科技网

Test-tube "mini-brains" used to study brain folds

Researchers from the Weizmann Institute of Science in the central Israeli city of Rehovot said that they have discovered a way to grow a miniature version of the human brain in a test tube that undergoes wrinkling in a similar way to a real brain. The researchers plan to continue developing their approach, in the belief that it could open new possibilities for understanding developmental disorders such as microcephaly, epilepsy and schizophrenia.

Source:stdaily.com

我国首创高效抑制乙肝病毒复制新药

杰华生物技术(青岛)有限公司近日宣布:其历时18年自主研发的一类新药乐复能已正式获得国家药品监督管理局颁发的一类新药证书和注册批件,批准其用于治疗慢性乙型肝炎。相较于现有药物,该药可更高效抑制乙肝病毒的复制。

来源:人民网

China launches "first-in-class" drug to battle chronic hepatitis B

Genova Biotech (Qingdao) Co,. Ltd. announced that its new pharmaceutical drug, Novaferon, was officially approved by National Medical Products Administration to treat hepatitis B and registered as the first-class new medicine. The drug, a novel recombinant protein injection, was the product of 18-year research and development of the company, which can more effectively inhibit virus replication.

Source: people. cn

俄研究用新方式改善基因疗法效果

如何使具有治疗作用的遗传物质顺利穿过靶细胞的内外膜,并且躲避细胞器的分解,是基因疗法成功与否的关键。近日,俄罗斯科研人员发现,用一种蛋白质制作"密封船"运送少量遗传物质,有望获得更佳疗效。俄联邦医学生物局下属莫斯科免疫研究所的专家日前在荷兰期刊《胶体与表面 B 辑:生物界面》上发表论文说,为探究上述转染效果的优劣,他们用氨基酸分子数不同且含有荧光物的胶原蛋白二胜肽、三胜肽、四胜肽,分别制成"密封船",并向其内部填充不同数量的小干扰 RNA,然后用这种复合体转染由人胚胎肾细胞衍生出的一种细胞。结果显示,三胜肽是最高效的材料,其转染效率是四胜肽脂质体的 20 倍。

来源:新华社

Russia conducts a research on improving the effect of gene therapy with a new method

It is key for gene therapy to make genetic materials with therapeutic action to pass through the inside and outside membranes of target cells while elude the decomposition of organelle. Recently, Russian researchers have discovered that it may have better therapy effect to produce "sealed vessel" with a protein to convey some genetic materials. Experts of Moscow Immune Research Institute, affiliated to Medical Biology Bureau of the Russian Federation Council, have published a paper on a Netherlands journal—Colloids and Surfaces B: Biointerfaces, and say that to explore the advantages and disadvantages of the effect of transfection, they have made "sealed vessels" from collagens dipeptide, tripeptide and tetrapeptide respectively with different numbers of amino acid molecules and with phosphor, and fill in them with different numbers of small interfering RNA, and use this complex to transfect the cell derived from human embryonic kidney cell. It shows that tripeptide is the most effective material whose transfection efficiency is 20 times that of tetrapeptide lipidosome.

Source: Xinhua News Agency

全球首创长效抗艾新药获批上市

近日,从前沿生物药业(南京)股份有限公司获悉,其自主研发的国家一类新药艾可宁(注射用艾博韦泰),获得国家药品监督管理局批准上市。艾可宁是全球第一个抗艾滋病长效融合抑制剂,由前沿生物完全自主研发,拥有全球原创知识产权。

来源:《经济观察报》

China launches world's first original long-acting anti-HIV drug

Albuvirtide (for injection), a new anti-HIV drug independently developed by Frontier Biotechnologies Inc. (Nanjing) has been accepted by National Medical Products Administration and entered the market. It is the world's long-acting HIV fusion inhibitor for treatment of HIV infection and AIDS, and is developed completely by Frontier Biotechnologies itself, which enjoys the intellectual property rights of the drug.

Source: *The Economic Observer*

T细胞免疫疗法成功应用于晚期乳癌

近日,英国《自然·医学》杂志在线发表了一项癌症学研究重磅进展:利用自身T细胞,美国一患者免疫系统调整后,完全彻底清除了乳腺癌细胞。这是T细胞免疫疗法首次成功应用于晚期乳腺癌,其也为所有常规治疗无效的晚期癌症提供了一种可能的治疗方法。这种方法在其他乳腺癌患者中获得成功的可能性较高。

来源:《科技日报》

T-cell immunotherapy succeeds in curing late-stage breast cancer

Recently, a woman in the United states has been completely cured of breast cancer after doctors tweaked her immune system with her own T-cells, enabling it to destroy the breast cancer cells. The treatment marks the first successful application of T-cell immunotherapy for late-stage breast cancer. It has the potential as a future treatment for cancers that have resisted all other forms of therapy. This treatment is probably effective for other breast cancer patients. The results of this work were published in the British journal *Nature Medicine*.

Source: *Science and Technology Daily*

复旦大学附属肿瘤医院"肺癌微创治疗3.0",创新理念获国际医学界认可

近日,被学界誉为外科学圣经的权威学术期刊《外科学年鉴》在"外科学展望"栏目中在线发表了复旦大学附属肿瘤医院肺癌研究团队在大量临床实践的基础上提出的关于"肺癌微创治疗3.0"概念的述评,为将来减少早期肺癌患者手术创伤的研究提供了新方向,也为今后世界各国在开展肺癌微创治疗时提供

了重要的理念和实践指导。

来源：大众医学网

"Minimally Invasive Thoracic Surgery 3.0", an innovative concept proposed by Fudan University Shanghai Cancer Center gains recognition from the international medical community

Recently, a review of the concept "Minimally Invasive Thoracic Surgery 3.0", produced by the lung cancer research team from Fudan University Shanghai Cancer Center, was published in *Annals of Surgery*, an authoritative medical journal hailed as the surgery bible, in its online column *Surgical Perspectives*. The article, which is based on massive clinical practices, not only points out a new direction for research in reducing the possibility of leaving scars to early-stage lung cancer patients, but also provides important theoretical and practical guidance for surgeons around the world to carry out minimally invasive surgeries in treating lung cancer.

Source: **popularmed. com**

3

航空篇

美海军研制新概念微型无人机集群,仅手掌大小

据物理学家组织网日前报道,美国海军研究实验室(NRL)一直在研究可堆叠微型无人机,其有效载荷可以自动配置网络后互相"联通"。实验室为其概念无人机取名"西卡德"(CICADA),意思是近距、隐蔽、自主、一次性使用的飞行器。该项目是五角大楼正在进行的使用无人机部署"先进技术群体行为"计划的一部分。国防系统的乔治·利奥波德说,美国海军正在推动研发先进技术,使这种小型无人机缩至手掌大小。

来源:《科技日报》

US Navy's new swarm of mini-drone concepts fits in the palm of a hand

According to a recent report by the PHYS. ORG, the U. S. Naval Research Laboratory(NRL) has long been developing an easily-stacked mini-drone, which with its payload can automatically access the Internet and stay connected. The drone was named CICADA, which stands for close-in, Covert, Autonomous, Disposable Aircraft. The project is part of Pentagon's efforts to carry out its Advanced Technology and Projects group plan. George Leopold from U. S. Defense Systems said that the U. S. Navy had worked for a long time on the palm-sized drone by promoting technology development.

Source: *Science and Technology Daily*

全球热浪或致飞机无法起飞

全球变暖导致的气温上升,将使得世界各地许多飞机在未来几十年里更加难以起飞。

这一结论来自最近一期《气候变化》杂志刊登的一篇研究报告。该报告指

出，在一天中最热的时候，10%到30%的满载飞机可能必须要清除一些燃料，减少一些货物或乘客，或者干脆等待气温降低之后才能正常起飞。

这份报告的首席作者、哥伦比亚大学博士生伊森·科菲尔表示："我们的研究结果表明，重量限制可能会让航空公司付出不容小觑的代价，并影响全球航空业务的发展。"

来源：科学网

Heat waves may disrupt airplanes' ability to take off

In the next few decades, the temperature rise caused by global warming will make it harder for airplanes around the world to take off.

This study appeared in a latest research report from *Climatic Change*. And it showed that 10%-30% of flights departing at the hottest time of a day would require some form of weight restriction, such as removal of some fuels, cargoes or passengers, or require the heat reduced to the normal level to take off.

"Our findings suggest weight restriction may cost the airlines a lot and affect the development of global aviation," said Ethan Coffel, the lead author of the research report and a doctoral student from Columbia University.

Source：ScienceNet. cn

国防科技大学学员打造防"黑飞"系统

近日，国防科技大学电子科学学院研究生学员研制的"对微型无人机被动探测与定位系统"，在第12届中国研究生电子设计竞赛全国总决赛中，一举获得团体特等奖。这款系统的独特之处，在于它能通过被动方式接收无人机遥控信号，对无人机及其操控者实施搜索、定位与跟踪，在电子地图上准确显示其位置，从而对无人机"黑飞"进行干扰、迫降或驱离，还能够搜寻到无人机操控者的位置，制止"黑飞"行为。

来源：科学网

Students in National University of Defense Technology developed an anti "black flight" system

Recently, "the passive detection and positioning system against micro unmanned air vehicles"(MUAV) developed by postgraduate students from National University of Defense Technology won the special team award in the national final of the 12th Chinese Postgraduate Electronic Design Competition. This system is special for it can receive the remote signals from MUAV by a passive way to search, locate and track MUAV and its operators and correctly mark the positions on electrical maps to interrupt, make crash landing of or expel "black flights" of MUAV, so as to stop "black flights".

Source: ScienceNet. cn

中国推首架商业两栖无人机 续航能超 2 000 公里

中国一家公司最近推出了一款新型两栖无人机,不仅能够在陆地上使用,还能够在海上使用。据该公司宣称,预计今年年底就能够从市场上买得到这款无人机。这架无人机被称为 U650,机身长度 5.85 米,翼展达到 12.4 米。据介绍,它的飞行范围超过 2000 公里,但是沉重的负载可能会缩短它的飞行范围。这架无人机在空中的飞行时间能够达到 15 小时以上,它完全由碳纤维打造,整机重量大约在 750 公斤,飞行速度能够达到 180 公里每小时。这款两栖无人机既可以民用也可以商用。

来源:网易科技

Cruising ability of China's first commercial amphibious drone exceeds 2 000 kilometers

A Chinese company has recently launched a new amphibious drone that can be used on land and at sea. According to the company, the drone is expected to be available on the market by the end of this year. The drone, known as the U650, is 5.85 meters long and has a wingspan of 12.4 meters. It is said to fly more than 2 000 kilometers, but the heavy loads may shorten its flight range. The drone, which can fly for more than 15 hours in the air, is made entirely of carbon fiber, weighing about 750 kilograms and flying at a speed of 180 kilometers per hour. The amphibious drone can be used for both civilian and commercial use.

Source: tech.163.com

法赛峰集团推出蛋形新发动机,颠覆传统飞机引擎设计

近日,法国航空发动机制造商赛峰集团展示了一款最新的发动机原型设计,并且声称它将在2030年之前装配到飞机上。这款开式转子发动机设计是在欧盟的支持下研发的,而且在法国马赛附近的一座基地建造了专门的设施进行测试。发动机的外形就像一枚细长的蛋,其背部有两排刀片,它的目标是比目前传统涡轮风扇发动机的燃耗降低15%。

来源:网易科技

French Safran Group launches new egg-shaped engine that subverts conventional aircraft engine design

Recently, Safran Group, the French aircraft engine manufacturer, has unveiled a new engine prototype design, and claimed that it would be assembled on the plane by 2030. The design of the open-rotor engine was developed under the auspices of the European Union, and a special facility was built for its testing at a base near Marseille, France. The engine is shaped like an elongated egg with two rows of blades on its back, and the goal is to cut fuel consumption by 15% compared with the current conventional turbo engine.

Source: tech.163.com

4

核能篇

我国核电重大专项取得标志性成果

"目前AP1000引进消化吸收基本完成,依托项目首台机组的热试主体工作已经完成,装料在即。CAP1400设计通过审查,关键试验全部完成,具备开工建设条件。高温气冷堆大部分主设备已安装就位,即将进入调试阶段。"在8月31日举办的大型先进压水堆和高温气冷堆国家科技重大专项新闻发布会上,核电重大专项管理实施办公室负责人、国家能源局核电司副司长秦志军介绍。

来源:新华社

China's nuclear power national major project achieves significant progress

"The introduction and adaption of AP1000 has now almost completed. The first unit of the project will soon be charged since the major work of its hot test has finished. The design of CAP1400 has been approved and all of its key tests have also been accomplished, so the project is ready to be put into construction. The main body of the High Temperature Gas-cooled Reactor (HTGR) has been installed and put into position, and its adjustment will soon begin." introduced Qin Zhijun, Director of the Nuclear Power Major Project Management and Implementation Office and Deputy Director of National Energy Administration Nuclear Power Department, in the press conference of the large advanced pressurized water reactor and high temperature gas-cooled reactor of National Science and Technology Major Project on August 31.

Source:Xinhua News Agency

日获取锆93核散裂反应基础数据

一个由日本九州大学、理化学研究所等机构49位科学家组成的联合研究小组，利用重离子加速器"RI 射束工厂"（RIBF），提取放射性核素锆 93（93Zr，原子序号 40、质量数 93、半衰期 153 万年）的不稳定核束，首次成功获取了其核散裂反应的基础数据。他们所采用的核转变新方法有助于降低核废料放射性并实现资源回收再利用。

来源：人民网

Japan obtains basic data of zirconium 93 spallation

A research group of 49 scientists from the Kyushu University, the Institute of Physical and Chemical Research and other Japanese institutes successfully obtained the basic data of radionuclide zirconium 93 (atomic number 40, mass number 93, half-life of 1.53 million years) for the first time by extracting the unstable nuclear beam of zirconium 93 with the heavy ion accelerator "RI Beam Factory" (RIBF). The new approach to nuclear transformation contributes to reducing the radioactivity of nuclear waste and recycling resources.

Source: people. cn

"华龙一号"全球首堆即将安装最大主设备

十九大代表、中核集团中国核动力研究设计院研究员王广金日前表示，"华龙一号"全球首堆示范工程——福清核电 5 号机组首台 ZH-65 型蒸汽发生器近日已运抵核电站自备码头，将择期安装。这是我国首个具有完全自主知识产权的蒸汽发生器，标志着我国已基本突破三代核电主设备设计、制造技术和工艺。

来源：《科技日报》

"HRP1000" to employ the largest primary device

Wang Guangjin, deputy to 19th CPC National Congress and researcher of

Nuclear Power Institute of China in China National Nuclear Corporation, once said, "HRP1000", the first demonstration nuclear power project—unit 5 in Fuqing nuclear power plant will install the first ZH-65 Vapor Generator on a selected day which have already arrived the plant-owned docks. This is the first vapor generator in China boasting completely independent intellectual property rights, which marks the general breakthrough in design, manufacturing technology and craft of the 3rd-generation nuclear power primary device.

Source: *Science and Technology Daily*

中国三代核电技术华龙一号完成英国第一阶段设计审查

11月16日,中国广核集团及其合作伙伴法国电力集团(EDF)发表声明称,英国核能监管办公室(ONR)和英国环境署(EA)当天发布联合声明,宣布华龙一号在英国的通用设计审查(GDA)第一阶段工作已经完成,正式进入第二阶段。

来源:新浪科技

China's third generation nuclear power technology Hualong One receives its first phase of GDA in the UK

On November 16, China General Nuclear Power Corporation (CGN) and its partner Électricité de France (EDF) announced that the UK Office for Nuclear Regulation (ONR) and the Environment Agency (EA) released a joint statement on the day that the first phase of the generic design assessment (GDA) of Hualong One in the UK had been completed and the second phase of its GDA had been officially launched.

Source: tech.sina.com.cn

科学家呼吁美国支持 ITER 项目

美国国家科学、工程和医学院日前警告说,美国在核聚变研究方面远远落后于世界水平,因此不应该放弃遭到该国众多议员反对的一项重大国际项目。

美国国家科学、工程和医学院在一份报告中指出,将资金从该项目中抽走将使美国科学家遭到孤立,同时给其他国家带来优势。该报告要求美国在资金有限的情况下重新绘制核聚变项目。

这一争论的焦点是美国参与的国际热核聚变反应堆(ITER)计划,即在法国建造的一个有 35 个国家参与的项目,目的是开发全世界第一个长期保持核聚变的装置。

来源:《中国科学报》

Experts called for the US to support ITER project

The United States was lagging far behind the world on fusion research and shouldn't abandon a major international project opposed by key senators, the National Academies of Sciences, Engineering and Medicine warned today.

Pulling money from the project would isolate U.S. scientists, give other countries an advantage and require the U.S. to redraw its fusion program at a time funding was limited, the National Academies report said.

At issue is U.S. participation in the International Thermonuclear Experimental Reactor, or ITER, a 35-nation project being built in France to develop the first device to maintain fusion for long periods of time.

Source: *China Science Daily*

俄科学家研制出基于镍-63 的大容量核电池,续航可超百年

近日由莫斯科物理技术学院、超硬和新型碳材料技术研究所及国家科学技

术大学 MISIS 联合开发的新式核电池,采用了基于镍-63 的设计,该放射性同位素的半衰期超过了 100 年。考虑到镍-63 的半衰期,该核电池拥有 3 300 mWh/g 的能量密度,是传统化学电池的 10 倍以上。

来源:36 氪

Russian scientists develop a high-capacity nuclear battery based on nickel-63 with a battery life of over 100 years

Recently, Moscow Institute of Physics and Technology (MIPT), the Technological Institute for Superhard and Novel Carbon Materials (TISNCM), and the National University of Science and Technology MISIS jointly developed a new nuclear battery based on nickel-63. The radioactive isotope has a half-life period of over 100 years. Considering of the half-life period of nickel-63, the nuclear battery has an energy density of 3 300mWh/g, which is 10 times higher than that of traditional chemical battery.

Source:36kr

钍能为下一代核反应堆提供动力

据《新科学家》杂志官网 8 月 27 日消息,荷兰核研究所近日进行了下一代熔盐核反应堆的第一次实验,这是半个世纪以来的首次实验,在探索钍燃料为下一代核反应堆提供动力的路上迈出了重要一步。

来源:人民网

Thorium could power the next generation of nuclear reactors

According to the report of newscientist.com on August 27, a Dutch nuclear research institute has just fired up the first experiment in nearly half a century on next-generation molten-salt nuclear reactors based on thorium, which is an important step in the exploration of using Thorium as power of next-generation nuclear reactors.

Source: people. cn

5

海洋篇

我国将建国家海底科学观测网

海底科学观测网是人类建立的第三种地球科学观测平台,通过它人类可以深入到海洋内部观测和认识海洋。目前,北美、西欧和日本等十几个国家都已经拥有海底观测网。日前,我国国家海底科学观测网正式被批复建立。

国家海底科学观测网是国家重大科技基础设施建设项目,将在我国东海和南海分别建立海底观测系统,实现中国东海和南海从海底向海面的全天候、实时和高分辨率的多界面立体综合观测,为深入认识东海和南海海洋环境提供长期连续观测数据和原位科学实验平台。

来源:中国网络电视台

China will build its ocean-floor scientific observation network

The Ocean-floor Scientific Observation Network, as one of the three Earth Observation Network founded by human beings, enables human to go deep into the sea, thus to observe and explore the sea. Up to now, over a dozen of countries have established their own ocean observation networks, including North America, Western Europe and Japan. Now, China is about to establish its own ocean observation network.

As a major scientific project of China's infrastructure construction, the Ocean-floor observation network will build the ocean-floor observation systems in both the East and South China Sea, where the system will offer a 24-hour real-time observation with high resolution, on multi-interfaces. This system will provide long-term continuous data and in-situ experiment platforms which will help us to gain insight into the environment of the two seas.

Source:CNTV. com

我国首次成功试航北极西北航道

近日,搭乘我国第八次北极科学考察队的"雪龙"号成功完成我国船舶北极西北航道首次试航。至此,"雪龙"号实现在北极三大航道(东北航道、西北航道、中央航道)的首次穿越,将直接推动我国船舶对北极航道的商业利用。

来源:《科技日报》

China's first successful trial voyage on Northwest Passage of North Pole

Recently, the 8th Chinese National Arctic Research Expedition successfully completed China's first ship trial in the Arctic Northwest Passage aboard "Xue Long". So far, "Xue Long" firstly finished its trial voyages through all three passages in the North Pole (Northeast Passage, Northwest Passage, Middle Passage), which directly promotes the commercial exploitation of North Pole passages by China's ships.

Source: *Science and Technology Daily*

箱形水母或将摧毁未来海洋

随着海洋变得愈发酸化,箱形水母可能开始吃更多东西。而它们贪婪的食欲会对海洋生态系统产生巨大影响。相关成果日前发表于《全球变化生物学》杂志。

科学家表示,海水酸化和箱形水母均减少了桡足类动物的数量,但两者共同导致的浮游动物死亡数量比单独导致的死亡数量之和多27%。其中,箱形水母会吃得更多:它们吞食了含有普通海水的水箱中近37%的桡足类动物,但在酸化海水中,这一比例达到近83%。

来源:科学网

Box jellyfish may destroy oceans in the future

As oceans become increasingly acidified, box jellyfish may start eating more and their voracious appetite will have a huge impact on marine ecosystem. The relevant research findings have been published in *Global Change Biology*.

Scientists said ocean acidification and box jellyfish have reduced the number of copepods, but the number of phytoplankton deaths jointly caused by them is 27% greater than the total number of deaths caused by them respectively. Box jellyfish eat more: they eat nearly 37% of copepods in tanks containing ordinary seawater, but in acidified seawater, the rate reaches nearly 83%.

Source: ScienceNet. cn

中国首艘载人潜水器支持母船"深海一号"开建

9月16日,我国首艘载人潜水器支持母船"深海一号"在武汉开工建造,这意味着"蛟龙号"载人潜水器将告别"向阳红09"船,迎来自己的专用支持母船。国家海洋局副局长孙书贤在开工仪式上表示:"'深海一号'建成后,将充分发挥'蛟龙号'的技术性能,大大提高我国深海精细调查能力,我国深海科考又添一国之利器。"

来源:中新网

China started to build Shenhai-1, the first mother ship for its manned submersibles

On September 16, China started to build its first mother ship for its manned submersibles in Wuhan, Hubei province. China's manned submersible Jiaolong, currently based on the Xiangyanghong 09, will have its own mother ship. At the kick-off ceremony, Sun Shuxian, Deputy Director of the State Oceanic Administration, addressed, "after its completion, Shenhai-1 will fully unleash the technical potential of Jiaolong, greatly boost China's capabilities in deep sea exploration and assist China in deep sea scientific expedition."

Source: chinanews. com

中俄海洋与气候联合研究中心成立

近日,中国国家海洋局第一海洋研究所-俄罗斯太平洋海洋研究所海洋与气候联合研究中心(以下简称"中俄海洋与气候联合研究中心")在俄罗斯符拉迪沃斯托克挂牌成立。该中心是中俄两国在科技创新合作不断加深背景下成立的第一个海洋科学研究领域的合作平台,标志着中俄海洋科技领域的合作进入新的阶段。

来源:科学网

Sino-Russian Joint Ocean and Climate Research Center established

Recently, the First Institute of Oceanography (FIO) of State Oceanic Administration (SOA) cooperated with the Pacific Ocean Research Institute of Russian Academy of Sciences to found the Sino-Russian Joint Ocean and Climate Research Center in Vladivostok. It was the first cooperation platform on oceanography between China and Russian in the context of their deepening relationship in the area of technological innovation, marking a new stage for cooperation in marine technologies between the two countries.

Source: ScienceNet. cn

我国首套 6 000 米级遥控潜水器创下潜纪录

日前,由中国科学院战略性先导科技专项"热带西太平洋海洋系统物质能量交换及其影响"支持,中科院沈阳自动化研究所主持,联合中科院海洋研究所共同研制的深海科考型遥控潜水器(ROV)圆满完成首次深海试验,顺利停靠惠州码头。

来源:中科院网站

China's first set of ROV of 6 000-meters breaks record

Recently, a remotely operated underwater vehicle (ROV) berthed in Huizhou port smoothly and successfully completed the deep sea trials for the first time, which was supported by strategic leading technology special project named "tropical western Pacific ocean system material energy exchange and influence" of Chinese Academy of Sciences, presided by the Shenyang Institute of Automation of CAS and jointly developed by Institute of Oceanology of CAS.

Source: www.cas.cn

"向阳红 01"船在南大西洋获取海底热液硫化物

当地时间 10 月 23 日晚,正执行中国首次环球海洋综合科考暨中国大洋 46 航次科考的"向阳红 01"船在南大西洋成功获取了海底热液硫化物。

大西洋航段首席科学家助理李兵表示,目前国际上对北大西洋中脊的研究已相对成熟,而对南大西洋中脊热液活动情况的研究尚在探索中。

来源:新华社

XIANG YANG HONG 01 gets submarine hydrothermal sulfide on the South Atlantic Ocean

XIANG YANG HONG 01 successfully obtained submarine hydrothermal sulfide on the South Atlantic Ocean on the night of October 23rd local time when it was carrying out China's first marine integrated scientific expedition and China's 46th marine voyage for scientific expedition.

Li Bing, assistant to the Chief Scientist of the Atlantic Ocean segment, said that the international research on the North Mid-Atlantic Ridge has been relatively mature while the study on the activities of the hydrothermal fluid along the South Mid-Atlantic Ridge is still under exploration.

Source: Xinhua News Agency

中国大洋45航次科考作业收官

随着科考队员近日将在5 200多米海底成功取样的箱式取样器回收至"向阳红03"科学考察船甲板,中国大洋45航次第三航段科考作业顺利收官,这也意味着大洋45航次的科考任务全部完成。目前,"向阳红03"船已驶离作业海域,踏上回国之路。

第三航段首席科学家黄浩说,第三航段大洋调查面广点多,取得了多项科考成果,包括首次在中东太平洋北纬10度断面开展多要素全方位调查,进一步深化区域生物多样性地理分布及其对全球变化响应的认识。

来源:新华社

China's 45th oceanic science expedition successfully concluded

China's scientific expedition researchers retrieved onto the deck of China's marine research vessel Xiangyanghong 03 the sampling boxes that had succeeded in collecting samples in more than 5 200 meters under the sea, marking the success completion of the 3rd part of the 45th expedition and also all the tasks planned for the journey. Now, Xiangyanghong 03, China's marine research vessel, had already left its operating sea, and was heading back home.

Huang Hao, the Chief Scientist of this 3rd part of the expedition said that this journey covered a wide range of targeted oceanic research areas and had obtained numerous scientific achievements, including the first multi-faceted research on the fracture located at 10th degree of Northern Latitude in the Middle East part of the Pacific Ocean, furthering the knowledge about the geographic distribution of biodiversity in the region and how it would impact on global change response.

Source: Xinhua News Agency

中国研制出水下永动机器人,将用于全球海洋观测

日前,我国研制出国内首个深海型海洋温差自供能漂流浮标样机,在理论上实现了"水下永动机器人"。其整体技术处于国际领先水平,将用于全球海洋观测计划(Argo 计划)。

Argo 计划旨在快速、准确、大范围收集全球海洋上层(从海面到 2 000 米深度)的海水剖面资料。该计划构想在全球大洋中每隔 3 个经纬度布放一个浮标,由数千个浮标组成庞大的海洋观测网,测量海水温度、盐度、压力等。

来源:《科技日报》

China developed underwater "perpetual motion robot" for Argo

China has recently developed a prototype for its fist deep-sea ocean thermal energy self-supply drifting float, an "underwater motion robot" with theoretically perpetual motion. Using the world's leading technologies, this robot is set to be applied in Array for Real-Time Geostrophic Oceanography (Argo).

Argo aims to quickly and accurately collect profiling data on the upper 2 000 m of the ocean in large scale. It plans to deploy several thousand of floats on an every 3° latitude × 3° longitude basis to form a vast ocean observing network, measuring the ocean's temperature, sanity, pressure, etc.

Source: *Science and Technology Daily*

中国大洋 49 航次科考完成首个站位作业

中国大洋 49 航次科考队 12 月 22 日抵达印度洋 90 度海岭中部以东的海域，成功完成本航次业务化工作的首个站位作业，即海气通量观测的第一站，布放投弃式气象漂流浮标和测波浮标各两套。

中国大洋协会相关负责人表示，这是我国首次在印度洋投放该类型的浮标，是我国在印度洋进行深远海海气界面环境观测保障及海气通量研究业务化工作的开端。

来源：新华社

COMRA's 49th ocean voyage for scientific research garners preliminary success

A group of scientific researchers with China Ocean Mineral Resources R&D Association (COMRA) reached the east of central Indian Ocean's ninety east ridge on Dec. 22, 2017, bringing an end to their first stage mission of fitting two sets of expendable meteorological drifting buoys and wave measuring buoy at the first leg of air-sea surface flux observations.

According to COMRA, this was the first time that China had successfully dropped buoys of this kind into the Indian Ocean, marking the beginning of China's work on environmental observation and sea air flux research in the deep sea of the India Ocean.

Source: Xinhua News Agency

国内首套万米全水深声学观测潜标实验成功

近日,由西北工业大学研制的国内首套万米全水深声学观测潜标在马里亚纳海沟挑战者深渊实验成功。此次实验由西工大航海学院海洋观测与探测技术研究团队牵头,与中国海洋大学、中国科学院声学研究所和国家海洋局第一海洋研究所合作,完成了万米全水深声学潜标的设计、研发、测试以及马里亚纳海沟声学观测实验方案的设计论证。

来源:中国新闻网

China's first 10 000-meter full-depth acoustic observation submersible buoy successfully tested

China's first 10 000-meter full-depth acoustic observation submersible buoy developed by Northwestern Polytechnical University was successfully tested recently in Challenger Deep, in the southern end of the Mariana Trench. The test was led by a team studying ocean observation and detection technologies from Northwestern Polytechnical University, in cooperation with Ocean University of China, the Institute of Acoustics of the Chinese Academy of Sciences and the First Institute of Oceanography of State Oceanic Administration. The design, R&D, testing of the 10 000-meter full-depth acoustic observation submersible buoy as well as the observation and experiment scheme in Mariana Trench have all been successfully conducted.

Source: chinanews.com

"向阳红01"船南极科考创下多项"第一"

"向阳红01"船圆满完成中国第34次南极考察暨中国首次环球海洋综合科考南极航段科考任务,抵达智利蓬塔港,海上考察历时46天,并创下多项"第一"。

本次南极科考中,"向阳红01"船主要在南极大西洋扇区进行了物理海洋与气象、海洋地质、海洋地球物理、海底地形与测绘、海洋化学与生物生态、海洋环境等学科的综合调查,超额完成计划任务。

来源:新华社

Science ship Xiangyanghong 01 makes unprecedented achievements in Antarctica

Xiangyanghong 01 successfully completed its scientific mission in Antarctica and arrived at the Port of Punta Arenas in Chile. It was China's 34th Antarctic expedition and a part of China's first maritime research expedition that integrates oceanic and polar research, and Xiangyanghong 01 has made many unprecedented achievements.

The ship overfulfilled its task during the 46-day mission. It conducted comprehensive surveys in the Atlantic sector of the Antarctica in various fields, including physical oceanography, meteorology, marine geology and geophysics, seabed topography and mapping, marine chemistry and ecology as well as marine environment.

Source: Xinhua News Agency

南海舰队:近距反击,舰艇一对一"搏击"

2月27日,从东印度洋驶入西太平洋的南海舰队远海训练编队展开了近距反击课目演练。演练开始后,扮演红方的导弹驱逐舰长沙舰率先发现了扮演蓝方的导弹护卫舰衡阳舰。长沙舰随即拉响战斗警报,雷达发现目标后迅速锁定。而衡阳舰突然高速机动,并利用主炮向长沙舰实施近距攻击。

来源:中国科技网

South China Sea Fleet: close counterattack and one-to-one warship "fight"

On February 27, the far-sea training formation of the South China Sea Fleet entered the West Pacific from the East Indian Ocean and conducted a close-range counterattack drill.

After the commencement of the drill, the missile destroyer "Changsha" which played the role of the red team spotted the missile frigate "Hengyang" which played the role of the blue team. Shortly after, "Changsha" raised the alarm, and the radar quickly locked the target after locating it. "Hengyang", on the other hand, used a high-speed maneuver and implemented a close-range attack upon "Changsha" by using the main armament.

Source: stdaily.com

潜龙三号完成南海航段最后一潜,两大突破成亮点

4月28日4时38分,"潜龙三号"在夜色中回到"大洋一号"母船甲板,顺利完成其试验性应用第二潜。航行38小时、航程121.3公里,这也是"潜龙三号"在"大洋一号"船综合海试B航段的第四潜和最后一潜。作为我国最先进的自主潜水器,"潜龙三号"此前完成了两个海上试验潜次,并在南海北部陆坡东沙西南海域完成了试验性应用第一潜。

来源:中新网

China's unmanned underwater vehicle Qianlong III completed its final dive into the South China Sea with two breakthroughs

At 4:38 a.m. on April 28, Qianlong III, an underwater drone, returned to the deck of its mother ship, Ocean No. 1, at night, thus successfully completing its second test dive. The submersible traveled a distance of approximately 75.4 miles during its 38-hour voyage. This was also Qianlong III's fourth and last test dive in the route where Ocean No. 1 was conducting its sea trial. As China's most advanced autonomous underwater vehicle, Qianlong III had previously completed two test dives, and also dived for the first time in the southeastern sea areas close to the Pratas Islands.

Source: chinanews.com

6

宇航篇

谷歌创始人打造世界最大飞船

据英国《每日邮报》5月26日报道,谷歌联合创始人谢尔盖·布林(Sergey Brin)正秘密打造世界上最大的飞船,长约200米,花费约1亿—1.5亿美元(约合人民币6.85亿—10.28亿元)。这艘飞船目前在硅谷NASA埃姆斯研究中心的2号飞机库中,占了飞机库的大部分空间。这艘飞船将有内部气囊,其中的氦气可产生浮力,且可以降落在任何地方。

来源:网易科技

Google founder is building the world's largest airship

According to *Daily Mail* on May 26, Google co-founder Sergey Brin has been secretly building the largest airship in the world. It is 200 meters long and costs about $100 to 150 million (equivalent to RMB 685 million to 1.028 billion). Now the craft is being built in Hanger 2 at the NASA Ames Research Center in Silicon Valley, taking up much of its space. It will be equipped with internal airbags filled with helium to produce the buoyancy, and can land anywhere.

Source:tech.163.com

美国首次启动接触太阳计划,将发射探测器观测日冕

美国宇航局宣布,计划于2018年向人类既熟悉又陌生的星球——太阳发射一个探测器;将在距离太阳表面650万公里的外大气层轨道,观测日冕的活动。这将是NASA第一个飞入日冕的探测器,也是人类首次近距离接触太阳。

来源:环球网

NASA's first mission to the sun: it is building a probe to 'touch the sun' in 2018

NASA's Parker Solar Probe will explore the atmosphere of the sun, a star that humans know only little, in a mission that begins in 2018. This is NASA's first mission to the sun and its outermost atmosphere, called the corona. The probe will come as close as 4 million miles (6.5 million kilometers) from the star's fiery surface.

Source: huanqiu.com

俄媒称中俄将签太空合作计划:中国有专长有资源

8月5日俄媒报道称,中俄两国将在秋季签署2018年—2022年的航天合作计划,包括月球研究和地球遥感探测领域的合作事宜。俄航天技术设备总公司宣布了这一消息。

该公司代表解释说,与中国伙伴的合作将包括如下领域:月球和外层空间研究、航天器和地面基础设施、元器件库和材料、地球遥感探测数据等。俄航天技术设备总公司和中方商业伙伴还将研究在国际空间站进行实验、从俄罗斯航天器传输地球遥感探测数据的问题。

来源:参考消息网

Russian media claims China and Russia are set to sign space cooperation program: China has the know-how and the resources

A Russian media reported on August 5 that China and Russia will sign an aerospace cooperation program covering research on the moon and terrestrial remote sensing. The headquarters of Russia's Aerospace Technology Equipment Company announced this news.

According to representatives of the company, cooperation between the two countries will cover researches on Moon and outer space, spacecraft and ground infrastructure, component banks and materials, and terrestrial remote sensing data, etc. The company and its Chinese partners will also conduct researches on issues such as performing experiments on the International Space Station and transmitting terrestrial remote sensing data from Russian spacecraft.

Source: cankaoxiaoxi. com

时速 112 公里！NASA 首次展示人类第一辆火星卡车

NASA 近日在佛罗里达州首次公开展示了可能用于未来载人火星登陆的太空卡车概念车。

这种卡车的外观相当科幻,有些类似地球上的全地形车,车轮采用了特殊的支撑结构设计,无需考虑地球与外星球的大气压力差。据介绍,这种火星卡车重量为 2 286 公斤,长 8.5 米,最高时速高达 112 公里。能够在火星上实现物资快速运输。

来源：环球网

NASA Exhibits First-Ever Space Truck for Mars Landing

Recently, NASA exhibited for the first time a prototype space truck in Florida that may be used for manned Mars landing in the future.

The truck looks quite imaginary, somewhat similar to all-terrain vehicles on earth. Its wheels are based on a special support structure, which makes you free from worry about the atmospheric pressure difference between the earth and the outer planet. According to reports, the truck is 2 286 kilograms in weight, 8.5 meters long, and its maximum speed is up to 112 kilometers. It may be able to transport materials rapidly on Mars.

Source: huanqiu.com

SpaceX 成功发射美空军无人太空飞机

9月7日，SpaceX 成功发射美国空军的实验用无人太空飞机 X-37B，标志着 SpaceX 成为除联合发射联盟以外，首家完成该任务的发射服务提供商。此次成功发射对于 SpaceX 来说，一大重要意义在于，有助于其将来获得更多来自美国国防部门的订单。

来源：环球网

SpaceX successfully launches the autonomous space drone of U.S. Air Force

On September 7, SpaceX successfully launched the X-37B, the autonomous space drone of U.S. Air Force. SpaceX thus become the second launch services supplier apart from United Launch Alliance that successfully fulfilled this task. This success is quite meaningful to the company because it may help SpaceX win more orders from US departments of national defense.

Source: huanqiu.com

科学家预测：至 2040 年或会有 100 人入住月球

欧洲科学家描绘出月球殖民的景象——2040 年之前，将会有 100 人住在月球，融冰为水、用 3D 打印建造房子与工具、吃着用月球土壤种出的植物和从事低重力、"会飞"的运动。

来源：人民网

Scientists predict: 100 people could live on the moon by 2040

A European scientist pictures out a future when moon is inhabited by human. By 2040, a hundred people will live on the Moon, melting ice for water, 3D-printing homes and tools, eating plants grown in lunar soil, and competing in low-gravity, 'flying' sports.

Source: people. cn

美国国家航空航天局:计划 2033 年抵达火星轨道

美国国家航空航天局官员近日在第 68 届国际宇航大会上透露,依托现有国际空间站,该机构的深空探索计划将分三步走,到 2033 年前后抵达火星轨道。

来源:新华网

NASA plans to reach Mars orbit in 2033

NASA officials recently said at the 68th International Astronautical Congress that the agency's deep space exploration program will be divided into three steps to reach the Martian orbit by 2033 by relying on the existing International Space Station.

Source: xinhuanet. com

中国计划 2030 年去火星采样

十九大代表、中国航天科技集团公司八院院长代守仑 10 月 20 日透露,我国计划在 2030 年前后实施火星采样返回、小行星探测、木星系探测等方案。

来源:《经济参考报》

China plans to take samples from Mars around 2030

Dai Shoulun, deputy to the 19th CPC National Congress and president of the Eighth Academy under China Aerospace Science and Technology Corporation (CASC), said on October 20 that China planned to take samples from Mars, exploring minor planets and the Jovian system around 2030.

Source: *Economic Information Daily*

NASA 的"双胞胎研究"证实太空旅行对人体影响甚大:改变基因表达方式

乘坐太空飞船长时间"旅行",对宇航员的影响远非此前所想。据《科学美国人》近日报道,美国国家航空航天局(NASA)的"双胞胎研究"项目的初步结果显示,太空旅行强烈地影响着基因的表达方式。

宇航员会在进入太空后发生肌肉萎缩、骨密度降低或视觉恶化等身体变化,NASA 希望更好地了解太空旅行对宇航员的所有生理和心理影响,为登陆火星或更遥远目的地的飞行任务做好准备。

来源:《科技日报》

NASA's "astronaut twins study" shows how spaceflight changes gene expression

The changes spaceflight induces in astronauts are much more than skin deep. Space travel strongly affects the way genes are expressed, preliminary results from NASA's "Twins Study" have revealed, according to a recent report in *Scientific American*.

Spaceflight also causes changes to astronauts' bodies on the macro level, including muscle atrophy, decreased bone density and visual deterioration.

NASA is keen to better understand all of the physiological and psychological impacts of spaceflight, so it can better prepare for crewed missions to Mars and other distant destinations.

Source: Science and Technology Daily

蓝色起源太空探索火箭引擎成功点火

近日,亚马逊创始人杰夫·贝索斯旗下太空公司蓝色起源(Blue Origin),首次为一种完全可重复使用的火箭引擎 BE-4 成功点火。这是美国 20 年来生产的最强大引擎。

著名的美国联合发射联盟也在考虑使用该引擎——过去 10 年里,联合发射联盟一直在依赖俄罗斯制造的火箭引擎来发动美国军方的阿特拉斯-5 型运载火箭,而 BE-4 引擎很有可能帮助美国政府摆脱依靠俄罗斯火箭引擎的历史。

来源:《科技日报》

Blue Origin successfully test-fired its rockets engines

Recently, Blue Origin, headed by Amazon founder Jeff Bezos, announced it had successfully conducted a hot-fire test of its BE-4 engine. It is the most powerful engine produced by the U.S. in the last two decades.

United Launch Alliance (ULA) is also considering using the engine. In the past decades, ULA relies on Russia-made engines to launch Atlas V rockets for the U.S. military. BE-4 engines may end U.S. reliance on Russian engines.

Source: Science and Technology Daily

NASA 披露离子发动机新突破,有望实现送人上火星

日前,来自 NASA 和美国密歇根大学的工程师们公布了一个在离子发动机

研发方面突破了纪录的测试,该离子发动机的设计初衷是让它实现带人类登上火星。这款被称为"霍尔推进器"(Hall Thruster)的离子发动机是目前正处于研发当中的三款"火星发动机"中的一款,它通过使用电场和磁场来离子化诸如氙气这样的气体,让它喷出离子,并进而产生出推动推进器前进的推力。

来源:网易科技

NASA reveals record-setting tests of radical ion engine that could take man to Mars

Engineers from NASA and the University of Michigan have revealed record breaking tests of a radical ion engine designed to get man to Mars. Known as "Hall Thruster", it is one of the three Mars engine prototypes currently in development, and uses electric and magnetic fields to ionize gases like xenon and expels the ions to produce thrust.

Source: tech. 163. com

2045年我国将建成航天强国

11月16日是我国运载火箭事业正式起步60周年纪念日,我国第一个导弹研究机构中国运载火箭技术研究院近日出炉的《2017—2045年航天运输系统发展路线图》,详细披露了我国未来航天运输系统路线图,其中提出到2045年,我国将全面建成航天强国。

来源:《中国青年报》

Building China into a space superpower by 2045

November 16 marks the 60th anniversary of the beginning of China's R&D of launch vehicle. On that day, China Academy of Launch Vehicle

Technology, China's first missile research institute, released the "Development Roadmap for Space Transportation System 2017-2045", which depicts in detail China's road to future space transportation system, and sets out the goal of building China into a space superpower by 2045.

Source: *China Youth Daily*

一箭三星，长征六号再战苍穹

11月21日12时50分，中国航天科技集团八院抓总研制的新一代运载火箭长征六号遥二火箭以一箭三星方式执行"吉林一号"卫星发射任务取得圆满成功。此次发射是长征六号火箭的第二次发射，是长征系列运载火箭的第255次发射，是八院抓总研制的长征系列火箭第86次飞行试验任务，也是中国新一代液体运载火箭首次参与商业发射。

来源：上海科技

Long March 6 set out again for space with 3 satellites

At 12:50 pm local time on November 21, China successfully launched the new Long March 6 Y2 carrier rocket, which completed the mission of sending three Jilin 1-series satellites in orbit. This marks the first commercial launch of China's new generation of liquid-propellant rocket, the second mission of the Long March 6, the 86th mission of the Long March series of rockets developed by the Shanghai Academy of Spaceflight Technology, and the 255th mission of all Long March series of rockets.

Source: stcsm.gov.cn

印度研发小型运载火箭瞄准微型卫星发射市场

印度空间研究组织近日说，印度目前正在研发一种造价约为传统运载火箭十分之一的小型运载火箭,以满足日益增长的通信卫星特别是微型卫星发射市场需求。

印度空间研究组织下属维克拉姆·萨拉巴伊航天中心主任斯万对媒体说,这种小型运载火箭预计于 2018 年底或 2019 年初研制成功,发射载荷为 500 至 700 公斤,起飞总重量约 100 吨,从组装到完成发射准备仅需 3 天,可将卫星送入近地轨道或太阳同步轨道。它有望大幅降低微型卫星发射成本。

来源:新华社

India develops a small launch vehicle for microsatellite launch market

The Indian Space Research Organization (ISRO) recently said that it is working on a small launch vehicle that costs around one-tenth of the traditional vehicles, so as to meet the growing demand for the market of communications satellites, especially of microsatellites.

K Sivan, director of Vikram Sarabhai Space Centre (VSSC) of ISRO told the media that the small launch vehicle is likely to be ready for launch probably by 2018-end or early-2019. This rocket will have the total payload capacity of 500 to 700 kg and its weight will be just 100 tonnes. It can be assembled in just three days and can launch satellites to the near-earth orbit or the polar sun-synchronous orbit. It is expected to significantly reduce the cost of launching microsatellites.

Source: Xinhua News Agency

SpaceX 再创历史,成首个执行 NASA 任务的私有公司

近日,埃隆·马斯克(Elon Musk)所拥有的火箭制造公司 SpaceX 创造了美国国家航空航天局(NASA)的历史,成为首家利用执行过发射任务的火箭给国际空间站执行补给任务的公司。

这是NASA首次允许一家私有企业执行这种任务,同样也是SpaceX公司第四次使用被称为"经过飞行验证的"助推器执行的发射任务,前三次发射也都是使用的猎鹰9号火箭。此次任务携带了2.5吨补给物资和科研设备,并将运送到国际空间站。

来源:新浪科技

SpaceX becomes the first private company to conduct NASA mission

Elon Musk's rocket company recently made NASA's new history, as SpaceX became the first company to launch a resupply mission to the International Space Station on a reused rocket.

It is the first time NASA has approved such a mission and the fourth time SpaceX has launched with what it says is a "flight proven" booster. Three commercial missions earlier this year reused Falcon 9 rockets. The mission brings about 2.5 tons of crew supplies and scientific payloads to the space station.

Source: tech.sina.com.cn

NASA宣布第四次"新边疆任务":探索彗星与土卫六

近日,NASA宣布了第四次"新边疆任务"的遴选结果:最终有两项任务进入决赛环节,一项是收集并带回彗星样本,另一项则是探索土卫六。第一项任务由康奈尔大学的史蒂夫·斯奎尔斯带领,名为"彗星宇宙生物学探索样本取回项目",简称 CAESAR。该任务将向丘留莫夫-格拉西缅科彗星发射一枚探测器,从彗星表面收集至少3.5盎司(约合100克)样本,然后将其带回地球。科学家将试着收集生命所需的有机化合物,借此理解彗星对地球生命的诞生作出了怎样的贡献。

来源:新浪科技

NASA announces its fourth New Horizons Mission to explore comet and Titan

NASA recently announced that it has selected two finalists for its fourth New Horizons Mission: one is to collect and bring back a sample from the comet; and the other is to explore Titan. The first task is named Comet Astrobiology Exploration Sample Return, or CAESAR, and led by Steve Squyres from Cornell University. A probe will be launched on comet Churyumov-Gerasimenko to collect a sample of at least 3.5 ounces (or approximately 100g) and bring it back to earth. Scientists will try to collect organic compounds required by life to reveal how the comet contributed to the origin of the Earth's life.

Source: tech. sina. com. cn

欧空局将发射航天器监测太阳风暴

近日,欧洲空间局(ESA)计划发射新航天器,监测可能导致地球通信瘫痪的巨大太阳风暴,该航天器可在具有破坏性的太阳风暴爆发前数天发出预警。

来源:人民网

ESA will launch a spacecraft to track solar storms

Recently, European Space Agency is planning for the launch of a new spacecraft to track violent solar storms that might disrupt telecommunications infrastructure worldwide. The spacecraft will release warning days before the breakout.

Source: people. cn

高度只有9.5米,世界最小日本航天火箭载入吉尼斯

据俄罗斯卫星网报道,日本宇宙航空研究开发机构称,日本制造的世界上最小的SS-520火箭被载入吉尼斯纪录。据悉,今年2月成功发射的SS-520是世界上能够将人造卫星送入轨道的最小火箭。它的高度只有9.5米,直径50厘米,重量2.6吨。

来源:中新网

Japan's 9.5-meter-high rocket included in the Guinness Book of Records

According to Sputnik, Japanese Aerospace Exploration Agency said the world's smallest rocket SS-520 made in Japan has been listed in the Guinness book of records. It is reported that SS-520, successfully launched in February 2018, is the world's smallest rocket that can deliver man-made satellite into orbit. It is 9.5 meters high, with a diameter of 50 centimeters and a weight of 2.6 tons.

Source: chinanews.cn

太空旅游新进展:"最大窗户"飞行器成功试飞

近日,由美国电子商务巨头亚马逊公司创始人杰夫·贝索斯创建的蓝色起源公司宣布,该公司于12月12日成功试飞并回收升级版"新谢泼德"亚轨道飞行器,新版飞行器的一个亮点是拥有太空飞行器中"最大的窗户"。"新谢泼德"飞行器集火箭与飞船于一体。蓝色起源公司提供的视频显示,"新谢泼德"从地面垂直起飞,飞到一定高度后火箭与飞船分离,火箭先行返回,在接近地面时一个发动机点火,着陆支架展开,成功在目标着陆场垂直降落。飞船也在降落伞的帮助下成功着陆。

来源:新浪科技

New progress in space tourism: successful trial flight of aircraft with "largest window"

Recently, Blue Origin founded by Jeff Bezos, founder of the US e-commerce giant Amazon, announced that it successfully tested and recuperated the upgraded version of the sub-orbiter "Shepard" on Dec. 12. A highlight of the new version aircraft is its "largest window" among all spacecrafts. "New Sheppard" aircraft integrates the rocket and spacecraft. The video from the Blue Origin shows that "New Sheppard" first takes off perpendicularly from the ground and after flying to a certain altitude, the rocket returns first. When approaching the ground, an engine fires and the landing bracket unfolds, successfully landing on the target landing field vertically. Later on, the spacecraft also lands with the help of a parachute.

Source: tech. sina. com. cn

7

交通篇

"十二五"国家科技支撑计划"大跨连续梁桥智能监测和诊断评价技术"项目通过验收

近日,"十二五"国家科技支撑计划——"大跨连续梁桥智能监测和诊断评价技术"项目顺利通过验收。项目通过时分/波分混合复用方法。采用超低反射率的低损耗光纤光栅阵列,实现了单根光纤复用2 000个以上的FBG传感点;通过maximally flat类型的可编程FIR数字低通滤波器,直接在采集电路的微控制器上研制了0—400Hz以内截止频率的低功率桥梁无线振动、动应变及动挠度传感器;并首次在大跨径连续梁桥上采用准分布式光纤光栅传感网(单光纤复用超2600个传感点)实现了混凝土应变、温度和裂缝实时监测。

来源:科技部

The project of the intelligent monitoring and diagnostic evaluation technology of the long-span continuous girder bridge passed the acceptance tests

Recently, the project of the intelligent monitoring and diagnostic evaluation technology of the long-span continuous girder bridge, one of the National Sci-Tech Support Plans of the 12th Five-Year Plan, passed the acceptance tests. By adopting the time/wavelength division multiplexing method and the optical fiber bragg grating array with ultra-low reflectivity and low loss, single optical fiber is able to multiplex more than 2 000 FBG sensor nodes. By using the maximally flat programmable FIR digital low-pass filter, low-power bridge wireless vibration, dynamic strain and dynamic deflection sensors with cut-off frequency of 0-400Hz were developed on the micro-controller of collecting circuit. Besides, it was the first time that the quasi-distributed FBG sensing network (single optical fiber multiplexes more than 2 600 FBG sensor nodes) was applied to the long-span continuous girder bridge, thus realizing the real-time monitoring of concrete strain, temperature and fissures.

Source: Ministry of Science and Technology

高通展示电动汽车无线充电技术，行驶中可充电

高通公司5月18日展示了一项"动态电动汽车充电"技术，可对行驶中的电动汽车进行无线充电。

业内人士称，该技术有望推动自动驾驶汽车的普及。将来的自动驾驶汽车需要支持自动充电功能，而无需人类的干预。因此，无线充电技术也是汽车厂商正在研究的一个重要领域。据悉，高通的无线充电硬件被嵌入到道路中，电动汽车从道路上驶过即可充电。

来源：新浪科技

Qualcomm showcases wireless charging for electric vehicles, which allows charging while driving

On May 18, Qualcomm Incorporate demonstrated its dynamic electric vehicle charging (DEVC) technology, which allows vehicles to charge while driving.

Experts believe that the technology will help accelerate the popularity of self-driving cars. As self-driving cars are expected to support self-charging without manual operations in the future, wireless charging has become an important area studied by automotive manufactures. It is said that the hardware of DEVC is embedded on pads through which electric cars can be charged while driving.

Source: tech.sina.com.cn

研究显示少量自动驾驶汽车有助交通畅通

美国研究人员近日发现，让少量自动驾驶车辆上路或可缓解交通堵塞现象，并有助降低事故风险和解决燃料效率低的问题。

在美国亚利桑那州图森市的一项野外试验中,一辆自动驾驶汽车与至少 20 辆人工驾驶汽车持续环绕一段轨道行驶。美国伊利诺伊大学厄巴纳－尚佩恩分校的研究人员发现,只要通过控制这辆自动驾驶汽车的行驶速度就能疏通交通,并使总油耗下降。研究负责人丹尼尔·沃克说,使用自动驾驶汽车来调节公路交通流是交通监控技术快速发展中的下一个创新。

来源:中国科学网

Research shows a few self-driving vehicles can alleviate traffic jam

U.S. researchers recently found out that a few self-driving vehicles on the road can alleviate phantom traffic jams as well as reduce accident risk level and improve fuel efficiency.

In a field experiment conducted in Tucson, Arizona, one self-driving vehicle circled a track with at least 20 manned vehicles. Researchers from University of Illinois at Urbana-Champaign found that by controlling the pace of this self-driving vehicle they can smooth out the traffic and reduce overall fuel consumption. The researcher in charge, Daniel Work said that the use of self-driving vehicle to regulate traffic flow is the next innovation in traffic monitoring technology development.

Source:minimouse.com.cn

首艘国产邮轮 2023 年交付使用

5 月 31 日,在沪举行的"一带一路"与邮轮经济发展专题座谈会上,中国船舶工业集团公司总经理吴强透露,首艘国产邮轮将于 2023 年交付使用,2024 年—2028 年,每年都将交付一艘。按照设计建造计划,首艘国产邮轮全长 323.6 米,型宽 37.2 米,设计吃水 8.25 米,有客房近 2 000 间,最大载客人数 5 000 人。

来源:《解放日报》

China's first home-made cruise liner due for delivery in 2023

China's first domestically manufactured cruise liner will be delivered in 2023, followed by a delivery rate of one vessel per year between 2024 and 2028, said Wu Qiang, general manager of China State Shipbuilding Corp. According to its blueprint, this first China-made cruise liner will be 323.6 meters long and 37.2 meters wide, with a maximum draught of 8.25 meters. It will have nearly 2 000 cabins and a maximum capacity of nearly 5 000 passengers.

Source: *Jiefang Daily*

全球第一艘无人船明年下水

《财富》网站近日报道,全球第一艘无人驾驶船舶"YARA Birkeland"号将于2018年开始下水航行,该船舶最初将被投放到挪威南部一条长37英里(约合59.5公里)的航线上,用于肥料运送。

"YARA Birkeland"号无人驾驶船舶的下水,被给予厚望,报道称它可能会成为全球航运史上的一个巨大转折点。无人驾驶船舶时代可能真的来了。

来源:新浪网

World's first unmanned vessel will be launched next year

The official website of *Fortune* recently reported that the world's first unmanned vessel "YARA Birkeland" will be launched in 2018. At first, the vessel will be put onto a 37-mile (about 59.5-km) long lane at the south of Norway for transporting fertilizer.

People have high hopes for the launch of "YARA Birkeland" which is called the big turning point of the history of global shipping by reports. The era of unmanned vessel may have come.

Source: sina.com.cn

英国考虑架设公路"顶篷"应对空气污染

随着汽车保有量上升,各国都要面对日益严重的车辆排放污染问题。英国正设想在公路上架设大型顶篷,用于吸收车辆排放污染物,以提升道路周边空气质量。据规划介绍,大型顶篷将会在污染水平较高路段架设,形成一个隧道状的构造。顶篷使用一种新型特殊材料制造,能吸收二氧化氮等车辆排放污染物。最终的设想是形成一个具有抑制污染物扩散功能的公路隧道,以解决空气污染问题给周边居民带来的健康困扰。

来源:科学网

Britain is considering using 'cantilevered canopies' to cope with air pollution

As more and more people have cars, every country has to deal with car emissions and air pollution that is deteriorating every day. Britain is considering covering motorways with cantilevered canopies to absorb car emissions so that the air quality nearby will be improved. According to the scheme, cantilevered canopies will be constructed over the most polluted sections of road to form a tunnel-like structure. Canopies contain special material that can absorb car emissions like nitrogen dioxide. The scheme aims to build a tunnel that can stop pollution from spreading so that the residents nearby will no longer be bothered by air pollution.

Source: ScienceNet.cn

国家高速列车青岛技术创新中心成立

国家高速列车青岛技术创新中心作为事业法人实体近日正式注册成立,标志着国内首个国家技术创新中心正式运行。

国家高速列车技术创新中心正式由科技部、国资委批复建设以来,青岛市与中车集团积极探索,积极落实科技部关于要在体制机制和管理模式等方面勇于开拓、先行先试,为我国全面开展技术创新中心建设提供可复制可推广经验的要求。在广泛调研、认真论证的基础上,提出了构建新型事业法人实体机构的技术创新中心管理体制和运行机制,由中车集团工业研究院有限公司和青岛市科技局共同发起开办国家高速列车技术创新中心;并在青岛市机构编制委员会办公室的协助支持下,顺利完成事业法人实体的注册工作。

来源:《科技日报》

China set up a National High-speed Train Technological Innovation Center in Qingdao

National (Qingdao) High-speed Train Technological Innovation Center has been officially registered as a legal entity recently, marking the official operation of the first national technology innovation center in China.

After receiving the reply from the Ministry of Science and Technology and State-owned Assets Supervision and Administration Commission of the State Council (SASAC), Qingdao Municipal Government and the CRRC Corporation Limited actively explored and piloted new and feasible solutions, such as adopting new systems and mechanisms and management models to build more national technology innovation centers nationwide. Based on abundant investigations and analysis, they proposed to build a National High-speed Train Technological Innovation Center as a public legal entity, adopting new management models and operation mechanisms. The center is co-sponsored by Research Institute of the CRRC and Science and Technology

日本研发老年人用低速自动驾驶汽车

近日,日本名古屋大学与丰田汽车合作,正在研发包括小型汽车、巴士在内的低速自动驾驶汽车,主要面向山区、偏远城镇的高龄人群,提供社区循环交通、共享车辆还车、自动代客泊车等服务,解决他们的最后一公里出行难问题。

来源:人民网

Japan develops low-speed self-driving cars for the elder

Recently, Nagoya University has been cooperated with Toyota to develop low-speed autonomous vehicles, including mini-cars and buses. These cars will provide services like community circulating cars, returning shared vehicles and automatic valet parking primarily for the elderly in mountainous areas and remote towns, helping them overcome the challenge of "last mile" travel.

Source: people. cn

日企展示可变形反弹行人的橡胶概念车

业内知名的橡胶、塑料和 LED 专业公司丰田合成株式会社将在东京车展上展示一款别致的概念车型。它的名字叫做 Flesby II,采用了类似乌龟的创意造型、以及可以变形的橡胶材质,旨在发生碰撞时反弹行人(或道路上的其他交通工具使用者),以减少对他们的伤害。

来源:人民网

Japan company to exhibit a rubbery concept car that can shift shapes and bounce off pedestrians

Rubber, plastics and LED specialist Toyoda Gosei will showcase a concept car, dubbed Flesby II, at Tokyo Motor Show 2017. The turtle-like concept features a creative exterior shell made out of shape-shifting rubbers which can bounce off pedestrians or other vehicles on the road in the event of contact to reduce harm.

Source: people. cn

首汽约车和百度达成战略合作,拟以自动驾驶引领智慧交通新时代

近日,首汽约车与百度战略合作发布会在北京举行。会上,首汽约车正式宣布与百度达成战略合作,未来双方将共同推动智慧交通的建设及车联网、自动驾驶的商业化运行——百度将向首汽约车提供包括 DuerOS 及 Apollo 平台在内的成套解决方案,而首汽约车将在自己的平台中进行自动驾驶的商业化运营。双方拟在现有基础上进一步展开合作,推动出行行业进入智慧交通时代。

来源:人民网

Shouqi Limousine & Chauffeur and Baidu achieved a strategic cooperation to lead a new smart transportation era with automatic drive

Recently, Shouqi Limousine & Chauffeur and Baidu Strategic Cooperation Conference was held in Beijing. During the conference, Shouqi Limousine & Chauffeur officially announced the strategic cooperation with Baidu. In future, the two parties will jointly promote the deployment of smart transportation and commercial operation of Internet of Vehicles and automatic drive-Baidu will provide the whole sets of solutions for Shouqi Limousine & Chauffeur including DuerOS and Apollo platform, while the latter will carry out commercial operation of automatic drive on its own platform. The two parties plan for a further cooperation on the current basis to push the traffic industry into the smart transportation era.

Source: people. com. cn

福特制造了一款防瞌睡的司机帽

福特公司开发了一种防瞌睡司机帽,这款设备中还有一个内置的加速度计和陀螺仪,它可以检测司机在整个驾驶过程中的头部运动,然后通过震动的元件以及更响亮的声音让司机清醒过来。

来源:环球网

Ford develops a hat that wakes drivers up with sound

American automaker Ford has developed a hat that can wake drivers up with sound. The hat has an inboard accelerometer and gyroscope that measure head movements throughout the driving process and then wake the driver up through vibrating components and louder sounds.

Source: huanqiu. com

俄公司最新飞行汽车酷炫来袭

近日,俄罗斯公司 Hoversurf 推出飞行汽车,这款汽车名为"Formula Project",为五座可升降空中出租车,装有 52 个微型涡轮推进器,可同直升机一样升入空中。同时,这款汽车的飞行翼为可折叠式,方便停靠普通车位。

来源:新浪科技

Russian company to build amazing flying cars

Recently, Russia's Hoversurf is launching a flying car called "Formula Project", which is a 5-seater taxi with 52 tiny turbine propulsion units and capable of taking off like a helicopter. Besides, the car also uses fold-away wings, so that it can be parked easily.

Source: tech.sina.com.cn

全球最大光伏公共充电站在沪投用,阴雨天可运营

近日,全球最大光伏公共充电站在上海落成并投入使用,它安装了超过1 000片高效光伏发电面板,日均可满足400辆电动汽车的充电需求。由于配置了大量储能装置,即使阴雨天也能正常运营,为电动汽车送上纯粹的绿电。

来源:上海科技

The world's largest public PV charging station commissioned in Shanghai, available even on rainy days

Recently, the world's largest public photovoltaic (PV) charging station has been put into use in Shanghai. Equipped with over 1 000 pieces of highly effective PV panels, the station is able to provide power for 400 electric EVs per day. Meanwhile, with massive power storage devices, the station can also work on cloudy and rainy days, totally delivering green power to every EV.

Source: stcsm.gov.cn

中俄深化高铁合作,联合组建高铁技术研发中心

日前,中车长客股份公司与俄罗斯快速干线股份公司、莫斯科交通大学等

单位组建的中俄高铁技术联合研发中心在长春揭牌。中车长客表示，未来将按照联合研发中心组建协议，积极与俄方协作开展好列车耐高寒、节能、运维等技术研究工作，同时培养国际化高水平的工程技术人员、整合技术标准，提升两国技术水平实力，为"中俄高铁合作项目"提供有力技术支撑。

来源：中国新闻网

China and Russia deepen cooperation to co-build High-speed Railway R&D Center

Recently, Sino-Russian High-speed Railway R&D Center jointly built by CRRC Changchun Railway Vehicle Co., Ltd., Russian High-speed Trunk Line Corporation, Moscow University of Transportation and other organizations was inaugurated in Changchun City. In accordance with the agreement on building the Center, CRRC Changchun Railway Vehicle said that they will actively conduct researches with Russian partners on technologies of resistance to severe cold, energy saving and operation of trains, train high-quality engineering technologists with international-level skills, integrate technology standards and enhance the technology strength of the both sides, so as to provide strong technology support for the Sino-Russian High-speed Railway Cooperation Program.

Source：chinanews.com

世界首艘智能船结束一周试航

日前，中国船舶工业集团公司（以下简称中船集团）建造的世界首艘智能船舶——中船"海豚"38 800吨智能散货船结束了为期一周的试航，回到中船黄埔文冲船舶有限公司码头。按照计划，该船将于12月初交付给船东。

来源：科学网

The one-week trial voyage of the world's first smart ship completed

The world's first smart ship built by China State Shipbuilding Corporation (CSSC) — 38 800-dwt bulk carrier "Dolphin" recently completed its one-week trial voyage and returned to the dock of CSSC Huangpu Wenchong Shipbuilding Company. According to plans, the ship will be delivered to its owner in early December.

Source: ScienceNet. cn

全球最大飞艇 Airlander 10 发生意外，两工作人员受伤

据拥有全球最大飞艇"Airlander 10"的混合空中飞艇公司（HAV）公司消息，全球最大飞艇"Airlander 10"在英国贝德福德郡脱离了停泊塔。

该公司表示，因飞艇拥有安全系统，所以他们很快使飞艇从空中降落，飞艇在落地时并未发生严重损坏。

来源：中国新闻网

World's largest airship Airlander 10 met with an incident, with two crew members injured

According to information from Hybrid Air Vehicles (HAV), its Airlander 10, the largest airship in the world, broke free from its mooring mast in Bedfordshire, England.

The company said that because of the safety system, the airship landed quickly and it was not seriously damaged when it landed.

Source: chinanews. com

智能无人公交车将服务冬奥会

11月17日,在张家港举行的"第四届中国汽车技术转移大会"上,清华大学机械学院副院长、清华大学汽车工程系主任杨殿阁表示,我国自主研发的智能无人公交车将服务2022年冬奥会。冬奥会智能车示范主要有三个车型,分别是传统纯电动车、燃料电池汽车和智能汽车。

来源:《科技日报》

Smart driverless buses to serve Winter Olympic Games

On November 17, at the Fourth China International Technology Transfer Convention held in Zhangjiagang City, Yang Diange, Vice Dean of School of Mechanical Engineering of Tsinghua University and Director of Department of Automotive Engineering of Tsinghua University, said the smart driverless buses independently developed by China will be commissioned in the 2022 Winter Olympic Games. The demonstrated buses mainly consist of three types, namely conventional pure electric vehicle, fuel cell vehicle and smart vehicle.

Source: *Science and Technology Daily*

国内最大新能源车光伏充电站落沪

国内最大的新能源汽车光伏超级充电站日前在上海松江正式对外运营,这也是首个实现绿色零排放的光伏充电站,预示着未来充电基础设施发展的全新模式。不同于传统的电网充电模式,该充电桩把光伏发电与充电技术相结合,将太阳光直接转化为电能,以此作为电动车的能源,实现真正意义上的零排放。

来源:《中国环境报》

China's largest PV charging station for new energy vehicles operates in Shanghai

China's largest PV super charging station for new energy vehicles has recently been put into operation in Songjiang District of Shanghai. It is the first green PV charging station with zero emission, indicating a brand-new development model of future charging infrastructure. Unlike traditional electricity grid charging model, the charging pole combines PV power generation and charging technology, and directly converts sunlight to electric energy, providing energy for electric vehicles and realizing real zero emission.

Source: *China Environment News*

充电仅需2分钟,世界首款氢能源电动自行车上路

位于法国下诺曼底大区的圣洛市政府于当地时间12月11日宣布,当天第一批氢能源电动自行车在当地正式投入使用。这款自行车由法国普拉格马工业公司(Pragma Industries)设计生产,该公司厂址位于法国南部沿海城市比亚里茨。公司销售总监克里斯多夫·布鲁略指出,这也是世界上首款商用氢能源电动自行车。

来源:环球网

First hydrogen-fueled bike takes two minutes to charge

On December 11, the first batch of hydrogen bicycles were put into production in Sint-Lô (Normandy, France). The bike was designed and manufactured by Pragma Industries, a French company located in the coastal city of Biarritz in southern France. It is the first commercially available electrically assisted bike, integrating the fuel cell technology, said Christophe Bruniau, sales manager at Pragma Industries.

Source: huanqiu. com

使用新技术,中国客机首次低能见度 150 米起飞

近日,一则客机在大雾中安全起飞的视频引发网友热议,不少网友惊叹真是"神级操作",也有网友担心雾中起飞是否安全。据悉,这次雾中起飞发生在济南遥墙国际机场,起飞的是一架搭载了 HUD(平视显示器)技术的波音 737-800 型飞机,这也是中国民航史上首次在能见度 150 米条件下实现安全起飞。

HUD 中文名称叫做平视显示器。HUD 就像一个透明的投影仪,起飞时会在飞行员眼前显示跑道的剩余长度、飞机的速度和目前的高度。使用 HUD 既能减轻飞行员的操作负荷,同时提高精准度,降低起飞能见度标准。

来源:《北京青年报》

New technology enables Chinese passenger aircraft to take off in a low visibility of 150 meters

Recently a passenger plane taking off in heavy fog has triggered warm discussion on social media. Though overwhelmed by the miraculous operation, some voice their concerns over safety. It is reported that this take-off occurred at Yaoqiang International Airport in Jinan. Equipped with a head-up display (HUD) system, the Boeing 737-800 plane took off safely in a low visibility of 150 meters for the first time in China, adding a milestone to civil aviation of China.

HUD is a transparent projector which could display information like the remaining length of runway, speed and height for pilots. HUD could streamline the operation for pilots, as well as enhance precision and allow takeoff in lower visibility.

Source: *Beijing Youth Daily*

奥迪宣布 Smart Energy Network：电动汽车的一体化家庭解决方案

伴随着特斯拉的风生水起，越来越多的传统汽车公司开始布局和推进全电动汽车业务。奥迪（Audi）公司1月22日正式宣布启动"Smart Energy Network"，是整合了家庭能源存储、太阳能发电以及电动汽车充电为一体的综合解决方案。奥迪称用户可以将 Smart Energy Network 认为是一座"虚拟发电厂"，降低对传统电网的依赖，通过太阳能等资源的调用来平衡电力消耗。目前该项目仍处于试验研发阶段，已经在英戈尔施塔特地区和苏黎世地区进行测试。

来源：新浪科技

Audi launched Smart Energy Network, an integrated household solution for EV

Tesla may have made waves with its Tesla Energy home batteries, but more luxury car makers are looking to do something similar as they make the jump to all-electric vehicles. Audi is one of the latest, as the company has just announced its own "Smart Energy Network" which combines home energy storage, solar power generation, and electric vehicle charging on Jan 22. Audi describes the Smart Energy Network as a kind of "virtual power plant," where the batteries not only reduce a homeowner's reliance on the electrical grid, but also communicate with each other and in turn balance out the demands for power consumption. At present, the project is still in the experimental research and development stage and has been tested in the Ingolstadt area and the Zurich region.

Source: tech.sina.com.cn

"飞行汽车"有望在 5 年内商用,时速最高可达 40 公里

日前,硅谷"飞行汽车"初创公司 Kitty Hawk CEO 塞巴斯蒂安·特隆在接受采访时表示,"飞行汽车"有望在 5 年内商用。据悉,特隆是 Google X"登月项目"实验室联合创始人之一,被誉为"谷歌自动驾驶汽车之父"。去年 4 月,特隆创建了 Kitty Hawk 公司,致力于开发消费级电动飞行汽车,并获得了谷歌联合创始人拉里·佩奇的投资。特隆表示,下月将发布下一阶段的研究方向。

来源:《广州日报》

Flying car with a fastest speed of 40 km/h may be available within 5 years

Flying cars could be in the air within five years, said the chief executive of Kitty Hawk, Sebastian Thrun, in an interview. Thrun was one of the founders of Google X, the search giant's moonshot lab, and also a pioneer of the company's driverless car project. In April last year, Thrun founded Kitty Hawk backed by Alphabet CEO Larry Page to develop electric flying cars. Thrun said that an announcement is due in March about the next stages of the project.

Source: *Guangzhou Daily*

伦敦将把所有公交车换成中国造? 英方运营商:这很棒

英国伦敦现在居住有近 900 万人口,现役的公交车大约一共 9 200 辆。而现在伦敦市长决心为治理空气污染下大力气,承诺至 2037 年将把伦敦所有公交车都升级成纯电动公交车。目前,已经有 51 辆中国比亚迪公司生产的纯电动巴士行驶在了伦敦街头,占当地全部纯电动巴士的九成以上。英国老牌公交运营商 Go-Ahead 伦敦总经理说:"中国制造正在帮助英国进行一场道路空气

清洁革命!事实上,纯电动公交消耗的电力甚至比比亚迪公司的设计预估值还要低,实在是太棒了。"

来源:新浪军事

Will London change all the buses to China-made ones? British operator: This is great

London, England, now has a population of 9 million citizens, and about 9 200 buses are in active service. The mayor of London is now determined to make great efforts to control air pollution and promise that all London buses will be upgraded to pure electric buses by 2037. At present, 51 pure electric buses produced by the Chinese BYD Co are running on the streets of London, accounting for more than 90% of all the local pure electric buses. "Made in China is helping Britain carry out a road air cleaning revolution," said the general manager of London's old bus operator, Go-Ahead London. "In fact, the electricity consumed by the pure electric bus is even lower than the BYD Co's design estimate, which is really great."

Source: mil. news. sina. com

重庆"魔幻"地铁站建在河中,民众垂钓捉虾泛舟

重庆轨道交通的"魔幻"站台"成员"众多,轨道交通 2 号线"李子坝站"穿楼而过,轨道交通 10 号线"红土地站"埋深 94.476 米,这两处"网红"地铁站被各地民众熟知。近日,"魔幻"地铁站又添新成员,轨道交通 6 号线"刘家坪站"站台的架空层建在一条弯弯曲曲的河流中,站台下每日都有民众垂钓泛舟。

来源:中新网

A metro station in Chongqing built across a river goes viral

Thanks to the geography of Chongqing in southwest China, Chongqing Rail Transit, branded as CRT, is quite a distinctive transit system in China with many of its stations built at inconceivable locations. For instance, Liziba station on Line 2 is located on the sixth to eighth floor of a 19-storey residential building. Hongtudi station on Line 10 is built 94.476 meters below the ground. The two metro stations have gone viral online. Recently another metro station of CRT, Liujiaping station on Line 6, shot to fame because the station stands right above a winding stream where residents come to fish and row every day.

Source: chinanews.com

打破西方垄断，又一个大国重器正在改变世界

高铁列车运行控制系统是高铁的"大脑和中枢神经"，是保障高铁列车准点发车、安全运行，确保高铁路网高效有序运营的大国重器！近日，国资委新闻中心宣布了一个重磅消息：中国高铁即将进入自动驾驶时代！值得每位中国人自豪的是，这项关键技术的突破，完全是中国自主研发，核心技术和产品100%国产化，并建立了中国的技术标准。

来源：凤凰网

China is making a difference worldwide by breaking monopoly of the West

The operation control system is the "brain and central nervous system" of high-speed trains, an important part that ensures on-time departure and safe operation of the trains and efficient and orderly operation of high-speed railway networks. Recently, the News Center of the State-owned Assets Supervision and Administration Commission of the State Council announced a piece of great news that China's high-speed train is about to enter an era of automatic driving. All Chinese people are proud that both core technologies and products were independently developed and China's technical standards have been established.

Source: ifeng. com

世界首条石墨烯改性路面在广西建成

近日,世界首条石墨烯复合橡胶改性沥青路面在广西南宁大桥建成,在世界上率先实现石墨烯在路桥高等级公路的商业化应用,打通了石墨烯产业从石墨烯宏量制备到规模化应用的产业链条,为石墨烯产业发展指明了新方向。

来源:人民网

World's first road paved with graphene modified asphalt completed in Guangxi

Recently, the world's first road paved with graphene composite rubber modified asphalt has been completed on Nanning Bridge in Guangxi Province. Therefore, China has taken the lead in achieving the commercial application of graphene in high-grade bridges and opened up the industrial chain, giving a new direction for the development of the graphene industry.

Source: people. cn

加州政府批准无人车接送客:须满足两个条件

加州政府最近启动了有关无人车接送消费者的两个试验性计划。无人车公司如果满足两个条件之一,即可以接送客人。第一个条件是无人车上配置了备份司机,在车辆出现意外时可以紧急操控,保障乘客安全。另外一个条件是如果没有配置备份司机,但是测试公司必须有专职的人员通过远程的方式监控车辆的运行。

来源:腾讯新闻

Government of California allows driverless cars to carry passengers under two conditions

Recently, Government of California has launched two pilot programs that allow driverless vehicles to carry passengers under two conditions. One is that a safety driver is behind the wheel. In emergency, the driver can operate the car to ensure the safety of passengers. The other is that the test company must monitor the cars remotely with specialists if a safety driver is not in place.

Source: news. qq. com

京津冀互通卡正式发售,京津冀加速联通

6月4日,"京津冀互通卡"面向石家庄市民正式发售。该卡不仅可以在北京、天津及河北的11个设区市刷卡乘坐公交和地铁,还可以在全国纳入"交通联合"范围的其他城市使用。

来源:新华网

Beijing-Tianjin-Hebei Interoperability Card comes out, to accelerate interconnection among 3 areas

On June 4, China's city Shijiazhuang started to sell the Beijing-Tianjin-

Hebei Interoperability Card to local residents. Reportedly, the card can be used to take public buses and subway trains in Beijing, Tianjin and 11 cities divided into districts in Hebei province, as well as other cities within the "Traffic Union".

Source: xinhuanet.com

地下 30 米"上海制造",武汉三阳路长江隧道贯通

6月9日,由隧道股份上海隧道承建的武汉三阳路长江隧道实现双线贯通,标志着国内最大直径盾构法隧道、中国首条公铁合建隧道全线贯通。

武汉三阳路隧道是中国第一条穿越复合地质土层的 15 米级超大直径盾构法隧道,需要穿越长江底石英含量高达 70% 的粉细砂层和富含黏土的强风化泥质粉砂岩地层,深达 30 米。

来源:东方网

30-meter-deep Sanyang Road Yangtze River Tunnel completed

The Sanyang Road Yangtze River Tunnel in Wuhan, built by STEC Shanghai Tunnel Engineering Company, was completed on June 9, marking the completion of the largest-diameter shield tunnel and also the first tunnel integrating roads and railways in China.

The Sanyang Road Tunnel is China's first shield tunnel with a diameter of 15 meters that passes through complex geological layers. The 30-meter-deep tunnel runs across a fine sand layer that's 70% quartz at the bottom of the Yangtze River, and a stratum of intensely weathered clay-rich argillaceous siltstone.

Source: eastday.com

马斯克:Roadster 将配备 10 个小型火箭推进器

北京时间 6 月 11 日上午消息,特斯拉 CEO 埃隆·马斯克在其推文中透露了下一代 Roadster 跑车的选装包信息。马斯克表示:新款跑车 Roadster 的 SpaceX 选装包将配备大约 10 个小型火箭推进器,紧密安装在车身周围。这些火箭推进器可以大幅提升加速度、最高时速、刹车和转弯性能,甚至可以让 Roadster 飞上天空。这辆汽车的性能将全面超越燃油跑车。

来源:新浪网

Musk: Roadster will be equipped with 10 small rocket thrusters

On the morning of June 11, Beijing time, Tesla CEO Elon Musk revealed information about the next-generation Roadster sports car's optional package in his tweet. Musk said that the new sports car Roadster's SpaceX optional package will be equipped with about 10 small SpaceX rocket thrusters, closely installed around the body. These rocket thrusters can greatly increase acceleration, top speed, braking and cornering performance, and even allow the Roadster to fly to the sky, allowing the car to surpass the performance of sports car using fuels.

Source: sina.com.cn

世界最大级别集装箱船在沪交付,成为"海上丝绸之路"的新使者

6 月 12 日,由中船集团自主设计建造的最大箱位集装箱船中远海运宇宙轮在江南造船(集团)有限责任公司正式交付。该船是江南造船为中远海运集团建造的六艘 21 000 箱超大型集装箱船的首制船。作为中远海运集装箱船队的核心旗舰,该船即将投入远东至欧洲精品航线营运,成为"海上丝绸之路"的新使者和新名片,为我国"一带一路"倡仪的实施提供坚强的运力保证。

来源:东方网

The world's largest container ship delivered in Shanghai, is to serve as the new messenger in the Maritime Silk Road

On June 12, COSCO Shipping's 'Universe' container ship, the largest container ship independently designed and manufactured by China State Shipbuilding Corporation (CSSC) was delivered at Jiangnan Shipyard (Group) Co., Ltd. The ship is the first of the six 21 000-TEU container ships Jiangnan Shipyard (Group) will have built for the COSCO Group. As the flagship of the COSCO container fleet, the vessel is about to be deployed in the route from the Far East to Europe, acting as the new messenger and new business card of the "Maritime Silk Road", and providing strong support for the implementation of China's "Belt and Road" Initiative.

Source: eastday.com

8

环境篇

全球变暖致苔藓快速生长,科学家:南极正在"变绿"

据英国《独立报》网站报道,自 1950 年以来,南极半岛的气温每 10 年上升大约 0.5 摄氏度,远高于全球平均水平。

英国研究人员对南极半岛横跨 1 000 公里范围内的 3 处地点进行了考察。根据他们的研究结果,1950 年以后,苔藓的生长速度是之前的四五倍。他们的研究结果发表在美国《细胞生物学杂志》上。

来源:参考消息网

Antarctic turning green as global warming triggers moss explosion

According to the website of *The Independent*, since 1950, temperatures in the Antarctic Peninsula have risen by about half a degree Celsius each decade-much faster than the global average.

And growth rates of moss after about 1950 have been running at four to five times the level before that year, according to a study by UK-based researchers who studied three sites across a 1 000km stretch of the peninsula. Their study was reported in an open-access paper in the journal *Cell Biology*.

Source:cankaoxiaoxi.com

人类竟一直在改造宇宙空间环境

发表在最新一期《空间科学评论》上的研究报告称,美国国家航空航天局(NASA)的范艾伦探测器发现了一个人造的"太空屏障"正在向外推动范艾伦辐射带。这一惊人事实,意味着我们人类不仅在改造地表,也在改造近太空环境。

范艾伦辐射带由被地球磁场捕获的带电粒子构成,是环绕地球的高能辐射带,经常因太阳风暴和其他空间天气事件而剧烈膨胀,会给卫星通信、GPS 定位系统和宇航员的人身安全造成一定威胁。

来源:人民网

Human Activity is Affecting the Space Around Earth

According to the research report published in the latest edition of *Space Science Reviews*, NASA's Van Allen Probes spotted a human-made barrier shrouding Earth that is pushing the Van Allen radiation belt further into space. This shocking discovery indicates that humans have not only shaped Earth's landscape, but the near-space environment as well.

The Van Allen belt is a high energy radiation zone of charged particles held in place by Earth's magnetic fields. Its drastic expansion, often caused by the solar storm and other space weather events, can pose certain threat to satellite communication, GPS navigation system, and safety of astronauts.

Source: people. cn

极端厄尔尼诺事件仍将显著增加

厄尔尼诺现象是指赤道中东太平洋的海温异常增暖，它与我们身边的极端天气现象息息相关。全球变暖如何影响厄尔尼诺？全球变暖是否会导致厄尔尼诺事件频发，对地球带来更大威胁？青岛海洋科学与技术国家实验室的一项最新科研成果对这些问题作出了解答，在全球气温 1.5 摄氏度增暖稳定后，极端厄尔尼诺事件发生频率仍至少持续增加 40%；即使在 2050 年以后的 100 年里，极端厄尔尼诺事件发生频率依旧将呈现显著的上升趋势。

来源：《人民日报》

Extreme El Nino events still to significantly increase

El Nino phenomenon means that the sea temperature in the eastern Pacific around equator rises abnormally, which is closely related to the extreme weather events affecting us. How dose global warming affect El Nino? Will global warming result in even higher occurrence rate of El Nino events and bring greater threats to Earth? The latest research results of Qingdao National Laboratory for Marine Science and Technology may offer answers to these questions. The research shows that as the global temperature comes to a stable situation after an increase of 1.5℃, the occurrence rate of extreme El Nino events is expected to continuously increase at least 40%; even during the century after 2050, the occurrence rate will still be on a marked rise.

Source: *People's Daily*

可可西里藏羚羊回迁，迁徙之谜至今未解

从可可西里国家级自然保护区管理局获悉，据工作人员观测，在可可西里卓乃湖集中产崽的藏羚羊于近期回迁，已陆续返至原栖息地。

中科院西北高原生物研究所研究员苏建平说，藏羚羊迁徙是世界上最为壮观的有蹄类动物大迁徙之一，每年它们都要成群结队翻过昆仑山，蹚过冰河，历经千难万阻，始终坚持不懈。其中究竟暗含着怎样的"生态密码"，仍待科学家持续探索。

来源：科学网

Tibetan antelopes return to original habitat, leaving migration mystery unsolved

According to the Administration of Kekexili National Reserve, the Tibetan antelopes, after giving birth to babies around Zhuonai Lake, are returning to their original habitat.

Su Jianping, researcher at Northwest Institute of Plateau Biology of Chinese Academy of Sciences, said that the Tibetan antelopes' migration is one of the world's most spectacular migrations of ungulates. Each year, they run in droves through the Kunlun Mountains and wade across the glaciers, persevering in the face of countless difficulties. What "ecological code" propels the migration still waits for scientists' exploration.

Source: ScienceNet. cn

欧洲每年 50 万未成年人死于空气污染

欧洲环保局发布最新报告称,尽管利用各种技术已让空气质量缓慢改善,但欧洲 41 个国家每年死于空气污染的未成年人数仍然超过 50 万。

来源:新华社

500 thousand juveniles die from air pollution every year in Europe

According to the latest report from European Environment Agency, more than 500 thousand juveniles in 41 countries die from air pollution every year in Europe although all kinds of technology has been used and the quality of air has been improved slowly.

Source: Xinhua News Agency

NASA 卫星:全球碳排放急剧上升 尤其在冬季

《科学》期刊近日援引环绕地球运行的 NASA 卫星数据指出,全球碳排放急剧上升,尤其是在冬季。

数据显示,在北半球随着季节改变,碳循环出现惊人的变化。在春天,植物会大量吸收二氧化碳;然而,到了冬季,植物吸收的二氧化碳量降到最低,且植物分解或腐化也产生二氧化碳排放到大气中。

来源:中国新闻网

NASA satellites: global carbon emissions climb sharply, especially in winter

Science recently quoted data collected from NASA's satellites orbiting the earth that carbon emissions climb sharply, especially in winter.

The data showed that seasonal changes in carbon cycle take place in the Northern Hemisphere. During spring months, plants absorb a substantial amount of carbon dioxide. However, in winter, when trees and plants begin to lose their leaves and decay, carbon dioxide is released in the atmosphere. This, combined with fewer trees and plants removing carbon dioxide from the atmosphere, allows concentrations to climb all winter.

Source: chinanews.com

研究表明地球工程不可半途而废

控制太阳辐射的地球工程,是逆转气候变化所带来的物理影响的潜在途径。但据英国《自然·生态与进化》杂志发表的最新研究,如果地球工程半途而废,对生物多样性造成的影响可能比气候变化带来的后果严重2~4倍。

为了实现《巴黎协定》设定的气温上升不超过2℃的目标,科学家建议,可以从大气层中大规模清除二氧化碳,或者使用气溶胶将阳光反射回太空。这些控制太阳辐射的地球工程,将能有效应对温室气体排放。

来源:《科技日报》

Research shows that geo-technology cannot be given up halfway

Geo-technology to control solar radiation is a potential way to reverse the physical impact of climate change. But according to a latest research published in the British journal *Nature Ecology & Evolution*, if geo-technology was given up halfway, the impact on biodiversity could be 2-4 times greater than the consequences of climate change.

To achieve the goal of limiting the increase in global temperatures to below 2 degrees centigrade, scientists suggest that carbon dioxide should be massively removed from the atmosphere, or aerosols should be used to reflect sunlight back into space. These efforts to control solar radiation will effectively address greenhouse gas emissions.

Source: *Science and Technology Daily*

重庆长江岸线生态复绿初见成效

重庆地处长江上游、三峡库区腹心地带,是全国重要的生态功能区。近年来,当地通过推进长江生态环境保护项目、植树造林、实施长江非法码头生态复绿等综合措施,使重庆长江岸线生态屏障区植被得以恢复。截至目前,长江三峡库区森林覆盖率已经达到50.2%。

来源:新华网

Ecological rehabilitation of ecological preservation areas along the Yangtze River achieve initial success

Chongqing, a city located in the upper reaches of the Yangtze River and the heart of the Three Gorges Dam area, is an important ecological area in China. In recent years, the local government has taken a series of measures, including promotion of ecological environmental protection projects, afforestation, and ecological rehabilitation of illegal wharves along the Yangtze River, so as to restore the vegetation of ecological preservation areas along the river. By now, the percentage of forest coverage in the Three Gorges Dam area has reached 50.2%.

Source: xinhuanet.com

9

娱乐篇

美国多家机构呼吁将有吸烟镜头电影定为"限制级"

美国多家健康机构 8 月 29 日联名呼吁,将有吸烟镜头的电影定为"限制级",以帮助防止青少年受不良影响养成吸烟习惯。

来源:《中国科学报》

US institutions call for marking films with smoking scenes as "restricted"

On August 29, numerous health organizations in the United States called for categorizing films with smoking scenes as "restricted", to protect teenagers from forming the habit of smoking under adverse influence.

Source: *China Science Daily*

微软公布新黑科技:Xbox 游戏不用下载完就能玩

近日,微软正在设计一款新的游戏管理系统,将使得 Xbox One 和 Xbox One X 游戏有更快的下载速度,并且占用的硬盘空间更小。该系统的内部代号为"Intelligent Delivery",它会将游戏内容分为几个标记的区块,届时玩家们玩游戏只需要下载他们想要的区块即可,不需要把完整游戏下载下来。

来源:逗游网

Microsoft releases new tech: Xbox users can play games without downloading the complete game package

Microsoft is designing a new game management system that will make Xbox One and Xbox One X games have a faster download speed, and take up less hard drive space. The new system—known internally as Intelligent

Delivery—splits game content into 'chunks' of data and then adds tags to them. Users only need to download chunks they'll actually need, as opposed to the complete game package.

Source: doyo. cn

4D 电影《熊猫滚滚》首映,科学性远超"功夫熊猫"

4D 科普电影《熊猫滚滚——寻找新家园》9 月 15 日公映,这是上海科技馆策划创作的第 10 部 4D 电影,也是 2017 年度继《蛟龙入海》《海洋传奇》后上映的第三部 4D 电影。

影片通过超写实全 CG 制作而成,包含超过 900 个模型元素,总计超过 9.5 亿个面及 5 000 万根毛发,共涉及 10 多种物种、30 多个角色制作、27 个场景制作以及 30 余个道具制作。在保证科学性的同时,影片逼真地将角色、场景融入有趣的情节中,并加入大量 4D 特效点,为观众打造了身临其境的观影体验。

来源:《上海科技报》

4D movie Panda Roller opens, far more scientific than "Kung Fu Panda"

The 4D popular science film Panda Roller — Journey to New Home made its public debut on September 15. It is Shanghai Science and Technology Museum's 10th 4D movie, and also the third one of this year, following the Dive with Ocean Dragon and the Sea Legend.

Created completely by the CG (computer graphics) technology, the ultra-realistic film involves the production of over 10 types of species, 30 plus roles and 27 scenes, boasting over 900 model elements, more than 950 million facades and 50 million hairs. While keeping its scientific features, the film also perfectly fuses the realistic roles and scenes with interesting plots, and adds a great number of special 4D effects, providing audience with the most immersive experience.

Source: *Shanghai Science and Technology*

"Magic Leap One"AR 眼镜正式发布

近日，Magic Leap 正式发布了其首款硬件产品——AR 眼镜 Magic Leap One。该产品是"创作者版本"(Creator Edition)，将于 2018 年开始发货。从其官网公布的图片来看，这款产品包含三个部分：一个 AR 眼镜、一个手柄和一个电池。这款眼镜的设计大胆抛弃了当下的极简设计风，采用了蒸汽朋克风格，可谓独树一帜。

来源：36 氪

"Magic Leap One" AR glasses officially released

Magic Leap recently launched its first hardware product Magic Leap One, a kind of AR glasses. The product is a Creator Edition and will start selling in 2018. According to pictures on the official website, the product consists of three parts: a pair of AR glasses, a control and a battery. The design adopts the unique steampunk style, shunning the prevailing minimalism.

Source: 36kr

小长假扫二维码就可阅读上海老建筑和特色街区

记者从上海市旅游局获悉，在外滩万国建筑博览群这一"明星"景区，黄浦区在外滩沿线 22 幢优秀历史保护建筑铭牌上都设置了二维码，并对南京东路街道辖区内 40 幢优秀历史保护建筑和 10 处里弄制作了木制二维码铭牌，内容以中英文介绍和图片为主。市民游客逛到这些建筑时，只要扫一下二维码就可以了解更多与这座建筑有关的故事。

来源：东方网

Scanning QR code enables tourists to read introductions to old buildings and unique neighborhoods in Shanghai

Our reporters learned from Shanghai Municipal Tourism Administration that in the "star" scenic area of foreign buildings in the Bund, QR codes have been placed on the nameplates of 22 outstanding historical buildings, and wooden QR nameplates mainly consisting of Chinese and English introductions and pictures have been made for 40 excellent historical buildings and 10 lanes in Nanjing East Road community. When visiting these buildings, tourists can find out more about the building by simply scanning the QR code.

Source: eastday.com

英国：拍照并分享有助于提升幸福感

英国兰开斯特大学一项研究显示，每天拍一张照片并分享到社交网站有助增强幸福感。

研究人员在《改善健康与社会包容的创造性实践》期刊发表的论文中写道，每天拍一张照片成为习惯有助减少孤独感，促进与他人沟通交流，让生活变得有目标、有意义，还有助于增加运动量。另外，研究人员发现，志愿者所晒照片中，76%在户外拍摄。

来源：新华社

UK study: taking a photo and posting it to social networking sites make you happier

According to a study conducted by Lancaster University in the United Kingdom, taking a photo every day and posting it to social networking sites can make you happier.

The researchers published an article in the journal *Creative Practices for Improving Health and Social Inclusion*, saying that developing a habit of taking a photo every day can help to reduce loneliness, promote communication with others, make life meaningful, and also increase the amount of exercise. In addition, they found that 76 percent of the photos posted by the volunteers were taken outdoors.

Source: Xinhua News Agency

中国文娱大数据在京发布，利用科技"脱水"明星数据

在影视娱乐行业，电影、电视剧、网剧及明星相关数据的伪造、虚报等已成为业内潜规则。2017—2018"金数据"中国文娱大数据从用户行为模式、发布内容特征和社交关系网络3个方面，对水军行为实现精准识别及对网络数据进行"脱水"，对"脱水"后具有商业价值和影响力的个人和团队授予表彰。据悉，"脱水数据"是第一次利用科技对影视娱乐行业的全面丈量，今后将继续致力于脱水数据的研究，让行业从业人员了解真实的影视作品效果以及明星商业价值。

来源：中新网

China Entertainment Big Data uses high technology to screen out false data

In the film and television entertainment industry, it is an unspoken rule to make a false report on the data related to films, television dramas, online dramas, and celebrities. The 2017-2018 "Gold Data" China Entertainment Big Data accurately identified water armies and screened out false data from three aspects—user behavior patterns, features of published contents, and social relationship networks, and commended the individuals and teams for their business value and influence.

It is reported that this is the first time that high technology has been used to fully judge the film and television entertainment industry. In the future, more efforts will be made to conduct research into screening out false data, so that industry professionals can understand the real effects of film and television works as well as business values of celebrities.

Source: chinanews. com

可口可乐推出透明可乐，日本将首发

据外媒报道，日本可口可乐公司将在今年6月11日于日本推出这款透明可口可乐，被称为"Coca-Cola Clear"，其包装和以往一样使用熟悉的塑料瓶装，只是在标签上增加了CLEAR字样。

来源：搜狐科技

Coca Cola releases a clear beverage in Japan

According to foreign media report, Coca-Cola Japan will release a clear beverage in Japan on June 11. The new beverage is called "Coca-Cola Clear" and it is packaged in the usual plastic bottles marked with the word "CLEAR".

Source: it. sohu. com

迪士尼将在苹果设备上用 AR 宣传星战电影

近日,迪士尼将会在 iPhone 以及 iPad 上,利用 AR 增强现实技术去宣传即将要上映的电影《星球大战:最后的绝地武士》。迪士尼希望用户可以扫描代码,然后使用 Star Wars App 去解锁和收集电影里的角色。

来源:**36 氪**

Disney will publicize Star Wars movie using AR on Apple devices

Disney is going to promote the upcoming "Star Wars: The Last Jedi" with AR on iPhone and iPad. In detail, Disney wants users to scan codes to unlock and collect the roles from the film with the Star Wars App.

Source: 36kr

10

出版篇

出版商威胁"研究之窗"删除数百万篇论文

数百万篇论文很快或将从世界上最大的学术社交网站——"研究之窗"(ResearchGate)消失。日前,5家出版商称它们成立了一个联盟,将开始要求"研究之窗"从其网站撤销研究论文,因为该网站侵犯了出版社的版权。该联盟一名发言人称,可能会有700万篇论文受到影响,第一批包含约10万篇文章的撤销通知可能会被"立即"发送出去。

来源:科学网

Publishers asked ResearchGate to delete millions of papers

Millions of papers might soon disappear from ResearchGate, the world's largest academic social network. Recently, five publishers said they formed a coalition that would start asking ResearchGate to withdraw research papers from its website which infringed the copyright of the publishers. A spokesman for the coalition said there might be 7 million papers affected, and the first revocation notice containing about 100 000 articles could be sent "immediately".

Source:ScienceNet.cn

我国科技论文国际影响力持续提升

10月31日,中国科学技术信息研究所在京发布"2017中国科技论文统计结果"。结果显示,我国国际论文被引用次数排名上升2位,列世界第2位。2007年至2017年(截至2017年10月),我国科技人员发表的国际论文共被引用1935万次,与2016年统计时比较,数量增加了29.9%,超越英国和德国前进到世界第2位。

来源:科学网

China's theses see constantly increasing global influence

On October 31, Institute of Scientific and Technical Information of China (ISTIC) issued *Statistics of China's Science and Technology Theses* in 2017 in Beijing. It is shown that the rank of China in the aspect of the times of China's theses being quoted worldwide moved up two spots to No. 2 in the world. From 2007 to October 2017, theses written by China's sci-tech professionals on international platforms have been quoted by 19.35 million times, a rise of 29.9% compared with the statistics obtained in 2016, making China rank No.2 in the world over the UK and Germany.

Source: ScienceNet. cn

11

材料篇

最细的纳米线可达原子厚度

你所能想象到的最细的线缆有多细？答案是一个原子！最近，英国剑桥大学和华威大学的研究人员成功将线缆缩小到了一串单一的原子（碲原子），制备出了真正的一维材料。为使碲原子稳定存在，研究人员将其固定在碳纳米管中，并且他们还发现：通过改变纳米管的直径，可以控制碲的其他性质。这项研究可能会使我们将来随身携带的设备变得非常小。

来源：《中国科学报》

The finest nanowires can reach atomic thickness

Can you imagine the thinnest cable? The answer is an atom! Researchers at Cambridge University and Warwick University have recently succeeded in narrowing the cable to a single set of atoms (tellurium atoms) to produce true one-dimensional materials. In order to stabilize the tellurium atoms, the researchers fixed them in carbon nanotubes, and they also found that other properties of tellurium could be controlled by changing the diameter of the nanotubes. This study may make our future portable devices quite small.

Source: *China Science Daily*

无溶剂石墨烯重防腐涂料研制成功

近日，扬州大学聚合物-无机微纳复合材料工程技术研究中心朱爱萍教授团队联合国内有关科研单位、企业，成功研制出无溶剂石墨烯重防腐涂料。目前，该产品已成功投产并实现工程示范应用。

来源：《科技日报》

Heavy-duty coating made from solvent free graphene successfully developed

The team led by Professor Zhu Aiping from the Engineering Research Center for Polymers-Inorganic Micronano Composites, Yangzhou University successfully developed the heavy-duty coating made from solvent free graphene, through joint efforts with relevant research institutes and enterprises in China. The newly invented product has been applied in production and realized demonstration engineering for application.

Source: *Science and Technology Daily*

碘化铯锡半导体热电性能独特

美国研究人员发现,一种名为碘化铯锡(CsSnI3)的晶体半导体材料具有独特的热电性能,能在保持高电导率的同时,隔绝大部分热量传递。他们在日前出版的美国《国家科学院学报》上发表文章指出,这种材料的热电性质独特,应用前景十分广阔。

来源:人民网

Unique Thermoelectric Property of CsSnI3

U. S. researchers have found that a crystal semiconductor material called CsSnI3 has a unique thermoelectric property that can maintain high conductivity while isolating most of the heat transfer. In a recent paper published in the *Proceedings of the National Academy of Sciences*, it is noted that the material has unique thermoelectric properties and the application prospects are very broad.

Source: people. com. cn

上海交大成功研制纳米陶铝合金,已用于天宫二号

近日,上海交通大学宣布新研制出纳米陶铝合金,兼具铝和陶瓷两者优点,比强度和比刚度甚至超过了"太空金属"钛合金。目前,该材料已经用于天宫一号、天宫二号、量子卫星、气象卫星等关键部件翱翔于太空。未来将走进民航、汽车等领域,有望引领材料轻量化革命。

来源:澎湃新闻

Newly developed nano ceramic aluminum alloy by Shanghai Jiaotong University has been applied in Tiangong-2

Recently Shanghai Jiaotong University has announced its successful development of nano ceramic aluminum alloy, a new material leveraging the properties of both ceramics and aluminum which is lighter but stronger than the most common space aviation material: titanium alloy. So far, the alloy has been used in the key components of Tiangong-1 and Tiangong-2, quantum satellites and meteorological satellites. And it is expected to be used in civil aviation and the automobile industries and thus lead to lighter materials reform.

Source: ThePaper. cn

"不知疲倦"的仿生智能薄膜问世

近日,华东师范大学张利东课题组与中国科学院深圳先进技术研究院杜学敏课题组合作,设计出了一种"不知疲倦"、快速响应的聚合物智能薄膜。8月1日,成果《丙酮分子刺激响应传感器的可控形变运动》发表在《先进材料》上。

来源:《科技日报》

Bionic thin film that is "inexhaustible" has been developed

Recently, a research group led by Zhang Lidong, a professor in East China Normal University cooperated with a research group led by Du Xuemin who works in Shenzhen Institutes of Advanced Technology, Chinese Academy of Sciences and developed an "inexhaustible" and responsive thin film made of polymers. They published an essay entitled *Vapomechanically Responsive Motion of Microchannel-Programmed Actuators* in *Advanced Materials*.

Source: *Science and Technology Daily*

全球首次实现非晶磁粉芯规模化生产

8月31日,从青岛市科技局获悉,青岛云路先进材料技术有限公司承担的青岛市自主创新重大专项"千吨级非晶磁粉芯的制备技术及产业化"通过了结题验收。

"青岛云路"公司已建成一条年产能1 000吨级非晶粉末生产线,形成具有自主知识产权的非晶磁粉芯产品全流程生产体系,实现世界上首次非晶磁粉芯的规模化生产;并成为该类产品中国市场第一大供应商,占据全球供应市场70%的份额。

来源:人民网

The globally first mass production of non-crystal magnetic powder cores realized

On August 31, Qingdao Science and Technology Bureau told us that the "Preparation Technology and Industrialization of One Kiloton of Non-crystal Magnetic Powder Cores", a major self-innovation project in Qingdao which was carried out by Qingdao Yunlu Advanced Material Technology Co., Ltd., had passed the final acceptance test.

Qingdao Yunlu has completed a non-crystal powder production line with a capacity of 1 kiloton and built an all-process production system of non-crystal magnetic powder core products with proprietary intellectual property rights, marking the first mass production of non-crystal magnetic powder cores in the world. The company has become the largest supplier of such products in the Chinese market and accounts for 70% of the global supply market.

Source: people. cn

中科院大连化物所复杂分子体系反应动力学研究获新进展

近日,中科院大连化物所研究员韩克利带领复杂分子体系反应动力学研究团队,在全无机钙钛矿光电探测器动力学研究中取得新进展。该研究团队发现,全无机钙钛矿微晶激发态载流子存在快速扩散行为,以此制备出的光电探测器具有超高灵敏度和快速时间响应。相关研究成果发表在《先进材料》上。

来源:科学网

Breakthroughs made in the Reaction Kinetics of Complex Molecular Systems in Dalian Institute of Chemical Physics

Recently, a research team on complex molecular system reaction kinetics led by Han Keli, a researcher in Dalian Institute of Chemical Physics, the Chinese Academy of Sciences, made new progress in the whole inorganic perovskite photodetector dynamics. The team found that the carrier in excited state of the whole inorganic perovskite microcrystalline can diffuse rapidly. Photodetectors produced on this could feature ultra-high sensitivity and fast time response. Related research results were published in *Advanced Materials*.

Source: ScienceNet. cn

新型高透光玻璃阻隔九成红外光

一块厚度为 6 毫米、泛着淡蓝色光泽的玻璃,既没有贴膜也没有任何遮挡,在强烈阳光照射下竟能阻隔 90% 的红外光,同时还能保持 70% 的高透光率……日前,南京安达玻璃技术有限公司内,一种具有自主知识产权的新型高透光高隔热浮法玻璃研制成功,节能指标刷新世界纪录,并通过住建部建材联合会技术鉴定。

来源:《科技日报》

New high transparent glass blocks 90% of infrared light

A piece of glass with thickness of 6 mm and tint of light blue can block 90% of the infrared light under the strong sunlight while maintaining 70% of the high transmittance rate in the condition of absence from the pad pasting or any shelter. Recently, Nanjing Anda Glass Technology Co., Ltd. has successfully developed a new type of high-transparent and high-permeability float glass with independent intellectual property rights, the energy-saving indicator of which created a new world record. This new creation has passed the technical appraisal of the National Housing and Urban Building Materials Association.

Source: *Science and Technology Daily*

可折叠有机电池问世,可用于起搏器等人体植入设备

近日,贝尔法斯特女王大学的科学家们研发出了新型柔韧有机电池,可以

取代医用植入设备（如起搏器）的刚性电池，是一大突破。

起搏器等装置目前使用的是刚性金属电池，可能会引起患者不适。有机电池的电量可达到常规电池的三倍，且由于其是可分解的，有机电池也有望具有环境效益。

来源：环球网

Flexible organic battery created to be applied in pacemakers

Recently, Queen's University Belfast scientists have designed a new flexible organic battery that could revolutionize how medical implants are powered.

Medical devices such as pacemakers are currently fitted with rigid metal based batteries, which can cause discomfort. The charge in the batteries is set to last three times as long as in their conventional counterparts. As it is decomposable, the organic battery is also expected to offer environmental benefits.

Source: huanqiu. com

人造肉之后人造皮也来了：不杀生 无污染

一家名叫 Modern Meadow 的美国公司近期在实验室里培养出了一种新型的人造皮革，他们为这种由胶原纤维制成的皮革取名为 Zoa。考虑到制皮传统方法其实就是把动物皮中非胶原的部分去除，这家公司采用了细胞培养胶原的方法：通过编辑基因序列，让细胞产生胶原纤维组织。总体上跟人造蜘蛛丝类似（人造蜘蛛丝的材料已经被 The North Face 用于大衣）。

这种实验室培养的皮革不会涉及动物，也没有鞣制过程可能带来的各种污染（比如 DMF）。据说 Modern Meadow 的工程师还能改变 Zoa 的各种属性，比如说让它变得更有弹力，更坚硬耐用，还能添加各种颜色。

来源：环球网

After artificial meat, artificial leather is coming too: no killing, no pollution

Modern Meadow, an American company, has recently developed a new type of artificial leather in the laboratory, which was made of collagen fibers and named Zoa. Considering that the traditional leather-making method is actually removing the non-collagenous part of the animal skin, the company uses the method of cell culture of collagen: let the cells produce collagen fibers by editing the gene sequence, which is generally similar to artificial spider silk (the material of artificial spider silk has been used for coat by The North Face).

Such lab-grown leather does not involve animals, nor does it have any pollution that may result from tanning processes (such as DMF). Modern Meadow engineers are said to be able to change the various attributes of Zoa, such as making it more resilient, harder and more durable, as well as adding a variety of colors.

Source: huanqiu. com

上海交大研发钙钛矿薄膜，比蝉翼薄数十倍

太阳能光伏技术是解决人类能源危机最具潜力的科技之一，然而目前太阳能光伏电池制备成本较高、工艺复杂，难以实现大规模应用。日前从上海交通大学获悉，上海交大材料科学与工程学院金属基复合材料国家重点实验室韩礼元教授团队的最新研究成果有望打破目前僵局。团队使用更加经济安全的新方法制备出比蝉翼还薄数十倍的大面积钙钛矿薄膜，向实现大规模低成本太阳能发电的目标迈出了重要的一步。该成果近日在国际著名学术期刊《自然》杂志在线发表。

来源：上海科技

Shanghai Jiaotong University (SJTU) developed perovskite film thinner than cicada's wings

The solar photovoltaic (PV) technology is seen as one of most potential technologies for tackling the energy crisis facing mankind; however, the large-scale application of this technology is still stagnant due to the high costs and complex process for making solar cells. According to SJTU, a research team led by Professor Han Liyuan at the State Key Lab of Metal Matrix Components of the university has published new research findings, which are expected to change this situation. The team used a new, safer and more economical method to make large-sized perovskite film that is several dozen times thinner than a cicada's wings, which marks a significant step forward towards the large-scale and low-cost solar power generation. The research findings have been published online in *Nature*.

Source: stcsm. gov. cn

修饰 DNA 可合成凝胶等全新材料

据物理学家组织网近日报道,美国斯克利普斯研究所化学家通过对 DNA 的核苷酸进行化学修饰,将 DNA 变成合成新型化学物质的平台。发表在德国《应用化学》杂志上的新研究证明,DNA 不止能储存遗传信息,还能用来研制药用物质或纳米材料。

来源:中国科技网

New materials like gel synthesized via DNA modifications

According to a report from Phys. Org, chemists at the Scripps Research Institute (TSRI) have turned DNA into a platform to synthesize new chemical materials by chemically modifying DNA nucleotides. A new study published in the chemistry journal *Angewandte Chemie* has shown that DNA not only stores genetic information, but also can be used to develop medicinal substances or nanomaterials.

Source: stdaily. com

中国学者仿萤火虫研制出"高亮发光"水凝胶,持续时间超 150 小时

近日,中国科学技术大学教授崔华、马明明等与南京大学教授王伟合作,模拟萤火虫生物发光,成功制备出一种可高强度和长时间化学发光的水凝胶,其发光在黑暗中肉眼可见,持续时间达 150 小时以上。国际权威学术期刊《自然·通讯》日前发表了该成果。

来源:新华社

Chinese scholars develop hydrogel that could illuminate for over 150 hours through simulating firefly bioluminescence

Professors Cui Hua and Ma Mingming from University of Science and Technology of China cooperated with Professor Wang Wei from Nanjing University in simulating firefly bioluminescence and succeeded in preparing a hydrogel with high-intensity and long-time chemiluminescence. The luminescence of the hydrogel is visible for more than 150 hours to naked eyes in the dark. This research has recently been published in *Nature Communications*, an international authoritative academic journal.

Source: Xinhua News Agency

史上最逼真人造肌肉问世,机器人会更逼真

近日,美国哥伦比亚大学的工程师研究出一种可以用于人形机器人的合成

肌肉。这种肌肉可承受比自身重量重 1 000 倍的压力,合成的软体肌肉通过 3D 打印制成,抛弃了之前模型所使用的外部压缩器和高压设备,还可模仿人体肌肉做出推、拉、弯曲和扭曲等动作。

来源:环球网

Most vivid artificial muscles created paves way for more lifelike robots

Recently engineers at Columbia University of the U. S. have created a 3D-printable synthetic soft muscle. The new material can lift 1 000 times its own weights, which doesn't need any external pumps, pressure-regulating equipment, or high voltage converters as previous muscles required. It can also replicate natural motion—push, pull, bend, twist.

Source: huanqiu. com

合肥工业大学研发智能水凝胶,一分钟实现 96% 自修复

日前,合肥工业大学科研人员成功设计一种新型材料,能在 1 分钟内实现 96% 的自修复。据介绍,这款可快速高效自修复的高性能仿生智能纳米复合水凝胶,具有多功能、优异机械性能等特点,应用前景广阔。

来源:中新网

Hefei University of Technology developed an intelligent hydrogel that enables 96% self-healing in a minute

Recently, researchers from Hefei University of Technology succeeded in developing a new-type material that enables 96% self-healing in a minute. It is learnt that this high-performance biomimetic intelligent nano-composite hydrogel can heal itself rapidly and efficiently, with various functions and superior mechanical properties. It has bright prospects for application.

Source: chinanews. com

新织物凉爽效果比棉织品高 55%

据最新一期美国化学学会期刊《ACS 纳米》报道,美国研究人员开发出一种新的热调节织物,其凉爽效果要比棉织品高出 55%。这种材料可由 3D 打印制造,为调节体温提供了一种更为简便、低成本的方式,降低了暑天使用空调的需求。

来源:《科技日报》

New fabric has a 55% greater cooling effect than cotton

According to a recent issue of *ACS Nano*, researchers have designed a thermal regulation textile that has a 55% greater cooling effect than cotton. The material can be fabricated using 3D printing, and could provide a simple, low-cost way to cool the human body and reduce the need for air conditioning on hot days.

Source: *Science and Technology Daily*

日本发明"机器人晶体":可像动物一样做屈伸运动

日本研究人员最近发明了一种可像尺蠖等动物一样屈伸运动的晶体材料,它可因加热和冷却而反复屈伸,能做出移动或翻滚等动作,所以被研究人员称为"机器人晶体"。日本东京工业大学和早稻田大学的研究人员在英国《自然·通讯》杂志上报告了相关成果。

来源:36 氪

Japanese invented "robot crystal": can do flexion and extension like animals

Japanese researchers recently invented a kind of crystal material that can bend and stretch like animals such as looper. It can be flexed and stretched repeatedly due to heating and cooling. It can make mobile or roll and so on. So it is called "robot crystal" by researchers. Researchers at the Tokyo Institute of Technology and the Waseda University reported the results in the journal *Nature communications*.

Source: 36kr

柔性新材料让电子皮肤更"智能"

美国斯坦福大学华人教授鲍哲南科研团队日前在英国《自然》杂志发表报告说,他们在柔性电子领域实现了制造工艺的新突破,首次成功开发出更易量产的高密度、高灵敏度可拉伸晶体管阵列,这一成果在电子皮肤等研究中具有突破性意义。

来源:新华网

New flexible material makes skin electronics more intelligent

A report published recently on the Britain journal *Nature* by a research group led by Chinese professor Zhe'nan Bao said that the researchers have achieved a breakthrough in manufacturing flexible electronics. They have successfully developed the first highly dense and sensitive stretchable transistor array that is more readily mass-produced. This groundbreaking research is of great significance for study into skin electronics.

Source: xinhuanet.com

我国半导体 SiC 单晶粉料和设备生产实现新突破

近日，在中国电子科技集团公司第二研究所生产大楼内，100 台碳化硅（SiC）单晶生长设备正在高速运行，SiC 单晶就在这 100 台设备里"奋力"生长。SiC 单晶是第三代半导体材料，以其特有的大禁带宽度、高临界击穿场强、高电子迁移率、高热导率等特性，成为制作高温、高频、大功率、抗辐照、短波发光及光电集成器件的理想材料，是新一代雷达、卫星通信、高压输变电、轨道交通、电动汽车、通信基站等重要领域的核心材料。

来源：《科技日报》

China makes new breakthroughs in producing SiC single crystal

Recently, 100 pieces of SiC single-crystal growth equipment have been operating rapidly in the production building of the Second Research Institute of China Electronics Technology Group Corporation. SiC single crystal is the third-generation material used for producing semiconductors. Featuring great forbidden band width, high critical breakdown field strength, great electron mobility, and high heat conductivity, it is an ideal material for producing high-temperature, high-frequency, high-power, anti-irradiation, short-wave luminescent and optoelectronic integrated devices. It is a major material in such areas as the new-generation radar, satellite communications, high-voltage power transmission, rail transportation, electric vehicles, and telecommunication base stations.

Source: *Science and Technology Daily*

可耐 3 000℃ 烧蚀陶瓷涂层及复合材料面世

近日，中南大学粉末冶金研究院粉末冶金国家重点实验室中国工程院院士黄伯云团队开发出了一种新型可耐3 000℃烧蚀的陶瓷涂层及复合材料,具有优越的抗烧蚀性和抗热震性,引发国际广泛关注。据悉,这是世界上首次合成该四元含硼碳化物单相超高温陶瓷材料,并制成涂层,与碳—碳材料完美"融合";而现行新材料领域,主流为二元化合物体系混合材料的研究。

来源:人民网

Composite ceramic coating resistant to 3 000℃ developed

Recently, a research team of Central South University has developed a new kind of composite ceramic coating with remarkable ablation and thermal shock resistance capacity, which can tolerate ultra-high temperature up to 3 000℃. The research is led by Huang Boyun, a member of China Engineering Academy, and conducted at the State Key Laboratory of Powder Metallurgy Research Institute (PMRI), Central South University. The new material has drawn attention worldwide. It is reported that it is the world's first synthesis of ceramic materials consisting of single-phase boron carbide that are resistant to ultra-high temperature, and are perfectly compatible with carbon-carbon material. In contrast, binary compounds are the main subjects in the current new materials research.

Source: people. cn

更耐用补牙材料研制成功

目前的补牙材料通常很硬,但比较脆,容易断裂。美国加利福尼亚大学圣巴巴拉分校研究人员开发的新材料同样坚硬,韧性则要高出50%,更加经久耐用,并且对细胞无毒。相关论文发表在《先进材料》杂志上。

来源:科学网

More durable dental filling materials are developed successfully

The current dental filling materials are usually hard, but relatively brittle and easy to break. Researchers at the University of California, Santa Barbara have developed new materials that are equally hard, yet 50% more ductile, making it move durable and non-toxic to cells. The paper is published in *Advanced Materials*.

Source: ScienceNet. cn

12

生物篇

科学家揭秘人类"第二大脑"的结构

来自斯坦福大学生物科技研究所的最新研究发表于《科学》杂志中,文章记录了对肠道中神经细胞的组织的理解,这个研究为肠道疾病的起源是一个全新的发现,其中包括肠易激综合征和慢性便秘。

由于肠道中存在着大量的神经元和复杂的连通性,它通常被人们称为人类的第二大脑;而且,其中存在的整个神经系统对于保持身体健康是至关重要的,因此了解这个组织的神经系统对于解决胃肠道疾病问题是至关重要的。通过试验,研究人员发现,控制着我们第二大脑的组织功能的并不仅仅是单一的肠道层,而是肠道壁的三维结构。

来源:新浪科技

Scientists have made an important step in understanding the organization of "second brain"

The latest research revealed the organization of nerve cells embedded within the gut that control its function-a discovery that could give insight into the origin of common gastrointestinal diseases, including irritable bowel syndrome and chronic constipation. The research was led by the Institute of Biological Science of Stanford University and published in *Science*.

Often known as the 'second brain' for its vast number of neurons and complex connectivity, the enteric nervous system has a crucial role in maintaining a healthy gut. Therefore, understanding how this neural mosaic is organized could help scientists find treatments for common gastrointestinal disorders. Researchers uncovered a set of rules that controlled the organization of the "second brain" not just along a single gut layer but across the 3D space of the gut wall.

Source: tech. sina. com. cn

全新微蛋白结构设计出炉

来自英国布里斯托大学的研究团队在本周出版的《自然·化学生物》杂志发表论文称,他们设计出一种比天然蛋白小很多的微蛋白,借此可以对蛋白质形成折叠结构并保持稳定的分子作用力"一探究竟",为设计生物医药所需的微小蛋白和微小分子等基本结构开辟了全新路径。

来源:《科技日报》

New structure design of mini-protein published

According to a thesis published by the research team from the University of Bristol in this week's *Nature Chemical Biology*, they designed the mini-protein structure which is much smaller than that of natural protein. This will allow scientists to unpick some of the molecular forces that assemble and stabilize protein structures, and offer new alternatives to designing basic structures needed by biological medicine, such as mini-protein and mini-molecule.

Source: *Science and Technology Daily*

果蝇的"内置指南针"找到

英国《自然》杂志近日发表论文称,美国科学家发现了生物的"内置指南针"——果蝇在导航过程中保持方向感所依赖的神经回路,以及转向神经元的"油门"和"刹车"。这项研究不仅能为研究其他动物的空间导航能力带来启发,更重要的是,还能加深我们对大脑如何将变化中的输入整合为持续活动的理解。

来源:《科技日报》

Internal compass guides fruit fly navigation

According to a paper published in *Nature*, scientists in the U.S. have found that a ring of cells in the middle of the fruit fly brain acts as a compass, and the "gas" as well as "brake" in sustaining a sense of direction. The research will not only serve as an inspiration on other researches into the internal navigation systems of other animals, but also deepen our understanding on how brain integrates the changing inputs into sustained activities.

Source: *Science and Technology Daily*

全球入侵物种数量在上升

一个国际研究团队在日前出版的《自然·通讯》上指出,在世界范围内,在过去200年里,新确定的外来物种数量在持续增长,所有的首次入侵记录,超过三分之一发生在1970到2014年。

出于这个原因,目前,世界各地正在建立各种法律法规,以减少新的外来物种的引入。"但是,我们的研究结果表明,过去的努力还不够有效以跟上正在进行的全球化。我们迫切需要实施更加有效预防政策。"研究者称。

来源:《科技日报》

Invasive species on the rise worldwide

An international research team has recently published a study on the new edition of *Nature Communication*. The study pointed out that, during the last 200 years, the number of new established alien species has grown continuously worldwide, with more than a third of all first introductions recorded between 1970 and 2014.

For this reason, various laws are currently in force globally attempting to mitigate the introduction of new alien species. "However our results show that the past efforts have not been effective enough to keep up with ongoing globalization. There is an urgent need to implement more effective prevention policies," said the researcher.

Source: *Science and Technology Daily*

研究发现鸟儿也懂"语法"

词序对语句含义很重要,比如"狼吃羊"和"羊吃狼"是两码事。科学家新近发现,一种野生的小鸟也掌握了这条语法规则,只会对顺序正确的鸣叫声有反应。

这种小鸟名为远东山雀。日本京都大学等机构研究人员说,成群的远东山雀遇到天敌时,会发出顺序如 ABC—D 的鸣叫声,其中 ABC 的含义是"有危险",D 的含义是"集合",平时它们会用 D 招呼亲友集合分享食物。这两个词按顺序组合时,远东山雀会聚集到一起围攻入侵者。

来源:科学网

Research finds out birds also know grammar

Word order matters a lot to the meaning of a sentence. For example, 'Wolf eats sheep' and 'Sheep eats wolf' are completely different. Recently, scientist have discovered that a wild bird is also a master of this grammatical rule as it only responds to tweets in correct orders.

According to researchers in Kyoto University, a parus minor, also called Japanese Tit, will tweet in an order of 'ABC—-D' when faced with natural enemies, in which 'ABC' means 'Danger' and 'D' means 'Get together'. It would also tweet 'D' to call for friends and families to share food. When those words are tweeted in a specific order, parus minors will gather around and attack intruders.

Source: ScienceNet. cn

广西发现珍稀雄王声猛蚁

近日,广西花坪自然保护区的技术人员与广西师范大学生科院的科研专家在保护区开展的蚁科多样性调查中,首次发现珍稀古老蚂蚁物种——雄王声猛蚁。

据了解,雄王声猛蚁堪称蚂蚁界的活化石,它的发现为探讨蚂蚁的演化历史和分布规律提供了新的证据,具有极高的科学价值。

来源:《科技日报》

Rare opamyrma hungvuong found in Guangxi

Recently, technical staff at Huaping Natural Reservation Area, Guangxi and scientists from the Life and Science College of Guangxi Normal University have first discovered an ancient ant species, opamyrma hungvuong in an ant diversity investigation conducted in the reservation area.

Opamyrma hungvuong is known as the living fossil in ant world, the discovery of which is of great scientific significance and will provide new insights in the ant evolution history and their distribution rules.

Source: *Science and Technology Daily*

最大鱼龙化石被"重新发现"

据国外媒体报道,英国和德国科学家近日在博物馆中"重新发现"了一具成年雌性鱼龙化石,化石长度为3至3.5米,是该类动物中最大的化石纪录。该化石20多年前发现于英格兰海岸,但直到最近才被科学家拿来研究。

鱼龙是一种类似鱼和海豚的大型海栖爬行动物。它们最早出现于约2.5亿年前,比恐龙稍微早一点(2.3亿年前),约9 000万年前灭绝,比恐龙早灭绝约2 500万年。有些鱼龙身体十分小,但有些鱼龙身体很大。

来源:《科技日报》

The largest Ichthyosaurus on record "rediscovered"

According to overseas media, scientists from the UK and Germany have "rediscovered" the largest Ichthyosaurus on record—estimated to be between 3 and 3.5 m. The new specimen was originally discovered off the coast of England, during the mid-1990s. However, the specimen remained unstudied until recent.

Ichthyosaurs were large marine reptiles resembling fish and dolphins. These reptiles appeared more than 250 million years ago, a little bit before the first dinosaurs, and became extinct about 90 million years ago, 25 million years before the extinction of dinosaurs. Ichthyosaurs ranges greatly in size from tiny to massive.

Source: *Science and Technology Daily*

食物中的RNA分子让蜜蜂长成工蜂

也许"人如其食"特别适用于雌性蜜蜂,这句西方谚语指饮食可反映一个人性格与生活环境。而雌性蜜蜂依据食物的不同,能长成不育的小个工蜂,也能变成多产的大块头蜂后。

之前,一些研究人员认为,蜂群供养年轻蜂后的食物中有一些特殊东西——一种名为蜂王浆的分泌物,这就让雌性蜜蜂最终出现分化,分别成为工蜂和蜂后。

但现在,一项新研究显示,工蜂幼虫体内有一种信号分子,抑制了其性发育。而普通工蜂的饮食主要是一种花粉和蜂蜜的混合物,这些"蜜蜂食料"里大量掺杂着一种微小核糖核酸(miRNA)。这些非编码的 RNA 分子能帮助调节蜜蜂的基因表达。

来源:科学网

The RNA molecules in the food can make the bees grow into worker bees

As a western proverb goes "We are what we eat", it refers to people's diet can reflect their personality and living environment. And this proverb is particularly applicable to the female bees. Based on what they eat, the female bees can grow into small worker bees with no fertility or big queen bees with a strong fertility.

Some researchers believed that the food fed on young queen bees had a special material, also known as royal jelly, which will grow the female bees into worker bees and queen bees.

But a new research shows that a signal molecule in larva worker bees will inhibit its sexual development. The common worker bees mainly eat a mixture of pollen and honey, which is mixed with a small RNA (miRNA). These non-coding RNA molecules can help regulate the gene expression of bees.

Source:ScienceNet.cn

美用抗体将成体细胞编程为多能干细胞

《自然·生物技术》9 月 11 日刊登了一项用全新方法培育干细胞的突破性研究。美国科学家建立了包含一亿种抗体的抗体库,并筛选出能替代转录因子的抗体,模拟自然发育过程,将普通成体细胞重新编程为诱导多能干细胞（iPSCs）。

来源：人民网

American scientists reprogrammed adult stem cells into iPSCs

On September 11, *Nature Biotechnology* published a groundbreaking research that cultivated stem cells in a brand new way. American scientists established an antibody library with 100 million kinds of antibodies, and then sifted out those being able to replace transcription factors to simulate the natural development process, thus reprogramming normal adult stem cells into induced pluripotent stem cells (iPSCs).

Source: people. cn

蒙古国发现巨型恐龙足迹化石

日本和蒙古国研究人员最近在蒙古国戈壁沙漠中发现了3个超过1米的巨型恐龙足迹化石，他们推测留下这些脚印的恐龙体长超过30米。

来源：《中国科学报》

Giant dinosaur footprint from Mongolia

A joint Japanese and Mongolian research team recently uncovered three well preserved natural casts of a giant dinosaur's foot measuring over one meters long in the Gobi Desert of Mongolia. They believed it was made by a dinosaur that might have exceeded thirty meters in length.

Source: *China Science Daily*

微生物在"全球大搬家",人类活动"功"不可没

9月15日,美国《科学》杂志刊登了中国科学院城市环境研究所及其国际团队的一篇论文,系统阐述了微生物通过人与动物、污水及其他物质的流通在全球范围的迁徙及其环境与生态效应。

文章指出,污水的处理促进了微生物和微生物携带基因的共同扩散。全球约有359 000平方公里的耕地依赖城市污水的灌溉,而80%的污水都只经过了简单处理甚至没有处理。废水含有高密度的微生物和可交换的基因,及大量化学污染物,包括金属、抗生素和消毒剂。细菌和化学污染物的共同迁移使细菌能够在新的环境中,通过突变和基因横向转移等获得适应性优势,主动地响应逐渐变化的环境。

来源:科学网

Human activities "contribute" to the "global relocation" of microorganisms

On September 15th, a paper was published in *Science* by the Institute of Urban Environment, Chinese Academy of Sciences and its international team, systematically explaining the global transporting of microbes and the consequent environmental and ecological effects as human beings and animals travelling and polluted water and other substances circulating.

The article pointed out that the waste water disposal facilitates the mutual diffusion of microorganisms and genes carried by them. There is 359 000 km^2 of cultivated land depending on the irrigation of urban sewage. However, 80% of sewage is simply processed or even not processed at all, containing high-density of microorganisms and commutative genes, and a great amount of chemical pollutants such as metallic substances, antibiotics and sanitizer. When moving with chemical pollutants together, bacteria can obtain adaptive advantages by mutation, lateral gene transfer and other methods so as to actively respond to the gradually changing environment.

Source: ScienceNet. cn

3 亿年海洋爬行动物曾有脊椎侧弯

动物王国中骨性错牙合畸形的例子屡见不鲜，比如四肢畸形或是脚趾数量异常。现在，研究人员报告了一种水生动物中发生的最古老的脊椎畸形案例，该畸形可能导致一只体长 80 厘米的海洋爬行动物方胸龙属（Stereosternum tumidium）脊柱侧凸。

这个化石发掘于巴西，距今约有 3 亿年，它表明该动物的第 18 个椎骨未能正常发育，这种畸形导致该方胸龙属动物脊椎弯曲，并可能限制它行动的灵活性。研究人员近日发表于美国《公共科学图书馆·综合》的文章中报告了该成果。

来源：科学网

This 300-million-year-old marine reptile had scoliosis

Examples of skeletal deformities abound in the animal kingdom — think malformed limbs or an abnormal number of toes. Now, researchers have reported the oldest record of a vertebral malformation in an aquatic animal, a deformity that likely led to scoliosis in the 80-centimeter-long marine reptile known as *Stereosternum tumidium*.

The fossils, unearthed in Brazil and roughly 300 million years old, reveal an 18th vertebra that failed to develop properly, a condition that curved this animal's spine and likely limited its flexibility, the researchers report this week in *PLOS ONE*.

Source: ScienceNet. cn

云南发现盲高原鳅新种丰富中国洞穴鱼类

中国科学院昆明动物研究所研究人员在云南省文山州西畴县西洒镇发现了一个眼盲的高原鳅新种,经过系统研究后以其采集地命名为西畴高原鳅,丰富了中国洞穴鱼类记录。

西畴高原鳅的主要鉴别特征如下:眼睛高度退化为一个细小的眼点,背鳍起点前于腹鳍起点,背鳍起点距离吻端的距离近于尾鳍基部,尾柄细长,身体光滑无鳞,鳔后室发达,长椭圆形,肠短,呈"Z"折叠于胃的后方。

来源:中新网

A new loach of the genus Triplophysa found in Yunnan Province, enriching the species of cave fish in China

A new species of blind triplophysa was found recently in Xisa Town of Xichou County in Yunnan Province, by researchers from Kunming Institute of Zoology (KIB), Chinese Academy of Sciences (CAS). After systematic examination, it is named after the place where it was collected—the Xichou County—as Triplophysa xichouensis, whose discovery helped enrich the species of cave fish found in China.

It can be distinguished from its congeners by the following characters: eyes highly degenerated to very tiny black dots; dorsal-fin origin closer to snout tip than to caudal-fin base and anterior to vertical line of pelvic-fin origin; body smooth and scaleless; lateral line complete and straight, long and oval; intestine short, bending in zigzag shape behind stomach.

Source: chinanews.com

研究发现地球生命并未如此大不同

所有看上去不同的物种实际上过着非常相似的生活。这种趋同表明,也许有朝一日,预测多少物种生活在特定的栖息地内将成为可能。相关成果日前发表于《美国博物学家》杂志。

科学家分析了4个大洲的134个蜥蜴物种。对于每个物种,他们分析了关于其生态学的50多个特征,诸如栖息地类型、觅食方式、繁殖产出以及对于捕食者的防御。研究人员反复发现不相关的蜥蜴出现在类似生态位上。在134个物种中,有100个出现这种情形。这远远超过随机发生的概率。例如,非洲变色龙拥有和美洲灌木变色龙相同的生活型。而澳大利亚棘蜥占据的生态位和北美角蜥几乎相同。

来源:科学网

Research shows life on Earth isn't that varied after all

Many seemingly different species actually live very similar lives. This convergence suggests that it may someday be possible to predict how many species live in a particular habitat. The research was recently published in *The American Naturalist*.

Scientists looked at 134 species on four continents. For each one, they examined more than 50 features of their niches, such as habitat type, hunting style, reproductive output and defenses against predators. Over and over, they saw pairs of unrelated lizards converge on similar niches. Out of the 134 species, 100 belonged to a convergent pair, far more than could have happened by chance. For example, African chameleons have ecological equivalents in the Americas called bush anoles, and Australia's thorny devil fills almost precisely the same niche as North America's horned lizards.

Source: ScienceNet. cn

中科院专家发现植物伪装术,同一物种在不同山头颜色不一

近日,中科院昆明植物研究所高山植物多样性研究组的孙航研究团队发

现，植物可以通过表型分异实现伪装色彩，局部适应周围环境，同一物种在不同山头颜色不一。

来源：澎湃新闻

CAS scientists discovered plants of the same species on different mountains have varied colors as camouflage

Recently, a research team led by Sun Hang from Kunming Institute of Botany of Chinese Academy of Sciences (CAS) has found that plants could change colors to blend in with surroundings as camouflage through phenotypic differentiation, which explains why plants of the same species on different mountains have different colors.

Source: ThePaper. cn

中国首次成功繁育全球最美蛇

近日，中科院与西华师范大学、四川省林科院合作，终于攻克繁育横斑锦蛇的难题，首批蛇蛋孵化成功。横斑锦蛇于约100年前首次被发现，但近百年来，被发现的活体不超过30条。

来源：看看新闻网

China succeeded in breeding the most beautiful snake for the first time

Recently, Chinese Academy of Sciences, with China West Normal University and Sichuan Academy of Forestry, succeeded in breeding pearl-banded ratsnake (Elaphe perlacea) with the hatch of the first batch of its eggs. First discovered by human in about 100 years ago, no more than 30 alive pearl-banded ratsnakes have been spotted since.

Source: kankanews. com

蜜蜂快速发现花朵之谜揭开

英国《自然》杂志近日发表的一篇动物学论文表明,蜜蜂和其他传粉者之所以能迅速发现花朵,是因为花瓣上纳米级图案产生的蓝色光环。这项研究表明,现存大多数开花植物群都有这种光环,但是不同系的植物可能各自独立进化出该特征。

来源:《科技日报》

Mystery of bees' quick finding of flowers is uncovered

In a zoology-focused paper recently published on *Nature*, it indicates that the reason why bees and other pollinators can find flowers so quickly is the blue halos generated by the nanoscale patterns on the petals. This research shows that most existing flowering plants have this kind of halo, while plants of different species may evolve this feature independently.

Source: *Science and Technology Daily*

中科院昆明植物所发现"蓝瘦香菇"家族新成员

中国科学院昆明植物研究所许建初研究组与 Peter E. Mortimer(南非籍)真菌研究团队合作在"蓝瘦香菇"成名一周年之际,发现了其家族粉褶菌的新种——勐宋粉褶菌。这项研究成果日前发表在《土耳其植物学杂志》上。

来源:科学网

A new member of entoloma sensu lato is discovered by Kunming Institute of Botany, Chinese Academy of Sciences

A research team led by Xu Jianchu of Kunming Institute of Botany,

Chinese Academy of Sciences, cooperating with a fungoid research team led by Peter E. Mortimer (a South African researcher), discovered a new member of entoloma sensu lato—entoloma mengsongense, a year after entoloma hochstetteri became famous in China.[①] Recently, the research result was published on *Turkish Journal of Botany*.

Source: ScienceNet. cn

深海鱼眼部发现新型视细胞

多国研究人员最新发现,生活在深海的"暗光鱼"眼部存在一种新型视细胞,可让这种鱼在昏暗条件下也拥有良好的视觉。

澳大利亚、沙特阿拉伯、挪威等国研究人员组成的科研团队在新一期美国《科学进展》杂志上报告了这一发现,认为这将有助于人们进一步了解动物的视觉系统。

来源:《科技日报》

A new type of cell has been found in the eyes of a deep-sea fish

Researchers of numerous countries have discovered a new type of cells in the eyes of a deep-sea fish, which enable mesophilic fish to have a good vision in dim environment.

Researchers from Australia, Saudi Arabia and Norway say that the discovery opens a new world of understanding about vision in a variety of light

---

① Due to its appearance, entoloma hochstetteri has acquired a Chinese nickname, "Lán shòu Xiāng gū", the literal meaning of which is a kind of blue and slender mushroom. It's also a popular internet buzzword, which is a homophonic pun derived from the Chinese expression "nán shòu xiǎng kū", meaning "feel sad and want to cry".

conditions. The result was published on *Science Advances*, an American journal.

Source: *Science and Technology Daily*

上海生科院等揭示 KDM5 亚家族组蛋白去甲基化酶的底物识别机制

近日，中国科学院植物逆境生物学研究中心杜嘉木课题组，中科院院士、中科院遗传与发育生物学研究所曹晓风课题组合作完成的论文，以 Structure of the Arabidopsis JMJ14‐H3K4me3 Complex Provides Insight into the Substrate Specificity of KDM5 Subfamily Histone Demethylases 为题，在线发表在 The Plant Cell 上，该研究利用结构生物学、生物化学和细胞生物学等手段，揭示了 KDM5 亚家族组蛋白去甲基化酶的底物识别机制。

来源：中科院网站

Chinese scientists discovered a recognition mechanism for Substrate of KDM5 Subfamily Histone Demethylases

Two research groups led respectively by Du Jiamu at Shanghai lnstitutes for Biological Sciences for Plant Stress Biology（PSC）and academician Cao Xiaofeng at the Institute of Genetics and Developmental Biology，Chinese Academy of Sciences（CAS），have recently published online in *The Plant Cell* a joint paper titled "Structure of the Arabidopsis JMJ14-H3K4me3 Complex Provides Insight into the Substrate Specificity of KDM5 Subfamily Histone Demethylases"，which used methods of structural biology，biochemistry and cytobiology to disclose a recognition mechanism for Substrate of KDM5 Subfamily Histone Demethylases.

Source: www.cas.cn

考古新发现！史前人类曾追杀 2 米高巨型树懒

据外媒报道,考古学家在美国新墨西哥州发现了一批化石,证明史前人类曾经与巨型树懒搏斗。科学家有望通过这一发现揭示远古人类狩猎的方式,而巨型树懒的灭绝,也极有可能与人类行为相关。

来源:中新网

New archaeological discovery about prehistoric men killing 2-meter-tall giant sloths

According to foreign media, archaeologists discovered a group of fossils in New Mexico, which proves that prehistoric humans used to fight with giant sloths. Scientists are expected to reveal the way ancient humans hunt through this discovery, and the extinction of giant sloths is also very likely to be related to human behaviors.

Source: chinanews.com

新研究称蜜蜂能理解"零"这个数学概念

据外媒 CNET 报道,科学家曾一度认为只有人类和一些灵长类动物等才能理解"零"这个概念。然而一项新的研究表明,蜜蜂也能理解"零"这个数学概念,它们比此前科学家认为的更加聪明;而这项研究结果也可能影响未来的人工智能设计。

来源:环球网

New study suggests bees understand the mathematical concept of zero

According to a report by CNET Networks Inc., scientists used to believe that only humans and some primates could understand the concept of zero. However, a new study suggests that bees could also understand the mathematical concept of zero and they are smarter than scientists used to think. The study could also have implications for the development of artificial intelligence.

Source: huanqiu.com

三峡发现世界最早动物足迹化石

近日,美国《科学》杂志子刊《科学进展》刊发了中美科学家在中国三峡地区发现距今5.4亿多年前动物足迹化石的研究成果。这些足迹由生活在寒武纪前的一种类似虾的动物留下,也是迄今发现的地球上最早的动物足迹化石。

来源:《北京青年报》

Scientists discover 'oldest animal fossil footprints on Earth' in southern China

Chinese and American scientists may have uncovered the earliest known fossil footprints in the Yangtze Gorges area of South China left by an animal on Earth, dating back at least 540 million years, according to a study published in the US journal *Science Advances*. The trackways are considered the earliest animal fossil footprints ever found on Earth made by animals living before the beginning of the Cambrian Period (541 mya-485.4 mya) that bore a resemblance to shrimps.

Source: *Beijing Youth Daily*

中美科学家首次在缅甸发现1亿年前热带蛙类

记者6月14日从中国地质大学(北京)了解到,中美两国科研团队首次在缅甸发现了中生代蛙类琥珀化石标本,鉴定并描述出一个全新的蛙类物种。该研究结果发表在国际知名学术刊物、自然集团旗下的《科学报告》上。本次发现的蛙类琥珀化石共有4件,由科学家们于2015年至2016年间陆续在缅甸发现,并在中国国家自然科学基金委及美国国家地理学会等项目资助下,完成了对这些化石的分析鉴定工作。

来源:《科技日报》

China and US scientists discover frogs in amber dating back to 100 million years ago in Myanmar

The reporter learned from the China University of Geosciences (Beijing) on June 14 that scientists from China and the United States for the first time discovered mesozoic frog fossil in Myanmar and described a brand new frog species. The findings were published in *Nature Scientific Reports*. A total of four frog amber fossils was discovered by scientists in Burma from 2015 to 2016. The study of these fossils was funded by the National Natural Science Foundation of China and the National Geographic Society.

Source: *Science and Technology Daily*

我国科学家成功繁育出濒危物种横斑玉斑蛇后代

历经3年,我国科学家人工饲养并繁育出濒危物种横斑玉斑蛇后代,结束了我国珍稀蛇类均由国外率先人工繁育成功的历史。横斑玉斑蛇有着"世界上最美蛇"的美誉。科学家们不仅成功繁育了横斑玉斑蛇后代,还破解了它为何难发现、其生活习性、栖息地等疑团。

来源:人民网

Chinese scientists succeed in reproducing Euprepiophis Perlacea

After 3 years' efforts, Chinese scientists successfully reproduced Euprepiophis Perlacea, ending the history that all rare snakes in the country were first artificially bred by foreign organizations. Researchers have not only bred this world's most beautiful snake species, but also found out information about its scarcity, life habits and habitats.

Source: people. com. cn

13

农业篇

上海探索校区、农区"双区联动"农业创新机制

上海正在探索大学校区与农业园区"双区联动"式的农业创新创业新机制。近日,上海交通大学新农村发展研究院与沪郊金山枫泾共建的农科实践基地正式开园,并且推出了首批农创实践项目。

据了解,这个校区、农区"双区联动"机制,其实是建立一个要素整合平台,让大学和科研院所的农业科技工作者、为农科技服务"特派员"带着科研成果和技术,与农业园区的农创项目以及"农"字号的投资意向进行多元结合。目前,在资源共享、信息互通、项目导入等前期工作的基础上,启动了首期120亩农地规模的农科实践基地,推出了生态型种养结合、功能性大米生产等农创项目。

来源:新华社

Shanghai explores co-development between the academia and agricultural parks for agricultural innovation mechanism

Shanghai is exploring a new agricultural innovation mechanism enabled by the co-development between higher education institutions and agricultural parks. Recently, the Institution of New Rural Area Development of Shanghai Jiao Tong University (SJTU) has jointly inaugurated an agricultural practice base with authorities of Fengjing Town in Jinshan District, Shanghai, and launched the first batch of agricultural innovation programs.

It is known that the co-development mechanism between the academia and the agricultural park aims to build a platform integrating all kinds of agricultural resources, which can enable diverse cooperation between agricultural and technological researchers in universities or research institutions and agricultural innovation programs in the park or investment intentions regarding agricultural programs, with the former serving as "specially deployed personnel" to contribute their research achievements and technologies. Currently, based on the sharing of resources and information and the introduction of programs, an 8-hectare practice base is put into operation in Phase I, with various agricultural innovation programs such as the bio-friendly integrated farming and livestock program, and the functional rice production program.

Source: Xinhua News Agency

我国学者研制出一种可回收的农药

中科院合肥物质科学研究院技术生物所吴正岩研究员课题组近期研制出一种可回收的 pH 控释农药,能显著提高农药利用率、减少农药使用量、降低农药引发的农业面源污染。国际化工学界知名期刊《化学工程》发表了该研究成果。

——来源:新浪新闻

Chinese scholars developed a recyclable pesticide

A project team led by researcher Wu Zhengyan from Institute of Technical Biology & Agriculture Engineering of Heifei Institutes of Physical Science, CAS recently developed a recyclable pH controlled-release pesticide which can significantly improve the efficiency of pesticides, reduce the dose of pesticides and mitigate the agricultural non-point source pollution caused by pesticides. The result is published on the famous international journal *Chemistry Engineering*.

Source: news. sina. com

咖啡最大产地的种植面积到 2050 年将缩减近 90%

若干研究已经预测,气候变化会使全球适合种植咖啡树的农田数量到 2050

年减半,而这主要是因为不断上升的气温。如今,对咖啡的最大产地——拉丁美洲进行的生态学建模显示了更严重的衰退:咖啡树的"栖息地"将缩减88%,损失尤其严重的是尼加拉瓜、洪都拉斯和委内瑞拉的地势低洼地区。

来源:科学网

Cultivated area of the biggest coffee producer will shrink by 90% in 2050

Several researches have predicted that climate change would cut the land suitable for planting coffee trees across the world into half by 2050, mainly caused by the rising temperature. At present, an ecological modeling of Latin America, the biggest coffee producer, indicates a more severe shrinkage, i.e. its habitant for coffee trees will decrease by 88%. The situation will be worse in low-lying areas in Nicaragua, Honduras and Venezuela.

Source: ScienceNet. cn

亩产620公斤我国海水稻研究取得重大突破

9月28日下午,青岛海水稻研究发展中心白泥地实验基地首批耐盐碱水稻开始收割评测,产量最高的达到亩产620.95公斤。专家认为,这意味着我国"海水稻"研究取得了一大重要突破。

耐盐碱水稻俗称海水稻,是一种可以长在滩涂和盐碱地的水稻。按照中国工程院院士袁隆平等专家的测算,亩产能提高到300公斤以上,"种海水稻就划得来,农民种植的积极性就会提高"。

来源:新华社

Research on sea-rice has made a major breakthrough, with a yield of 620 kg per mu

On the afternoon of September 28, the first batch of saline and alkaline-resistant sea-rice was harvested at Qingdao Sea-Rice Research and Development Center's Bainidi experimental base, with the highest yield amounting to 620.95 kg per mu (~667 m^2). Experts believe it is a major breakthrough in the sea-rice research.

The sea-rice, known for its resistance to saline and alkaline, can grow in the intertidal zone and saline-alkali soil. According to Yuan Longping, academician of Chinese Academy of Engineering, when the yield increases to over 300 kg per mu, "it is worthwhile to grow such rice and the farmers will be more willing to do so".

Source: Xinhua News Agency

宜家 Space10 实验室推出室内农场　植物生长速度较传统方法快三倍

近日,宜家创新实验室 Space 10 展示了实验性室内农场 LOKAL。宜家旨在通过这个系统解决现实世界的问题,使人们能够在室内无阳光或土壤的地方种植和收获自己的食物。这个垂直小农场的原型是一个水培系统,而不是土壤,作物在充满适量矿物质营养物质的水中生长。Lokal 使用可堆放的托盘和气候控制盒,在 LED 灯下种植蔬菜,使得室内植物生长速度比传统方法快三倍。

来源:36 氪

IKEA's Space10 Innovation Lab launches indoor farm, growing plants three times faster than traditional method

Recently, IKEA's Space10 Innovation Lab demonstrated its experimental indoor farm LOKAL. IKEA aims to solve real-world problems with this system through enabling people to grow and harvest their own food indoor without sun or soil. The prototype of this vertical small farm is a hydroponic system, not the soil; and the crop grows in water added appropriate amount of mineral nutrients. Lokal uses stacking trays and climate control boxes to grow vegetables under LED lights, making indoor plants grow three times faster than using traditional methods.

Source: 36kr

中国首个农业全产业链人工智能工程"农业大脑"正式启动

中国首个农业全产业链人工智能工程"农业大脑"在武汉正式启动。据悉,"农业大脑"是基于农业全产业链传感矩阵的人工智能决策体系,将为农业全产业链提供数据支撑。据农业大脑主创人张磊介绍,"农业大脑"工程的核心采用物联网、云计算、人工智能等技术,通过把传感器嵌入到农业研、供、产、销、服务等各个环节,系统分析土壤和气候等数据,最终作出最合理、最经济、最高效率的实施与决策。

来源:人民网

China launched the first industry chain-wide AI project "Agriculture Brain"

China recently officially launched in Wuhan its first industry chain-wide AI project "Agriculture Brain". It is learned that the Brain is an AI decision

-making system powered by industry-wide sensing matrices, and set to provide data support for the entire agricultural industry chain. According to one of the developers of the Brain, Zhang Lei, the core of the project is supported by technologies such as IoT, cloud computing and AI, which enables the Brain to make systematic analysis of the soil and climate data via sensors embedded in all sectors of the agriculture industry, including research, supply, production, sales and services, thus helping make and implement decisions in the most reasonable, economical and efficient manner.

Source: people. cn

沪研成果有望助人远离镉大米

日前,《自然·通讯》在线发表了中科院分子植物科学卓越创新中心植物生理生态研究所龚继明研究组的一项科研成果。该论文揭示了一种关键植物蛋白(CAL1)通过分泌和长途运输,从而调控水稻中重金属镉积累的新机制,从概念上验证了"修复型"水稻的培育理念。

来源:《解放日报》

Shanghai scientists breed a rice variety that can lower cadmium accumulation

Recently, *Nature Communications* published a research by Gong Jiming of the Institute of Plant Physiology and Ecology, Chinese Academy of Sciences. The paper reveals a new mechanism by which a protein named CAL1 lower cadmium accumulation in rice through secretion and long-distance transport, thus making the cultivation of rice varieties that produce safe grains while remediating paddy soils possible.

Source: *Jeifang Daily*

14

基因篇

中国科学家发现水稻高产关键基因

如何进一步提高水稻的单产,这是关乎国计民生的重要课题。中国科学家8月4日在《细胞研究》上发表报告说,他们发现一个关键基因能调控水稻"理想株型"并有潜力增加其产量,这将有助未来培育出更高产量的水稻品种。

来源:新华社

Chinese scientists found key gene of rice associated with higher grain yield

How to further improve rice yield is a crucial issue concerning national interest and people's livelihood. Chinese scientists published a paper on *Cell Research* on August 4, saying that they found a key gene which can control and adjust rice to grow into an "ideal plant architecture" and is potential to increase rice yield. This finding will help cultivate new types of rice with higher grain yield.

Source: **Xinhua News Agency**

新工具帮科学家实现染色体复杂构象可视化

染色体的功能远不止保持 DNA 整齐有序,这种基因组是由 DNA 和蛋白质组成的复合物,有许多不同的结构和构象。这些结构和构象可能会影响周围基因的表达。在某些构象中,线性 DNA 中相距较远的两个序列可能实际上非常靠近,并影响彼此的活性;而在其他形式中,这两个序列又可能相距甚远。

美国麻省理工学院研究生 Erez Aiden 与同事共同开发了一种能在基因组水平上揭示染色体折叠方式的新工具。这种名为 Hi-C 的技术不仅能详细描述影响基因表达的 DNA 环和结构域,甚至还能将复杂的基因组拼接在一起。

来源:《中国科学报》

New tool helps scientists to realize the visualization of complex conformations of chromosomes

The functions of chromosome can be far beyond keeping DNA in order. This genome, a sort of compound consisting of DNA and proteins, can have different structures and conformations which may affect the expression of surrounding genes. In certain conformations, two distant sequences in a linear DNA can actually be close to each other and have mutual effects on their activity. While in other conformations, these two sequences may be far away from each other.

Erez Aiden, a graduate student of MIT, US, and his colleagues developed a new tool that can unveil the folding ways of chromosomes on genome level. This technology named Hi-C can not only elaborate DNA loops and structure domains that affect gene expression, but also match complex genomes together.

Source: *China Science Daily*

英国首次利用基因技术编辑人类胚胎

近日,英国弗朗西斯·克里克研究所宣布通过基因编辑技术展示了人类胚胎早期发育阶段一种关键基因的作用机制,这有助科学家破解胚胎发育的一些未解之谜,从而改进体外受精等生殖辅助技术。这是英国首次实施人类胚胎基因编辑。由于牵扯道德伦理问题,人类胚胎研究一直存在争议,此前只有中美两国实施过人类胚胎基因编辑。

来源:新华社

UK scientists edit genes in human embryos for the first time

Recently, researchers from the Francis Crick Institute used genome editing technology to reveal the role of a key gene in human embryos in the first few days of development. This could help them understand some of the unsolved mysteries about embryonic development and improve assisted reproductive technology like in vitro fertilization. This is the first time that the UK has ever conducted a genome editing. Studies on human embryos have been controversial since they may cause the confusion of morality and ethics. Only China and America have done such an editing before.

Source: Xinhua News Agency

转基因小麦被用于制作腹腔友好型面包

那些不吃谷蛋白的人很快就能吃上适合自己的面包了。每100人中间可能会有1人会对食用谷蛋白产生危险的免疫反应，现在一种不会产生这种谷蛋白的小麦品系已经出现。

据悉，一些人的免疫系统对谷蛋白会产生不同的反应，这会损伤肠壁并导致腹泻、呕吐、营养不良，甚至是肠癌。为此，西班牙科尔多瓦市可持续农业研究所的 Francisco Barro 团队设法去除它们。研究人员利用转基因技术去除了小麦中90%以上的醇溶朊。

来源：科学网

Genetically modified wheat used to make coeliac-friendly bread

People forced to avoid gluten could soon have their bread (and cake) and eat it. Now there are strains of wheat that do not produce the forms of gluten that trigger a dangerous immune reaction in as many as 1 in 100 people.

It is learnt that some people's immune systems respond incorrectly to gluten, which damages the gut lining and can lead to diarrhoea, vomiting, malnutrition, and even gut cancers. So, Francisco Barro's team at the Institute for Sustainable Agriculture in Cordoba, Spain, set about getting rid of them. They used a genetic modification technique to remove 90 per cent of the gliadins, the main culprit of such a response, in wheat.

Source: ScienceNet. cn

首个针对中国地区古人类全基因组研究成果发布

首个针对中国地区古人类的全基因组研究成果近日在《当代生物学》杂志上发表，题目为"四万年前亚洲人为欧亚早期人群结构提供新洞见"。这项研究分析了距今四万年前出土于北京房山田园洞的一具男性个体的基因组，发现东亚早期人群组成十分复杂。

来源：新华社

The first-ever genome-wide study of ancient humans in China published

The first-ever genome-wide study of ancient humans in China, titled "An Asian Man Unearthed Living 40 000 Years Ago Gives an Insight into the Study of the Early Eurasian Population Structure", was recently published on the *Current Biology*. The study analyzed the genome of a male individual unearthed living 40 000 years ago in the Tianyuan Cave of Fangshan, Beijing, and found that the early population structure in East Asia was very complicated.

Source: Xinhua News Agency

美研究发现改造玉米基因方式，使其更富营养价值

近日，美国研究人员称，他们发现了一种改造玉米基因的方式，可以生产出

肉类才含有的一种氨基酸,为玉米增加营养价值。同行审议刊物《国家科学院院刊》发布一份报告,宣布了这一突破。

来源:中新网

America finds out the method to modify corn's gene to make it more nutritious

Recently, some American researchers claimed that they have found a method to modify corn's gene that can make corn generate an amino acid only contained in meat, increasing its nutritional value. *Proceedings of the National Academy of Sciences of the United States of America*, a peer review publication, has published a report announcing the breakthrough.

Source: chinanews. com

科学家能"剪出"蝴蝶翅膀颜色

蝴蝶翅膀上有绚丽而复杂的图案,从令人难忘的眼点图案到美丽的蓝色条纹,研究人员曾认为这是复杂基因共同协调作用才形成的最终图案模式。但近日发表的两个研究揭示,两个基因在决定蝴蝶翅膀的条纹和颜色方面起着巨大作用。关闭这些基因就会扰乱蝴蝶图案,甚至让它们黯然失色。相关论文近日刊登于美国《国家科学院院刊》。

来源:科学网

Scientists can "cut out" color of butterfly wings

Butterfly wings have gorgeous and complex patterns from its unforgettable eyespot patterns to beautiful blue stripes, which researchers used to believe are a combined work of complex genes. However, two recent studies published have revealed that two genes have played a significant role in deciding the stripe and color of butterfly wings. By turning off them, the pattern of butterfly wings should be disturbed or even eclipsed. Related papers have been published on *Proceedings of the National Academy of Sciences of the United States of America*.

Source: ScienceNet.cn

中科院科学家培育出基因编辑瘦肉猪

中国科学家10月23日宣布,他们利用基因编辑方法培育出一批健康的瘦肉猪,比正常猪脂肪少24%。

这项工作由中国科学院动物研究所赵建国领导完成,论文发表在新一期美国《国家科学院院刊》上。一些专家认为,这是一个重要进展。但也有人怀疑民众对基因编辑瘦肉猪的接受程度。

来源:新华社

CAS scientists successfully fostered gene-edited lean-meat pigs

Chinese scientists have announced on Oct 23rd that they have successfully fostered healthy lean-meat pigs with gene-editing technology, of which fat is 24% less than normal pigs.

This work is led and done by Zhao Jianguo from the Institute of Zoology, Chinese Academy of Sciences and the paper has been published on the latest *Proceedings of the National Academy of Sciences* of the USA. Some experts believe this is a significant step forward, but some are also concerned about public acceptance towards gene-edited lean-meat pigs.

Source: Xinhua News Agency

北大 7 位学者历时 7 年刷新 DNA 测序精度

日前,北京大学黄岩谊教授带领的团队在《自然·生物技术》期刊上在线发表《基于信息理论来修正错误的高准确度荧光产生 DNA 测序方法》,这标志着我国学者已成功刷新 DNA 信息解读的精确程度,从根本上提高了测序方法本身的精度,打破了国外在基因测序领域的技术垄断,极大推动了我国生命科学与医学的研究发展;同时,今后有望为婴儿基因突变检测、循环肿瘤 DNA 等测序临床医学应用的进一步发展提供更好的工具。

来源:科学网

Peking University scholars upgrade DNA sequencing accuracy

Recently, the team headed by Prof. Huang Yanyi at Peking University published online in the *Nature Biotechnology* the article *Highly accurate fluorogenic DNA sequencing with information theory-based error correction*. The publication marks Chinese scholars' upgrading of accuracy in interpreting DNA information, breaks the monopoly of foreign technology in gene sequencing, and propels significantly China's life science and medicine research. In addition, it is expected to provide better instrument for fetus gene mutation testing, circulating tumor cells sequencing and other clinical applications.

Source:ScienceNet. cn

上海科学家首绘水稻基因组图谱

近日,《自然·遗传学》杂志在线发表了中科院分子植物科学卓越创新中心/植物生理生态研究所和上海师范大学生命与环境科学学院黄学辉教授团队题为"泛基因组分析揭示栽培稻和野生稻中基因组变异"的研究论文;首次绘制了栽培稻-野生稻的泛基因组图谱,并系统鉴定了涵盖各类群水稻的编码基因集,为我国进一步培育优良水稻品种打下理论基础。

来源:《新民晚报》

Shanghai-based scientists first map the genome of rice

Recently, *Nature Genetics* published a study entitled "Pan-genome analysis highlights the extent of genomic variation in cultivated and wild rice" conducted by a team led by Professor Huang Xuehui with researchers from CAS Center for Excellence in Molecular Plant Sciences, Institute of Plant Physiology and Ecology and College of Life and Environmental Sciences, Shanghai Normal University. The team has mapped the genome of cultivated and wild rice for the first time, and systemically investigated the whole set of coding genes, laying a theoretical foundation for further cultivation of excellent rice varieties.

Source: *Xinmin Evening News*

超 100 个基因在"操纵"人类头发颜色

记者从中国科学院获悉,由该院北京基因组研究所联合多国科研机构科学家的一项最新研究发现,影响人类头发颜色的基因超过 100 个,这打破了"人类头发颜色主要由几个已知的基因决定"的原有认知。该研究成果已于近期在国际学术期刊《自然·遗传学》上发表。

来源:《中国青年报》

Over 100 genes found to affect human hair color

More than 100 genes have been found to affect human hair color, according to a recent research done by scientists at Beijing Institute of Genomics of Chinese Academy of Sciences (CAS), in partnership with overseas institutions. The new discoveries have broadened the scope of people's knowledge about hair-related genes since previously scientists knew only a couple of genes that influenced hair color. The study was recently published in the journal *Nature Genetics*.

Source:*China Youth Daily*

15

通信篇

印度少年创造世界最轻卫星,仅重 64 克

近日,印度一名 18 岁少年设计制造了世界上最轻的卫星,命名 KalamSat,美国国家航空航天局(NASA)计划于 6 月将其发射升空并送入轨道。印度青少年 Rifath Sharook 开发的这个卫星重 64 克,并在 NASA 和教育机构 I Doodle Learning(我涂鸦学习)举办的"Cubes in Space"比赛中荣获冠军。

来源:环球网

Indian Teen Builds World's "Lightest Satellite"

An 18-year-old Indian teenager has built what is thought could be the world's lightest satellite, which is named KalamSat and will be launched at a NASA facility in the US in June. Rifath Sharook, the Indian teen, developed this 64-gram satellite. His project was selected in a challenge called Cubes in Space, organized by education company I Doodle Learning with support from NASA.

Source:huanqiu.com

中国两部委投 1.6 亿元,用四颗空间科学卫星撬动大批原始创新

国家自然科学基金委-中国科学院空间科学卫星科学研究联合基金合作协议日前在京签署。该协议旨在进一步加强中科院和基金委的合作,共同支持全国范围的科研队伍,充分利用中科院空间先导专项支持的首批 4 颗空间科学卫星平台,即暗物质粒子探测卫星、实践十号返回式科学实验卫星、量子科学实验卫星和硬 X 射线调制望远镜卫星,开展前沿领域和综合交叉领域研究,以最大程度发挥空间科学卫星的效能,促进原始创新成果的产出。

来源:人民网

CAS and NSFC jointly invest 160 million in 4 space satellites to galvanize original innovations

National Natural Science Foundation of China (NSFC) and Chinese Academy of Sciences (CAS) recently signed the Cooperation Agreement on Joint Funding for Space Science and Satellite Science Research in Beijing. The agreement is intended to further strengthen cooperation between CAS and NSFC, provide support for research teams all over China, and make full use of the first batch of the 4 space satellite platforms supported by the Strategic Priority Research Programs of CAS, namely Dark Matter Particle Explorer, SJ-10 Retrievable Space Science Probe, Quantum Experiments at Space Scale, and Hard X-ray Modulation Telescope, so as to conduct research in cutting-edge areas and cross-sector areas, maximize the efficacy of space satellites and increase original innovation results.

Source: people.cn

中国首款四通道 GNSS 宽带射频芯片"天鹰"发布

中国首款四通道 GNSS 宽带射频芯片——"天鹰"5月23日(由合众思壮)发布,这是继去年发布的星基增强基带芯片"天琴"之后,又一款面世的中国精度星基增强芯片。

据了解,随着北斗全球系统的建设以及欧洲伽利略系统开始逐步提供服务,越来越多的导航频率和信号可以提供使用,特别是对于改善高精度定位的多模多频接收机定位性能提供了丰富的信号及频率资源。这对于采用传统的窄带射频接收前端技术的多模多频接收机提出了挑战,在接收机板卡尺寸日益小型化的需求下,中国首款四通道 GNSS 宽带射频芯片——"天鹰"应运而生。

来源:《人民日报》

UniStrong launches China's first four-channel GNSS wideband RF chip

On May 23, 2017, UniStrong launched China's first four-channel GNSS wideband RF chip named "Aquila", which is another ChinaCM product for satellite based augmentation systems following the "Lyra" baseband chip released last year.

With the BeiDou Navigation Satellite System under construction and the Galileo system starting to provide services, more frequencies and signals will be available for satellite navigation, which can be particularly leveraged by multi-mode and multi-frequency (MMMF) receivers to improve their performance in high-accuracy positioning. Therefore, MMMF receivers that adopt the traditional narrowband FR receiving technology now face new challenges. In order to meet the need of these receivers and further downsize receiver boards, "Aquila" was created as China's first four-channel GNSS wideband RF chip.

Source: *People's Daily*

我国北斗导航有了基准服务系统

5月27日上午,国家测绘地理信息局举行新闻发布会,宣布"全国卫星导航定位基准服务系统"正式启用,将面向社会公众提供开放的实时亚米级的导航定位服务,以及面向专业用户提供实时厘米级和事后毫米级的服务,全面提升我国卫星导航定位服务的能力和水平。

来源:人民网

Beidou navigation spatio-temporal reference service system officially launched

On May 27, National Administration of Surveying, Mapping and Geoinformation held a press conference to announce the official launch of the "National Satellite Navigation and Positioning Service System", which will improve Chinese satellite navigation and positioning service capacity and level on a comprehensive scale. The system will provide the public with real-time navigation and positioning services at less than 1-meter accuracy level and the professional users with real-time centimetric service and non-real time millimetric service.

Source: people. com. cn

手机要"甩开"电池了

最近,美国华盛顿大学的研究人员发明了一款无需电池的手机,这款手机所需的能量来源于周围环境的无线电信号或光线中。这一重大发明,或许有望使手机没电时因没有充电器或充电线而无法刷朋友圈带来的焦虑成为历史。

来源:《中国科学报》

Cellphones may become cell-free

Recently, researchers from the University of Washington in the US invented a cellphone that can operate without batteries, using the energy from radio signals or light in its surroundings, a major invention that could make the anxiety of not being able to update your WeChat moments when your phone is dead with no chargers or cables at hand a thing in the past.

Source: *Chinese Science Daily*

中国量子保密通信"京沪干线"具备开通条件

近日,中国量子保密通信"京沪干线"项目获得评审专家组认可,评语称"完成了预期的技术验证和应用示范任务,同意通过技术验收"。这意味着,世界首条量子保密通信骨干线路已具备开通条件,中国在量子技术的实用化和产业化方面继续走在世界前列。

来源:科学网

Quantum security teleportation "Beijing-Shanghai Main Line" qualified for operation

China's security teleportation "Beijing-Shanghai Main Line" project has received recognition from assessment panel. The expert panel remarked that "the project has finished the pre-defined tasks of technological validation and application demonstration, thus can pass the technical acceptance." This means that the world's first quantum security teleportation main line are ready to be put into operation and China continues to lead the world in terms of the application and industrialization of quantum technologies.

Source:ScienceNet.cn

国家食药监体系98家单位接入微信辟谣中心,携手打击网络谣言

近期,国家食药监总局及98个地方各级食药监管部门的微信公众号接入微信辟谣中心,开启政企合作打击网络谣言的新模式,实现食药监部门专业性、权威性与微信平台辟谣能力的有效结合,携手共建健康、绿色的网络环境。据了解,仅2017年初至今,第三方机构已拦截100余万谣言文章,辟谣信息触达2 100余万人次。

来源:腾讯科技

China Food and Drug Administration and 98 local counterparts join WeChat Rumor Refuting Center to combat online rumors

Recently, the WeChat Official Accounts of China Food and Drug Administration and 98 local food and drug supervision departments at all levels join the WeChat Rumor Refuting Center to combat online rumors in a new manner of government-enterprise cooperation. The center combines the expertise and authority of China Food and Drug Administration with the rumor refuting capacity of WeChat, contributing to a healthy and green online environment. It is said that more than one million online rumor articles read by more than 21 million people have been intercepted by third-party organizations since early 2017.

Source: tech.qq.com

IBM 发布云迁移服务:120TB 数据塞入拉杆箱

近日,IBM 推出了一款"拉杆箱"——Cloud Mass Data Migration,里面是一套容量 120TB 的存储系统,可以让用户快速地将本地数据上传到 IBM 的云存储中。该系统使用方式很简单,客户提交"批量数据迁移"需求,IBM 就会发来这个拉杆箱,将本地数据上传并加密后再运回 IBM,IBM 再将里面的数据导入云存储平台,然后销毁"拉杆箱"里的数据。在此之前,IBM 云用户通过网络上传海量数据需要几周甚至几个月时间,而且会占用巨大的宽带,而现在只需 7 天。

来源:快科技

IBM launches Cloud Mass Data Migration service, packing 120TB of data into a carry-on bag

Recently, IBM released a "carry-on bag" — Cloud Mass Data Migration, which contains a 120TB storage system, allowing users to quickly migrate local data to IBM's cloud platform. The system is easy to use: a customer submits a "mass data migration" request; in response, IBM then ships this pre-configured bag. The encrypted data is then stored and returned to IBM, which transfers the data to its cloud object storage platform, and then erases the data in the "bag". IBM cloud users used to spend weeks or months to upload massive data to the cloud platform, which could occupy a big bandwidth; but now they could move their data in just 7 days.

Source: mydrivers.com

专家：中国5G技术有望领先全球进入预商用状态

业内预计，随着明年5G第一阶段标准的确定，包括芯片、系统厂商，以及下游终端应用企业，将会全面投入5G的产业化进程中，产业热潮有望形成。大唐移动公司总经理马建成判断，明年，中国有望领先全球进入预商用状态，"现在系统设备已经达到小型化和低成本这样一个接近于实用状态，我们预计明年，中国应该能率先进入预商用的状态。"

来源：新华网

Experts: China 5G technology is expected to lead the world into the pre-commercial state

As is forecast in the industry, with the determination of 5G standard of the first stage in the next year, chip manufacturers, system vendors, and downstream terminal applications will fully invest in the 5G industrialization process and the industry boom is expected to form. Ma Jiancheng, general manager of Datang Mobile said that China is expected to lead the world into the pre-commercial state during next year. "Now system equipment has achieved miniaturization and low cost which is close to the practical condition. We predict that China would take the lead in entering the pre-commercial state in the next year", commented by Ma Jiancheng.

Source: Xinhuanet.com

"引路"4号卫星发射成功,日版GPS体系建成

10月10日早晨7点左右,日本政府在鹿儿岛县种子岛宇宙中心使用H2A火箭36号机发射了旨在构建日本版卫星定位系统(GPS)的准天顶卫星"引路"4号。

来源:中国新闻网

Japan launches Michibiki No. 4 satellite to build a Japanese GPS

At 7:00 a.m. local time on the morning of October 10, Japan successfully launched an H2A rocket carrying the Michibiki No. 4 satellite, a quasi-zenith satellite at the Tanegashima Space Center, in Kagoshima Prefecture, in southwestern Japan, with an aim to build a "Japanese GPS".

Source: chinanews.com

量子计算云平台"中国版"启动

10月11日,量子计算云平台"中国版"正式启动。这一云平台,由中科院与阿里云合作发布。据介绍,这是为用户提供量子计算的起点,希望推动量子计算产业化,实现三方面的愿景:一是提升现有计算,包括提升机器学习、组合优化等性能,带动基于这些核心计算的业务;二是赋能新兴产业,营造量子信息技术的生态系统;三是扩充安全,加强已有的量子加密通信技术,使用量子卫星,推出基于量子密码的安全计算。

来源:新华社

Quantum computing cloud platform released in China

A research institute of Chinese Academy of Sciences (CAS) and Alibaba Cloud, Alibaba's cloud computing subsidiary, released a cloud platform for quantum computing on October 11. According to a briefing, the platform was the first step in providing users with quantum computing, and it would help industrialize quantum computing and achieve three visions: the first was to improve the performance of the existing computing, including that of machine learning and combinatorial optimization, so as to push forward the business based on those core computing; the second was to develop emerging industries and build an ecosystem for quantum information technology; the third was to tighten up security by enhancing the quantum existing cryptographic communication technology, and using quantum satellites to launch quantum cryptography-based secure computing.

Source: Xinhua News Agency

遥感光谱拍照识别大地物质成分

提到地质勘探、环境调查，人们首先联想到的往往是研究人员在现场取样，在实验室运用物理化学方法进行检测的场景。如今只要拍张照，便能识别出大面积区域内待检测物质的成分。近日从南京理工大学获悉，该校与南京地质调查中心联合建设的江苏省光谱成像与智能感知重点实验室研制的"遥感地质应用微型高光谱成像仪与数据分析系统"将这一设想变为了现实。

来源：人民网

Remote sensing spectral imaging technique identifies material compositions of land

At the mention of geological prospecting and environmental surveys, the first thing come to our mind is the scene that researchers take samples on the site and detect them in labs with physical and chemical methods. But today, we only need to take a picture to identify compositions of substances to be detected in a large area. It is learned from Nanjing University of Science and Technology that Jiangsu Key Laboratory of Spectral Imaging and Intelligent Sense, an institute jointly established by NUST and Nanjing Geological Survey, developed "a micro hyperspectral imager and a data analysis system for remote-sensing geological application" to realize the vision above.

Source: people. com. cn

北斗系统在国产客机应用试飞成功

10月10日至14日,在山东东营机场,我国自主研发的北斗卫星导航系统首次在我国完全自主设计并制造的支线客机 ARJ21—700 飞机 103 架机上进行了测试试飞,试验取得圆满成功。这次不寻常的飞行试验,正式拉开了国产卫星导航系统在国产民用客机应用的序幕。

来源:人民网

Domestic passenger planes with Beidou system made a successful trial flight

From October 10 to 14, at Dongying Shengli International Airport, Chinese-developed Beidou Satellites Navigation System made its first trial flight on 103 ARJ21-700 feeder liners that was independently designed and manufactured by China and achieved a complete success. This unusual trial flight officially kicked off the application of domestic satellite navigation system to domestic civil airplanes.

Source: people. cn

我国碳卫星数据向全球用户免费开放

中国新一代静止轨道气象卫星"风云四号"和首颗全球二氧化碳监测科学实验卫星(简称"碳卫星")的数据产品将对全球用户免费开放!

近日,在地球观测组织(GEO)第14届全会"中国日"活动上,中国代表宣布了这一重大消息。碳卫星数据产品率先正式开放共享。至此,中国成为继日本、美国之后,第三个可以提供碳卫星数据的国家。

来源:《科技日报》

China to freely share the data of its carbon satellite with global users

The data products of China's new generation of geostationary orbit meteorological satellite "FY-4" and China's first scientific satellite for monitoring global carbon dioxide ("carbon satellite" for short) will be freely accessible for global users.

This big news was announced by Chinese reprehensive at the China Day event during the 14th Plenary Meeting of the Group on Earth Observations (GEO). The data products of carbon satellite would first be shared. By now, China has become the third country (following Japan and the US) that can provide carbon satellite data.

Source: *Science and Technology Daily*

张江微小卫星创新研究院已发射22颗卫星,北斗三号近期发射

我国北斗三号全球组网卫星将于近期发射,太空中将会迎来又一颗从中科院微小卫星创新研究院"升空"的小卫星。近年来,从新一代北斗导航卫星首发星、暗物质粒子探测卫星,到世界首颗量子科学实验卫星、我国首颗全球二氧化碳监测卫星,坐落在张江的微小卫星创新研究院,先后研制和发射了22颗卫

星,在创新中取得一系列重大成果,实现了一次次"零"的突破。

来源:上海科技

Zhangjiang Micro Satellite Innovation Institute has launched 22 satellites, Beidou-3 to be launched soon

The Micro Satellite Innovation Institute of the Chinese Academy of Sciences, which is located in Zhangjiang, Shanghai, will launch another small satellite named "Beidou-3" in the near future. In recent years, the institute has developed and launched a total of 22 satellites, including the first generation of the Beidou Navigation Satellite System, the dark matter particle detection satellite, the world's first quantum science experimental satellite, and China's first global carbon dioxide monitoring satellite. By now, the institute has made a series of significant innovations and breakthroughs in the development of satellites.

Source:stcsm. gov. cn

新平台有望给遥感相机安上国产"视网膜"

11月12日从中国航天科技集团五院508所获悉,该所探测器技术实验室正在着力建立系统的光电探测器应用验证测试平台,打通探测器从设计研制到工程应用的"最后一公里",促进国产探测器的快速在轨成功使用。

空间光学遥感一直是我国航天发展的重点领域之一。光电探测器作为光学遥感器的核心器件,其技术水平决定着遥感器的性能指标,研制能力已成为遥感器研制能力的核心体现之一。长期以来,我国光电探测器大量依赖国外进口,制约了空间光学遥感整体能力的发展。

来源:《科技日报》

New platform is expected to install indigenous "retina" to remote sensing camera

On the 12th of November, it was reported that the Detector Laboratory of China Academy of Space Technology is trying its best to establish a systematic testing and verification platform for the application of photoelectric detectors as its efforts to open the "last mile" from design and development to engineering application so as to put domestic detectors to use in a rapid manner.

Spatial optical remote sensing has been one of the key development areas in China's space industry. As the core device of an optical remote sensor, the photoelectric detector determines the performance index of the remote sensor, and the research and development capability of such detector have become the key factor in the development capability of the sensor. For a long time, China's photoelectric detectors rely heavily on foreign imports, which can severely restrict the overall development capability of space optical remote sensing.

Source: *Science and Technology Daily*

北斗应用质量认证体系建设启动

在北斗车联网认证联盟的组织协调下,国家卫星应用产品质量监督检验中心、中国质量认证中心、中检南方等检测认证机构启动了北斗应用质量认证体系建设。中国科学院院士、航天科技集团高级技术顾问孙家栋认为,北斗系统很快就将完成全球组网,提供全球服务,在这样一个关键时期启动北斗应用质量认证体系建设,非常及时必要。

来源:新华社

China initiates the development of a quality assurance system for Beidou applications

Under the auspices of Beidou Vehicle Networking Certification Alliance, multiple institutes, including National Center for Quality Supervision and Inspection for Applied Satellite Products, China Quality Certification Center and CCIC Southern Electronic Product Testing (Shenzhen) Company have embarked on the development of a quality assurance system for Beidou applications. Sun Jiadong, Academician of the Chinese Academy of Sciences (CAS) and Senior Technical Adviser of China Aerospace Science and Technology Corporation (CASC) holds that the Beidou Navigation Satellite System is projected to soon accomplish a full-scale coverage, serving global customers upon its completion. In that sense, it's highly imperative and relevant that we launch a quality assurance system for Beidou applications at such a critical point.

Source: Xinhua News Agency

英特尔发布商用 5G 新品

11月17日,英特尔推出首个支持 5G 新空口(5G NR)的多模商用调制解调器家族,英特尔 XMM 8000 系列,以及英特尔最新 LTE 调制解调器——英特尔 XMM 7660。英特尔还宣布已经成功实现了基于英特尔 5G 调制解调器的完整端到端 5G 连接,而这款早期 5G 芯片是英特尔发展史上的一座关键里程碑。

来源:新浪科技

Intel unveils its first commercial 5G modem

Intel unveiled its first 5G New Radio (5G NR) modem suite, the XMM

8000 series featuring multi-modal functionality, and its newest 4G/LTE modem, XMM 7660 on November 17. The company also announced that it had already completed end-to-end 5G network connection based on its previous 5G modem, a milestone in Intel's history.

Source: tech.sina.com

混合型量子网络实现信息可靠传送

《自然》杂志在线版 11 月 22 日刊登了量子通信研究的一项里程碑式成果：西班牙光子科学研究所（ICFO）科学家用两种完全不同的量子节点，建立了一种混合型量子通信网络，并在两个节点间成功实现了光量子通信。新研究首次证明，不同量子节点组成的混合型量子网络，能像相同量子节点间一样进行可靠的量子信息传送。

来源：《科技日报》

"Hybrid" quantum network achieves reliable transfers of quantum information

A landmark study on quantum communication was published in *Nature* online on November 22. ICFO researchers have achieved a "hybrid" quantum network link and demonstrated photonic quantum communication between two very distinct quantum nodes. The study demonstrated for the first time that transfers of quantum information made by a "hybrid" quantum network composed of different quantum nodes are as reliable as those between identical nodes.

Source: Science and Technology Daily

室内定位导航需求极大

全球有四大卫星导航系统，但室内却无卫星信号。与此同时，人们有80%的时间在室内，室内定位导航需求极大。据科技行业咨询公司IDTechEx日前预测，2024年，室内定位产品市场规模将超过100亿美元。

众所周知，高精度智能混合定位和室内复杂空间的导航一直是国际导航与位置服务领域的研究难题。

来源：上海科技

Demand for indoor GPS navigation soars

There are four global navigation satellite systems in the world, but there is no satellite signal indoors. Meanwhile, people spend 80% of their lifetime staying indoors, so there is great demand for indoor GPS navigation. As predicted by IDTechEx, a consulting company in science and technology industry, the market scale of indoor GPS navigation will exceed 10 billion US dollars by 2024.

It is known that high-accurate and intelligent hybrid positioning and complicated indoor space have always been a challenge in the global navigation and position service field.

Source: stcsm.gov.cn

谷歌利用光束技术为印度农村地区提供互联网服务

谷歌近日宣布，将利用光束技术将互联网普及到印度安得拉邦的农村地区。确切而言，Google X实验室正与安得拉邦电信运营商FiberNet合作，使用"自由空间光通信技术"来提供互联网服务。该技术利用光束来传递高速、高容量的长距离网络连接。目前，通过与FiberNet合作，Google X实验室已建立了约 2 000 个 FSOC 连接，希望为 1 200 万个家庭，以及数千家政府机构和私人企业提供宽带连接。

来源：新浪科技

Google uses light beams to connect rural India to the Internet

Google recently announced that it will use light beams to connect rural areas of India's Andhra Pradesh into the Internet. In partnership with Andhra Pradesh's telecom operator FiberNet, Google X is using Free Space Optical Communications (FSOC) to connect far-flung regions of the state. It involves using beams of light to deliver high-speed, high-capacity connectivity over long distances. By now, Google X has set up some 2 000 FSOC links in partnership with FiberNet, as part of the state's plan to bring broadband connectivity to 12 million households and thousands of government offices and private enterprises.

Source：tech. sina. com. cn

欧洲伽利略导航系统 4 颗新卫星升空

欧洲伽利略卫星导航系统第 19、20、21 和 22 颗卫星由一枚阿丽亚娜 5 型火箭从法属圭亚那库鲁航天中心发射成功。欧洲航天局表示，此次成功发射意味着距该系统全部卫星组网并实现覆盖全球的导航服务只差明年的最后一次发射。

据悉，这 4 颗导航卫星由德国 OHB-System 集团公司和英国萨里卫星技术公司设计建造，每颗卫星重约 715 公斤。

来源：新华网

4 new Galileo satellites lift off

Another 4 Galileo satellites, No. 19, 20, 21 and 22, were launched successfully by an Ariane 5 from Kourou in French Guiana. The European Space Agency (ESA) stated that this launch indicates the final lift-off expected next year in realizing the whole system networking and offering global navigation services.

It is reported that the four satellites, made together by OHB System AG of Germany and Surrey Satellite Technology Ltd (SSTL) of UK, weigh approximately 715kg each.

Source: xinhuanet.com

国内首个陆路内河海上一体气象导航正式上线

日前,一款精准便捷的"气象安全导航"已正式上线。该导航由浙江省气象局自主研发,是国内首个集陆路导航和内河、海上导航为一体的气象导航软件,填补了国内水陆交通气象保障空白。据了解,目前"气象安全导航"数据已经接入浙江省沿海七大港区、主要港口和航线预报,无缝连接长江黄金水道,通过将气象大数据与行业大数据叠加应用,真正实现了海陆、行业动态关联。仅航线预报一项,就使舟山客运航线通航时间增加20%,直接经济效益超2 000万元人民币。

来源:中国新闻网

China's first integrated weather routing debuts

Recently, China's first weather routing was launched. Designed by Zhejiang Meteorological Bureau, the software covers land, inland waters and seas, filling China's gap in weather guidance for land and water transport. At present it has been connected with the province's major ports and dovetailed with the Yangtze River. The application of big data on meteorology and transport has realized in the real sense dynamic synergy of land and sea and different industries. In the single aspect of route forecast, it increases Zhoushan's transport time by 20%, bringing a direct economic profit of over 20 million RMB.

Source: chinanews.com

我国成功发射陆地勘查卫星二号

12月23日12时14分,我国在酒泉卫星发射中心用长征二号丁运载火箭,成功将陆地勘查卫星二号发射升空,卫星进入预定轨道,发射任务获得圆满成功。据介绍,这颗卫星主要用于开展陆地资源遥感勘查。这次任务是长征系列运载火箭的第259次飞行。

来源:新华社

China launches land exploration satellite

China launched a land exploration satellite into a preset orbit from the Jiuquan Satellite Launch Center in the Gobi desert, northwest China's Gansu Province, at 12:14 p.m. Beijing Time on Dec. 23, 2017. A Long March-2D rocket carried the satellite into space. The satellite is mainly used for remote sensing exploration of land resources. The launch was the 259th mission of the Long March rocket series.

Source: Xinhua News Agency

全球最小手机 Zanco Tiny T1 发布

美国 Kickstarter 众筹平台上架一款全球最小手机 Zanco Tiny T1。此款手机由 Clubit New Media 公司研发,手机长 47 毫米,比大拇指还小。Tiny T1 最多可存储 300 个联系人、50 条短信及 50 个通话记录,可用来打电话和发短信。除此之外,该手机支持 nano-SIM 卡,搭载 OLED 显示屏,并设置有 13 个语音指令,待机时间长达 3 天。

来源:36 氪

World's smallest mobile phone Zanco Tiny T1 launched

American crowdfunding platform Kickstarter launched the world's smallest mobile phone, known as Zanco Tiny T1. Developed by Clubit New Media, this device is only 47 millimeters, smaller than a thumb finger, and can make phone calls and send texts with a maximum storage of 300 contacts, 50 texts, and 50 call logs. With an OLED display and up to three-day standby time, it supports nano-SIM cards and is set with 13 voice commands.

Source:36kr

国内首颗"环保型"微纳卫星——"淮安号"恩来星发射成功

近日,南京理工大学研制的"淮安号"恩来星在酒泉卫星发射中心由"长征 11 号"运载火箭成功搭载发射升空,当日 13 时 48 分在新疆喀什基地收到了第一轨信号,功能运行正常,进入在轨测试阶段。"淮安号"恩来星采用两单元结构,重量 2.475 千克,结构、电源、通信等分系统采用了南理工廖文和教授带领的微纳卫星研究团队研制的具有自主知识产权的立方体卫星平台。光学相机由南理工电光学院光电成像与信息处理实验室自主研制,采用了 OV 系列高性能 CMOS 传感器和专用图像压缩 DSP 微处理器进行图像的压缩处理,可实现大视场对地成像探测。

来源:《科技日报》

China's first environmentally-friendly micro-satellite, "Huaian" Enlai Satellite, launched into space successfully

Last Friday, the satellite named after late Premier Zhou Enlai was successfully launched from Jiuquan Satellite Launch Center, carried by a CZ-11 solid fuel rocket. At 13:48 on the same day, Kashi Base in Xinjiang received the signal from the first orbit, showing all functions working correctly and starting in-orbit tests. "Huaian" Enlai Satellite has a two-unit structure, weighing 2.475 kilograms. It adopts patents on structure, power supply as well as communication systems from the Cubic Satellite Platform developed by the nano-satellite research team led by Liao Wenhe, a professor in Nanjing University of Science and Technology (NJUST). It is also equipped with optical cameras developed by School of Electronic and Optical Engineering, NJUST, with CMOS sensors and DSP microprocessors for picture compression, making it possible to shoot space pictures of the earth in a wider range.

Source: *Science and Technology Daily*

我国商用卫星物联网计划启动

日前,记者从中科院西安光机所获悉,由该所投资孵化企业——九天微星发起的卫星物联网计划已正式启动,试图解决网络局限带来的诸多问题并开拓新的服务领域。这个计划的启动标志着我国商业航天模式开始了新的探索。九天微星计划于今年下半年发射一箭七星"瓢虫系列",以验证物联网通信关键技术和多卫星组网能力,并开展商用试运营。一箭七星"瓢虫系列"涵盖研发设计、频率协调、发射许可、在轨运营,是目前中国民营商业航天领域规模最大、复杂程度最高的试商用项目。为确保未来物联网用户的低成本、低功耗与可靠连接,九天微星正与西安光机所展开光学载荷前沿技术的合作研发。

来源:《科技日报》

China launched a commercial satellite IoT program

According to reports, Commsat, a company backed by Xi'an Institute of Optics and Precision Mechanics (XIOPM), Chinese Academy of Sciences, has officially launched the satellite IoT program, seeking to address various issues due to the limit of network and explore new service area. The launch of this program marks a new exploration for China's commercial space model. In the second half of this year, Commsat plans to launch the "Ladybug Rocket Series", carrying seven satellites to verify the key technologies of IoT communications and multi-satellite networking capability and conduct commercial trial operation. The Ladybug Series includes R&D, frequency coordination, launch approval and on-orbit operation, and is currently the largest and most complex commercial trial project in China's private commercial aerospace sector. In order to ensure cost-effective, power-efficient and reliable connection for future IoT users, Commsat is cooperating with XIOPM to develop state-of-the-art technologies in optical load.

Source: *Science and Technology Daily*

上海布局研发新一代"中国芯"

上海首批市级科技重大专项之一"硅光子市级重大专项"项目启动会近日在张江实验室举行。硅光子技术让光子作为信息载体,实现信号传输的安全性和可靠性,是有望颠覆传统光电子产业的前瞻性技术。为此,市政府将其列入重大专项,予以全力支持,力争在上海形成完整的硅基光互连芯片产业链,打造世界级硅光子基地。

来源:解放网

Shanghai plans to develop the next generation of "China chips"

"Key Municipal Project on Silicon Photonics", one of the first batch of key projects of Shanghai, was launched in Zhangjiang Lab recently. Enabling photons to act as carriers of information, silicon photonics realizes safe and reliable data transfer and is a cutting-edge technology expected to subvert traditional optoelectronics industry. Therefore, Shanghai Municipal People's Government list it into a key project and gives it full support, striving to form a complete industrial chain of silicon-based optical on-chip interconnects and build a world-class silicon photonics base in Shanghai.

Source: jfdaily.com

我国高分六号卫星成功发射

6月2日,我国在酒泉卫星发射中心用长征二号丁运载火箭成功发射高分专项高分六号卫星。高分六号卫星是一颗低轨光学遥感卫星,也是我国首颗实现精准农业观测的高分卫星。它将与在轨的高分一号卫星组网运行,大幅提高对农业、林业、草原等资源的监测能力。

来源:新华网

China's Gaofen-6 satellite successfully launched

On June 2, China's Gaofen-6 satellite was successfully launched by a Long March-2D rocket at Jiuquan Satellite Launch Center. The low-altitude optical remote-sensing satellite is the first high-resolution satellite in China to achieve accurate agricultural observation. It will work together with Gaofen-1 satellite to significantly improve the capabilities of monitoring agriculture, forestry, grassland and other resources.

Source: xinhuanet.com

四维超纠缠态光子室外首次传输成功

近日,奥地利科学家成功在两个相距 1 200 米的屋顶间传送了超纠缠态光子,首次在实验室以外的现实世界证明了超纠缠态光子传输的可行性。发表在最新一期《自然·通讯》杂志的这一研究成果,向实现基于卫星系统快速安全传输量子信息的全球化量子网络迈出了重要一步。

来源:《科技日报》

The first successful outdoor transmission of four-dimensional hyperentangled photons

Austrian scientists have successfully transmitted hyperentangled photons between rooftops that are 1 200 meters apart, which, for the first time, proves that hyperentanglement transmission is feasible outside laboratory. The result has been published on the latest issue of *Nature Communications*. It marks a big progress toward the global quantum network in which quantum information is transmitted quickly and securely based on satellite system.

Source: *Science and Technology Daily*

美国研制出新型无线电天线

美国东北大学的研究者日前研发出一种新型的无线电天线,体积比现有的无线电天线小 100 倍,其运行频率适用于蜂窝网络和 WiFi 信号。据悉,这种新型的无线电天线可以集成到宽仅为 1mm 的芯片上,接收无线电信号的方式是首先将无线电波转化为声波,再转化为电信号,发送信号的时候反过来进行这个过程。

来源:**IT** 之家

US developed a new radio antenna

Researchers from Northeastern University of US developed a new radio antenna 100 times smaller than currently available antennas and with a running frequency suitable for cellular network and Wi-Fi signals. It is learned that this new type of antenna can be integrated onto a 1mm-wide chip. When receiving radio signals, the antenna firstly converts radio waves into acoustic waves, then into electrical signals; when sending signals, it will go through the process in a reversed way.

Source: ithome.com

16

物理篇

欧洲强子对撞机新型加速器建成：快 3 倍

欧洲核研究组织（CERN）于本月正式建成了用于大型强子对撞机的新型粒子加速器 Linac 4。据介绍，Linac 4 将作为大型强子对撞机 LHC 加速环上的首个加速器，其使命是替代自 1978 年服役至今的 Linac 2 加速器，为粒子对撞实验提供更高频率的加速。目前，Linac 4 加速器被安装在地下 12 米的建筑当中，总长度约 90 米，开周期长达 10 年。Linac 4 可以将氢负离子加速到 160 MeV，这是 Linac 2 的 3 倍。能够为 LHC 对撞机输出更大能量的粒子。

来源：环球网

CERN Has Completed its New LHC Accelerator: 3 Times More Powerful Than its Predecessor

This month, European Organization for Nuclear Research (CERN) has completed the Linac 4 which is the newest accelerator for Large Hadron Collider (LHC). Linac 4 will replace Linac 2 which has been in service since 1978, and become the first step in CERN's accelerator chain, delivering acceleration with higher frequency to a wide range of experiments. Linac 4 is an almost 90-meter-long machine sitting 12 meters below the ground. It took nearly 10 years to build. Linac 4 can bring negative hydrogen ions up to 160 MeV, which is more than three times the energy of its predecessor. This will enable delivery of particles with higher energy to the LHC.

Source: huanqiu. com

5 颗小行星即将掠过地球

近日，来自美国喷气推进实验室的科学家列出了 5 颗需要人类在明年特别关注的小行星，并且其中 1 颗将离地球非常近。据悉，这些小行星的直径最小的只有8米，最大的则有90米，它们跟地球的距离将短至3个月球距离。

1个月球距离指的是地球和月球相隔的距离，约有23.89万英里（38.4万公里）。这听起来好像很远，但在浩瀚的太空中却是一个非常近的距离。

率先登场的是一颗叫做2017 BS5的小行星，它是当中体积最大的，这也是它第一次掠过地球。它将预计在今年7月23日以跟地球3.15个月球距离飞过。

来源：环球网

5 asteroids coming close the earth

Recently, scientists from the American Jet Propulsion Laboratory have listed five small asteroids that require special attention next year, and one of them will be very close to the Earth. It is reported that the smallest diameter of these asteroids is only 8 meters, the largest 90 meters. They will be less than 3 moon distances from the Earth.

Lunar distance is the average distance from the center of Earth to the center of the Moon, about 384 000 km. This may sound far but in the mass universe it is quite near.

The first and largest near earth asteroid is 2017 BS5. This is the first time it makes its trip past our planet. It is expected to fly by within 3.15 lunar distances on July 23rd, 2017.

Source: huanqiu. com

澳无线电望远镜捕捉到来自狮子座罕见信号

据澳大利亚"新快网"5月24日报道，近日，仅启动几天的澳大利亚平方千米阵列望远镜探测器（ASKAP）捕捉到来自狮子座的罕见"快速无线电暴"。据悉，快速无线电暴一般持续时间仅仅几毫秒，释放出巨大能量，科学家目前尚不清楚其发生原因。

来源：环球网

Australian Radio Telescope captures rare signals from Leo

According to Australian media on May 24th, Australian Square Kilometers Array Pathfinder (ASKAP), starting only a few days ago, captured rare "fast radio bursts" from Leo. The fast radio bursts usually only lasted a few milliseconds, releasing great energy. Scientists are still not clear as to the cause of this event.

Source：huanqiu.com

木星天空充满电子流、氨气和巨大风暴

科学家一直知道木星是一个充满风暴的地方。但自从美国宇航局（NASA）的"朱诺"号探测器在去年7月抵达太阳系的这个最大的行星之后，科学家发现那里的风暴比此前认为的更加剧烈。

研究人员在5月25日发表于《科学》的文章中表示，去年8月"朱诺"号首次绕轨运行时捕捉到的木星极地的首个细节图揭示了混乱的风暴漩涡，其中一些直径可达1 400公里。

来源：人民网

Jupiter's skies are peppered with electron streams, ammonia plumes, and massive storms

Scientists have long known that Jupiter is a stormy place. But since NASA's Juno probe reached the solar system's largest planet last July, they've found it to be a far more tempestuous place than they realized.

The first-ever detailed look at Jupiter's polar regions-captured during Juno's first orbit last August-reveals chaotic swirls of storms, some measuring up to 1 400 kilometers across, researchers reported in *Science* on May 25.

Source: people. cn

320 光年外的神秘"泡沫塑料行星"：帮助发现外星生命

天文学家最新发现一颗神秘气态行星，将成为勘测类地行星大气层的"黄金标准"。这颗行星的密度接近于聚苯乙烯泡沫塑料，同时，它将有助于科学家未来搜寻潜在生命迹象的星球。

来源：新浪科技

Mysterious "styrofoam planet" found 320 light years away: may help study other planets for signs of life

Astronomers have recently discovered a mysterious gaseous planet that will become the "gold standard" for surveying the atmospheres of Earth-like planets. The density of this planet is close to that of polystyrene foam. Moreover, it will assist scientists in searching for planets with potential signs of life in the future.

Source: tech. sina. com. cn

冰行星宜居性认知或被颠覆

日前《自然·地球科学》杂志在线刊登北京大学杨军和胡永云教授等的研究成果：冰行星或冰卫星很可能将来是非宜居的。该研究表明，随着恒星辐射的增强，这类固态星体将直接进入极端炎热的"温室逃逸状态"，而不是进入液态水存在阶段。

来源：人民网

The habitability of icy planets may be challenged

Recently, a study published on the online version of the journal *Nature Geoscience*, conducted by Yang Jun, Hu Yongyun and other professors at Peking University in China, shows that icy planets or moons may very likely be not habitable in the future. According to the study, as the stellar fluxes increase, the snowball bodies may directly transit to "runaway greenhouse," instead of becoming liquid water.

Source: people. com. cn

紫外线打印"神奇纸张"可重复使用 80 次

据英国《每日邮报》报道,日前美国加州大学河滨分校和中国山东大学的研究人员合作已开发出使用紫外线印刷的纸张,免除对墨水的需求。并且这种轻巧纸张具有和传统纸张一样的外观和手感,但只要加热到 120 摄氏度以上就能擦除字迹,因此可重复使用 80 次以上。

来源:人民网

The "magic" paper that can be printed with UV light and reused up to 80 times

According the *Daily Mail* in the UK, researchers based at the University of California, Riverside in the US and Shandong University in China have jointly developed paper that can be printed with ultra violet rays, eliminating the need for ink. The light-printable paper has the same feel and appearance as conventional paper, but can be erased by heating to 120℃ and reused more than 80 times.

Source: people. com. cn

夸克胶子等离子体"整体极化"理论获证

宇宙在最初诞生的百万分之几秒内以"夸克胶子等离子体"的形式存在,这种类似"电浆"的状态被认为是固体、液体、气体之后的第四种物质形态。近日,我国科学家首次提出的夸克胶子等离子体"整体极化"理论,被美国布鲁克海文实验室重离子碰撞实验证实,该实验室 RHIC-STAR 国际合作组织发言人许长补教授认为,超流体中相对论量子"整体极化"的提出和被证实是近年来世界高能核物理领域里的最重要突破。该实验结果已作为封面文章发表在 8 月 3 日出版的《自然》杂志上。

来源:《科技日报》

The Global Polarization theory of quark-gluon plasma has been confirmed

In the first microseconds of the Universe, it existed in the form of quark-gluon plasma, which behaves like an "electrical fluid" and is considered to be the fourth state of matter after solids, liquids and gases. Recently, the Global Polarization theory of quark-gluon plasma, a theory first proposed by Chinese scientists, has been confirmed in the high-energy heavy-ion collisions conducted at the Brookhaven National Laboratory (BNL) in the United States. Professor Xu Changbu, speaker of the Star collaboration at RHIC, BNL, believes that the proposal and confirmation of the Global Polarization theory of relativistic quantum in super fluid is the most important breakthrough in recent years in the field of high energy nuclear physics. The results have been published as the cover story in the August 3rd issue of *Nature*.

Source: *Science and Technology Daily*

上海超强超短激光首次实验

最近几天,在张江综合性国家科学中心内,超强超短激光实验装置正在进行首次实验。中科院上海光学精密机械研究所的沈百飞团队在上海超强超短激光实验装置试用5拍瓦级(1拍瓦=1 000万亿瓦)激光脉冲,这是科研团队首次用这么大功率的激光进行实验,力争下周让这个装置加速产生高能质子束,并"打"在肿瘤细胞切片等样品上。

与此同时,上海超强超短激光实验装置大楼内,科研人员正在安装调试设备,确保今年底实现10拍瓦激光脉冲输出,成为"世界第一"。

来源:上海观察

Shanghai launches first ultra-short super-intense laser experiment

These days in Zhangjiang National Comprehensive Science Center the ultra-short intense laser experimental facility is in its first trial. Led by Shen Baifei from Shanghai Institute of Optics and Fine Mechanics, Chinese Academy of Sciences, the team tries with 5 petawatt-class laser pulses, such high-power lasers used for the first time ever by the team. They strive to accelerate the apparatus and produce high-energy proton beam next week, and cast on samples such as tumor cell sections.

In the meantime, within the experimental building, researchers are installing and adjusting devices to ensure laser pulse output of 10 petawatt by the end of this year, aiming to be the world first.

Source: Shanghai Observer

中科大研究发现地球内核边界局部存在"糊状层"

近日,中国科学技术大学地震与地球内部物理实验室温联星教授研究组,利用地震观测资料首次发现地球内核边界在局部区域存在"糊状层"。研究结果显示,地磁场驱动力随区域变化,地球外核成分接近铁和轻元素的共晶组成物的成分,因而在大部分地区形成了无糊状层的尖锐内核界面;而在局部地区,地球外核偏离铁和轻元素的共晶组成物的成分,形成了局部糊状层。

来源:新浪科技

USTC found "paste layers" in the Earth kernel boundary

Recently, the Earthquakes & Earth Interior research team of the University of Science and Technology of China (USTC), led by Professor Wen Lianxing, has revealed the existence of a "paste layer" in the Earth kernel boundary for the first time, using seismic observations. The research shows due to variations of geomagnetic field driving forces in different regions, the outer region of the Earth nucleus contains eutectic compositions of iron and light elements, thus forming a sharp kernel layer without a paste layer. However in several local areas, the eutectic compositions there devoid of iron and light elements form a paste layer.

Source: tech. sina. com. cn

最新合成图像现蟹状星云"真实面目"

目前,天文学家基于5个不同望远镜的观测图像,合成了一张接近完整的蟹状星云电磁波谱图像,呈现出蟹状星云的详细结构。

蟹状星云是一颗恒星爆炸之后的残骸,差不多1 000年前照亮夜空,它非常明亮,地球在6 500光年之遥就能观测到。研究人员使用甚大望远镜和哈勃太空望远镜的观测数据,结合其他几个望远镜观测数据,从不同波长范围整合观测结果,从而有助于提高我们对该星云复杂内部运行状况的认知。

来源:新浪科技

A new look at the Crab Nebula

Earlier this week, astronomers produced a new and highly-detailed image of the Crab Nebula by combining data from 5 different telescopes.

The Crab Nebula, the result of a bright supernova explosion illuminating the night sky nearly a thousand years ago, is some 6 500 light-years from Earth. Researchers used data collected from the Very Large Telescope (VLT), Hubble Space Telescope, and several other telescopes, compared these new images at different wavelengths, and provided us with a wealth of new details about the Crab Nebula.

Source: tech. sina. com. cn

激光可迅速清除土壤中污染物

美国东北大学的研究人员在美国《应用物理学杂志》新一期上报告说,他们用多孔二氧化硅材料模拟土壤,使其受到有机化合物 DDE 的污染,然后用高能红外激光束照射,发现 DDE 从土壤中消失了。

DDE 是杀虫剂滴滴涕(DDT)的主要代谢产物之一,能损害动物的生殖系统。研究人员说,激光照射能在局部产生数千摄氏度的高温,足以破坏 DDE 分子的化学键,使其分解成水和二氧化碳等。

来源:新华社

Laser may remove soil contaminants

A study published on Journal of *Applied Physics* by researchers of Northeastern University of the U. S. reports that laser light could remove contaminants in the soil. The researchers conducted a test that uses simulated soil made from porous silica. They contaminated their artificial soil with a carcinogenic chemical called DDE, which is one of the main metabolites of DDT and is harmful to animals' reproductive system. After the contaminated artificial soil shined with high-powered infrared laser, the DDE was immediately no longer present. The laser light heats up the pollutant locally, reaching temperatures up to several thousands of degrees Celsius. This heat is sufficient to break the chemical bonds of the pollutant, fragmenting DDE into carbon dioxide, water, etc.

Source: Xinhua News Agency

我制成世界首个集成自由电子光源芯片

清华大学电子工程系黄翊东教授团队成员刘仿副教授,带领科研人员日前研制出了集成自由电子光源的芯片,在国际上首次实现了无阈值切伦科夫辐射,是我国科学家率先实现的重大理论突破,加速了自由电子激光器小型化进程。相关研究论文近期发布在国际权威期刊《自然·光子》上。

来源:人民网

China makes first integrated chip of free-electron light source

Associate Professor Liu Fang, member of a team headed by Professor Huang Yidong at Department of Electric Engineering of Tsinghua University, led a group of researchers and succeeded in producing the integrated chip of free-electron light source. This is the first time that Chinese scientists realize non-threshold Cherenkov radiation in the international arena, which is a major theoretical breakthrough accelerating the progress of miniaturization of free-electron laser. The relevant paper was published in *Nature Photonics*.

Source: people. com. cn

全球最大 X 射线激光器在德国汉堡投入使用

近日,全球最大的 X 射线激光器 European XFEL(欧洲 X 射线自由电子激光)在汉堡大都市区正式投入使用。共有 11 个欧洲国家参与研发了这一造价达 12.2 亿欧元的激光器。

据介绍,European XFEL 是世界上最大的激光设施:每秒可发射多达 27 000 个脉冲,亮度比传统的同步加速器光源亮度高出十亿倍。激光器的成功研发,开辟了全新的研究领域,有助于突破当前的科学知识界限。

来源:中国新闻网

Biggest X-ray laser in the world put into use in Hamburg, Germany

Recently, the European X-ray free electron laser (European XFEL), the biggest X-ray laser in the world, has been commissioned in Hamburg, Germany. Scientists from 11 European countries have worked together to build this laser valued at EUR 1.22 billion.

According to report, European XFEL can generate 27 000 X-ray laser flashes per second, and its laser light is extremely intense and a billion times brighter than that of conventional synchrotron light sources. The advent of this laser can help scientists to venture into new scientific fields and push the boundary of science.

Source:chinanews. com

太阳迎来两次 X 级耀斑:级数强达 X9.3

近日,NASA 的太阳动力学观测卫星捕捉到了两个 X 级耀斑——特别是第二个异常抢眼。据悉,第一个耀斑级数为 X2.2,第二个则有 X9.3,数字越高,耀斑发出的光就越强。NASA 表示,X9.3 耀斑是目前太阳周期中出现的最大的一个。

来源：环球网

Sun unleashes two powerful solar flares categorized as X2.2 and X9.3

Recently, NASA's Solar Dynamics Observatory captured two strong solar flares. The first one was categorized as an X2.2, while the second is more intense, categorized as an X9.3. Higher numbers correspond to stronger flares. NASA said the X9.3-class flare is the largest one in the solar cycle so far.

Source: huanqiu. com

英国自由电子激光加速器 CLARA 成功产生第一枚电子

近日,英国科技设施研究理事会的达斯伯瑞实验室(Daresbury Laboratory)正在建造的自由电子激光加速器(FEL)成功射出了第一枚自由电子,标志着由英国人设计建造的紧凑线性加速器 CLARA 可以正常工作。CLARA 即将投入运行,为人类探索世界打开一个新的窗口。

来源：人民网

The British free electron laser (FEL) CLARA successfully generated the first electron

Recently, the first free electron was successfully ejected by FEL, which is being constructed by the Daresbury Laboratory of Science and Technology Facilities Research Council of UK. It demonstrates that the compact linear accelerator CLARA, designed and constructed by the British, can work normally. CLARA will soon be put into operation and open a new window for the mankind to explore the world.

Source: people. com. cn

科学家发现氧含量最低的矮星系

科学家近日发现,天猫座中一个只是最近才开始制造恒星的小型星系拥有在形成恒星的星系中迄今见到的最低氧含量。这使其成为探测宇宙大爆炸所产生化学元素的最好地方。

来自乌克兰基辅重点天文台的 Yuri Izotov 和同事一直在寻找和含有极少氧气的原始星系相像且能形成恒星的星系。"它们极其罕见。"来自美国弗吉尼亚大学的 Trinh Thuan 表示,这是因为形成恒星的星系拥有在诞生后很快爆炸的巨大恒星,从而使氧含量增加。

来源:科学网

Scientists find dwarf galaxy with lowest oxygen level

Scientists recently discovered that a small galaxy in the Lynxmko that started forming stars just recently has the lowest oxygen level than any other star-forming galaxies, making it the best place to detect chemical elements generated by the big bang.

Yuri Izotov and his colleagues from a key observatory in Kiev, Ukraine have been looking for galaxies that resemble primitive galaxies with little oxygen and can form stars. "They are extremely rare." Trinh Thuan from the University of Virginia in the United States said this was because star-forming galaxies had massive stars that explode shortly after their birth, thus increasing the oxygen content.

Source: ScienceNet. cn

我科学家研制设备"透视"10万米垂直大气层

中国科学院大气物理研究所近日牵头研制完成一套"多波段多大气成分主被动综合探测系统"(简称APSOS),能够对近地100千米高度的垂直大气层进行多要素连续观测。此种形式的大气观测系统在国际上尚属首例。

来源:人民网

Chinese scientists develop facility to observe atmosphere 100km above the ground

The Atmospheric Profiling Synthetic Observation System (APSOS), a project led by the Institute of Atmospheric Physics, Chinese Academy of Sciences, has completed recently. The APSOS can conduct continuous observation of multiple elements in the atmosphere 100km above the ground, which is the first observation system of its kind in the world.

Source: people.com.cn

任意子的分数统计特性被证实

从中国科学技术大学获悉,该校潘建伟教授及其同事在国际上首次通过量子调控的方法,在超冷原子体系中发现了拓扑量子物态中的准粒子——任意子,证实了任意子的分数统计特性,向着实现拓扑量子计算的方向迈出了重要一步。日前,国际权威学术期刊《自然·物理学》在线发表了这项重要研究成果。

来源:《科技日报》

Anionic fractional statistics verified by Chinese scientists

Professor Pan Jianwei and his colleagues from University of Science and

Technology of China for the first time found the quasi-particle-the anyon, in the topological quantum state in a super-cold atomic system with quantum control thus demonstrated anionic fractional statistics, a huge step toward topological quantum computing. The findings were published online at *Nature Physics*, a monthly, peer reviewed, scientific journal.

Source: *Science and Technology Daily*

锂—液态多硫流动电池实现"再生"

锂—液态多硫流动电池理论上适合用于电网大规模储能,然而这种电池在循环过程中容量容易降低,无法真正获得应用。历时多年,美国斯坦福大学崔屹教授课题组日前找到恢复电容的"再生"之术,有望解决电网大规模储能难题。

来源:《科技日报》

Reactivation of lithium polysulfide flow battery is now possible

The lithium polysulfide flow battery is theoretically suitable for grid-scale energy storage. However, the practical application of such batteries was impossible due to the capacity degradation during cycling. With many years of efforts, a research group led by Professor Yi Cui of Stanford University has recently found a battery "reactivation" strategy, which is expected to address the problem besetting the grid-scale energy storage.

Source: *Science and Technology Daily*

反射光谱显示月球浅表或含大量水

据英国《每日邮报》官网近日消息,德国科学家分析月球测绘数据后认为,月球地幔中富含大量水，未来向月球移民或许将因此变得容易许多。这一结论同时也让"月球是否有水"的争论再起波澜。

报道称，来自德国多特蒙德技术大学的一组研究人员，从月球浅表反射的光谱中搜寻水的线索，他们通过观察哪些波长的光被月球浅表吸收或反射，来了解相应存在着哪些矿物质和化合物。他们在最近一期《科学进步》杂志上发表论文称，整个月球浅表都有水存在，而且在一天中的任何时候都不会消失。

来源：《科技日报》

Reflectance spectrum indicates a deep reservoir of water beneath the moon's surface

According to the news on the official website of *Daily Mail*, German scientists believe there is plenty of water in the lunar mantle after analyzing data from the Moon Mapping Mission, which may make it easier for the future human settlement on the moon. This conclusion sets the debate of whether there is water on the moon on fire again.

The report said that a group of researchers from Technical University of Dortmund, Germany searched for clues of water in the spectrum of light reflected from the moon's surface. By looking at which wavelengths of light are absorbed or reflected by the surface, they could get an idea of which minerals and other compounds are present. In a paper published in *Science Advances*, they pointed out that there is water present across the whole surface of the moon, at all times of the day.

Source: *Science and Technology Daily*

中国散裂中子源低温系统完成首轮运行

8月16日至9月13日，中国散裂中子源（CSNS）低温系统进行了为期4周的首轮运行,并完成了首次打靶。

首轮运行的结果表明,运行状态满足工作联系单《慢化器反射体与低温系统的接口条件及要求》的技术指标。

来源:中国科学院高能物理研究所

The cryogenic system for China Spallation Neutron Source finished its first operation

From August 16th to September 13th, the cryogenic system for China Spallation Neutron Source (CSNS) conducted the first 4-week operation and first targeting.

The result of the first operation shows that the running status meets the technical indicators of the work contact list "Interface Conditions and Requirements of Moderator Reflector and Cryogenic System".

Source: Institute of High Energy Physics, Chinese Academy of Sciences

超高能宇宙射线来自银河系外

一个国际科研团队近日表示,他们首次证实那些地球上探测到的超高能宇宙射线不是来自银河系内,而是源自银河系之外的遥远星系。

由来自18个国家400多名科学家组成的一个科研团队,在新一期美国《科学》杂志上报告说,他们发现,这些宇宙射线从太空射向地球的方向分布并不均匀,而是偏向于来自某特定方位,而这个方位与银河系中心方向偏差120度;说明超高能宇宙射线不是像一些科学家认为的那样来自银河系内。

来源:人民网

Scientists discover highest energy cosmic rays from deep space

An international scientific research team recently declared that they have finally pinned down the point of origin of the highest energy cosmic rays hitting Earth. And it isn't from anything inside the Milky Way but rather from a galaxy far, far away.

In an article to be published in the journal *Science*, a group of more than 400 scientists from 18 nations describe how they detected an anisotropy, an asymmetry in the cosmic particles' distribution of arrival directions as they approach the Earth. The prominent arrival direction is from a broad area of the sky about 120 degrees away from the direction that points to the center of our Milky Way galaxy, where some scientists have hypothesized the rays may originate.

Source: people. com. cn

我首台高平均功率太赫兹自由电子激光饱和出光

由我国科学家自主研发的国内首台高平均功率太赫兹自由电子激光装置,日前在四川成都首次饱和出光。经第三方检测,实验真实可靠且装置运行稳定。我国太赫兹源从此正式进入自由电子激光时代。

来源: 人民网

China obtains the first lasing of the CTFEL facility with high average power

China's first lasing of the CAEP THz FEL (CTFEL) facility with high average power, which was independently researched and developed by Chinese scientists, was obtained for the first time in Chengdu, Sichuan province. Through the third-party testing, the experiment is true and reliable and the facility is in the stable operation. From this time on, China's terahertz source officially enters into the era of FEL.

Source: people. com. cn

小行星撞击曾触发地壳物质循环

据英国《自然·地球科学》杂志 9 月 24 日在线发表的一篇论文称,澳大利亚科学家最新进行的数字模拟显示,40 多亿年前小行星撞击地球,触发了地球地壳物质循环。该研究对早期地球构造作用静止的假设提出了挑战。

来源:《科技日报》

Asteroid impact in early earth period may have triggered the first material cycle in earth crust

According to a paper published online by *Nature Geoscience* on September 24, Australian scientists found in their latest digital simulation that asteroid impact 4 billion years ago may have triggered material cycle in earth crust. This research challenges the assumption of static tectonism in early period of earth.

Source: *Science and Technology Daily*

太阳系"曝光"首个"双重身份"天体

据探索频道旗下"探求者"网站 9 月 24 日消息,天文学家通过哈勃太空望远镜,在太阳系中确认了全新怪异天体——一对相互绕转的小行星"双胞胎"。更惊人的是,它们虽身为小行星,却拥有彗星才有的结构,即明亮的光晕(彗发)以及长长的尘埃尾(彗尾)。这是人们发现的首个此类天体,未来将作为一个非常重要的研究系统。

来源:人民网

The first Solar System objects with "binary identities" spotted

Seeker, a website affiliated to Discovery Channel, reported on September 24 that astronomers have spotted new and bizarre objects in Solar System—a pair of asteroids orbiting around each other. Though appeared to be asteroids, they have the structures that are unique to comet, namely the bright halo (coma) and the long tail of material (comet tail). These are the first objects of this kind ever spotted by humans, and will become a very important research subject in the future.

Source: people. cn

比水轻！新方法设计出超轻铝晶体

据物理学家组织网近日报道，美国犹他州立大学（USU）和俄罗斯南联邦大学的科学家，利用计算机模型设计出比水还轻的超轻晶体铝。发表在最新一期《物理化学杂志》网络版的这一重大突破性成果，有望用于航天飞机和汽车等领域制造超轻部件。

来源：科学网

Aluminum crystal lighter than water designed with new methods

The Phys. org recently reported that scientists from America's Utah State University (USU) and Russia's Southern Federal University have jointly designed a new kind of aluminum crystal structure that is lighter than water by using computational modeling. Published on the online edition of *The Journal of Physical Chemistry*, this new achievement is expected to be applied to the manufacturing of ultra-light components in fields such as space shuttle and automobiles.

Source: ScienceNet. cn

中国启动建设全球首个综合极端条件实验装置,大科学装置将有大作为

由中国科学院物理研究所等建设的综合极端条件实验装置,日前在北京市怀柔科学城正式开工。该工程拟通过 5 年左右时间,建成国际上首个集极低温、超高压、强磁场和超快光场等极端条件为一体的用户装置,极大提升我国在物质科学及相关领域的基础研究与应用基础研究综合实力。

来源:人民网

China to start building the world's first comprehensive extreme conditions experimental device: large scientific device will be a big hit

The comprehensive extreme conditions experimental devices built by the Institute of Physics of Chinese Academy of Sciences and other organizations recently was formally started in science city of Huairou in Beijing. The project intends to build an user device with the world's first set of extremely low temperature, ultra-high pressure, strong magnetic field and ultra-fast light field and other extreme conditions within 5 years, which will greatly enhance the basic research and application basic research comprehensive strength of our country in material science and other related fields.

Source: people.com.cn

30 多亿年前月球存在过大气层

据物理学家组织网近日报道,美国国家航空航天局(NASA)的一项新研究表明,月球在古代曾有过大气层。约 30 亿年前到 40 亿年前,月球上强烈的火山爆发喷出了大量气体,这些气体喷射到月球表面的速度快过逃逸到太空的速度,从而形成了月球的大气层。

来源:《科技日报》

Moon had an atmosphere 3-4 billion years ago

According to the Phys. org, NASA has found that moon had an atmosphere in ancient times. About three to four billion years ago, intense volcanic eruptions spewed gases above the surface faster than they could escape to space, forming the atmosphere of moon.

Source: *Science and Technology Daily*

火星赤道附近区域发现大量氢分子

15年前,美国"奥德赛"火星探测器在火星上空观测到以火星南极为中心的高纬度地区地下有大量氢分子存在。日前一个国际研究团队重新分析了以往数据后发现,在火星赤道附近区域也存在大量氢分子。

由美国约翰·霍普金斯大学的杰克·威尔逊领衔的团队,对2002年至2009年"奥德赛"探测器上的中子谱仪采集的数据进行了重新分析,并通过图像重建技术将上述数据的空间分辨率从520公里提升至290公里。研究人员意外发现,在火星赤道附近区域有大量的氢分子,这意味着可能有水冰存在。

来源:新华网

A large number of hydrogen molecules found near the equator of the Mars

Fifteen years ago, the United States' "Odyssey" Mars probe discovered that there exist a lot of hydrogen molecules in high latitudes centered at the Mars South Pole. Recently, an international research team reanalyzed the previous data and found that there were a lot of hydrogen molecules in the vicinity of the equator of Mars.

The team, led by Jack Wilson of Johns Hopkins University in the United

States, reanalyzed the data collected with the neutron spectrometer of Odyssey detector from the 2002 to 2009 and enhanced the spatial resolution of these data from 520 km to 290 km using image reconstruction technology. Researchers have accidentally discovered that there is a lot of hydrogen molecules near the equator of Mars, which means that there may be water ice.

Source: xinhuanet. com

黑洞吞噬物质，讲究"细嚼慢咽"

几乎每个星系中心都存在一个超大质量黑洞。最新研究发现，这些黑洞在吞噬周围物质时，心急吃不了热豆腐，因为如果吞噬物质速度太快，有可能反而将这些物质推开。中科院南美天文中心博士后克劳迪奥·里奇团队的这项发现，发表在近日出版的《自然》杂志上。

来源：《科技日报》

The Black Hole is slow in devouring materials

There is a supermassive black hole in the center of almost every galaxy. Newest researches have revealed that black holes are not in a hurry in devouring materials surrounding it, or else materials might be pushed away. This was found out by the team led by Claudio Ricci, a postdoctoral fellow at Chinese Academy of Sciences South America Center for Astronomy and published in recent issue of *Nature*.

Source: *Science and Technology Daily*

科学家将光子弯曲至被实际通信使用的波长

几十年来，光子纠缠在量子计算和通信中的潜力一直为人所知。然而，妨碍其直接应用的其中一个问题是,很多光子纠缠平台并未在大多数通信形式使用的范围内运行。

一个国际团队展示了一种新的纳米尺度技术,从而开始解开纠缠光子之谜。该技术利用半导体量子点将光子弯曲至如今流行的C波段标准使用的波长,他们在日前出版的美国物理联合会所属《应用物理快报》上报告了这一成果。

来源:科学网

Researchers bend wavelengths of entangled photons to those used in telecommunications

The potential for photon entanglement in quantum computing and communications has been known for decades. One of the issues impeding its immediate application is the fact that many photon entanglement platforms do not operate within the range used by most forms of telecommunication.

An international team of researchers has started to unravel the mystery of entangled photons, demonstrating a new nanoscale technique that uses semiconductor quantum dots to bend photons to the wavelengths used by today's popular C-band standards. They reported their work this week in *Applied Physics Letters*, a subsidiary of the American Institute of Physics.

Source: ScienceNet.cn

零折射率波导让光驻波首次"现形"

据物理学家组织网日前报道,美国科学家研发出可与目前的硅光子技术兼容的零折射率波导,而且他们还借此观察到了一种此前被认为不能观察到的物理学现象——光的驻波。这一研究发表在美国化学学会旗下《光子学》杂志上。

来源:人民网

A zero-index waveguide: researchers directly observe infinitely long wavelengths for the first time

According to phys. org, American researchers have developed a zero-index waveguide compatible with current silicon photonic technologies. In doing so, the team observed a physical phenomenon that is usually unobservable — a standing wave of light. The research is published in ACS *Photonics*.

Source: people. cn

海王星以外矮行星拥有自己的环系统

英国《自然》杂志10月11日在线发表的一篇最新天文学报告称,欧洲科学家利用多达12架望远镜发现,一颗位于海王星轨道以外、名为妊神星的矮行星竟拥有自己的环系统。这项发现为人们打开了海王星外区域的研究新通道。

来源:《科技日报》

A dwarf planet located beyond Neptune has a ring to it

According to a latest astronomical paper published online on the *Nature* on October 11, European scientists observed from twelve telescopes that a dwarf planet beyond Neptune called Haumea has a ring to it. The discovery has offered us a new possibility for carrying out research into the space beyond Neptune.

Source: *Science and Technology Daily*

中科院等破解类星体宽线区之谜

日前，国际期刊《自然·天文》在线发表了一项中国科学院关于类星体宽发射线区起源的研究成果。

在该研究中，科研人员提出了宽线区起源于尘埃环的理论，建立了中心超大质量黑洞、吸积盘、宽线区和尘埃环之间的物理联系，诠释了宽线区谱线轮廓的物理意义，揭开了困扰天文学家长达 70 多年的活动星系核和类星体的宽线区起源和物理结构的核心谜题。基于这个理论，人们可从谱线轮廓准确地获得超大质量黑洞附近的电离气体空间分布和动力学，使得目前误差高达半个数量级的黑洞质量测量精度有望大幅度提高。

来源：科学网

CAS solved the puzzle about the origin of quasar broad emission line regions

Recently, the international journal *Nature Astronomy* published an on-line research paper on the origin of quasar broad emission line regions produced by Chinese Academy of Sciences (CAS).

In this paper, scientific researchers proposed that broad emission line regions originated from the dust ring, established the physical relationship between a super massive black hole at the center of the Milky Way galaxy, an accretion disk, broad emission line regions, and the dust ring, explained the physical significance of the line contour of broad emission line regions, and solved the puzzle about the origin and physical structure of broad emission line regions of active galactic nuclei and quasars that has perplexed astronomers for as long as over 70 years. Based on this theory, it is possible to get the accurate spatial distribution and dynamics of ionized gases near the super massive black hole from the line contour, so that the measurement accuracy of the black hole's mass, which has an error of up to half an order of magnitude, is expected to be greatly improved.

Source: ScienceNet. cn

科学家实现用激光驱动水流

中外科学家携手解决了一项困扰科学界多年的难题——用激光驱动宏观物质运动。科学家在现实条件下，首次实现了用脉冲激光在纯水中驱动水流持续高速运动。

这一研究成果近日发表在《科学》杂志的子刊《科学进展》上。由电子科技大学、河南工程学院、美国休斯敦大学等中外高校组成的联合科研团队在普通的金纳米颗粒非线性光学性质实验中，意外发现了一种奇特的光声流体效应。在玻璃容器中，经过一段时间纳秒激光的照射，金纳米颗粒水分散液会形成高速流动的流场。该流场方向与激光传播方向一致，长度可贯穿整个 10 毫米玻璃器皿，在 120 毫瓦激光照射下，流速可达 4 厘米/秒，流场可持续近小时之久。

来源：新华社

Scientists successfully harnessed laser to generate a water flow

Using laser to drive the motion of macro materials had been a challenge scientifically for years. But with the collaboration among Chinese and foreign scientists, the problem was solved. They generated a steady-state high-speed water flow by a pulsed laser beam in pure water under factual conditions.

The research result has recently been published in *Science Advances*, one of the subordinate academic series of *Science*. A joint research team, consisting of scientists from University of Electric Science and Technology of China, Henan University of Engineering, University of Huston and other colleges and universities at home and abroad, accidentally discovered a peculiar optofluidic principle during the regular no-linear optical property experiment of gold nanoparticles. After being exposed under nanoparticle-assisted laser for some time in a glass container, the aqueous dispersion liquid of gold nanoparticles will form a high-speed flow field which has the same directions as the directions of laser propagation and can penetrate a 10 mm-long glass container. Being exposed under the laser power of 120 mW, the speed of the water flow can reach 4 cm/s, and its flow field can last for nearly an hour.

Source: Xinhua News Agency

"钙钛矿"探测器大幅减少 X 射线剂量

近日,华中科技大学武汉光电国家实验室(筹)研发出一种新型钙钛矿辐射探测器,该探测器具有高灵敏度、无铅化特点,且其材料相比制造闪烁晶体所用的稀土材料更加低廉易制取,应用到医学和安检成像领域,可大幅减少 X 射线剂量对人体的伤害。

来源:《科技日报》

"Perovskite" probe can significantly reduce X-ray doses

Wuhan National Laboratory For Optoelectronics, Huazhong University of Science and Technology of China has recently developed a new type of Perovskite radiation probe featuring high sensitivity and non-lead. The new probe is made from materials cheaper than the rare earth material for producing scintillation crystals. When applied in the imaging of medicine and security check, the probe can greatly reduce the harm of X-ray doses to human body.

Source: *Science and Technology Daily*

中子星碰撞，黄金抛向太空

美国宇航局（NASA）日前发布中子星碰撞时产生的超美粉色云团照片。引人关注的重点是，云团包含超级多的黄金和铂金。

专家表示，当中子星碰撞时，高温高密度且不断膨胀的碎片云从两个中子星上剥落，形成了图中粉色的云团。在这个云团中，形成了大量的宇宙超重金属，其中包含相当于数百个地球质量的黄金和铂金。

来源：《新京报》

Neutron stars collided and produced much gold

NASA recently published a picture of an extraordinarily beautiful pink cloud cluster taken during a collision between two neutron stars. Noticeably, the cloud cluster contained a huge amount of gold and platinum.

According to experts, when the neutron stars collided, high-temperature, high-density and ever-expanding pannus peeled off from the neutron stars and formed a cloud cluster in the picture above. In this cloud cluster was a large number of heavy elements, including gold and platinum that together were equal to the quality of hundreds of earth planets.

Source: *The Beijing News*

国家重点研发计划项目"高精度原子光钟"启动

近日，国家重点研发计划项目"高精度原子光钟"项目正式启动。

据介绍，"高精度原子光钟"项目旨在解决在高精度时频体系方面制约我国科技发展的若干"瓶颈"问题，发展具有自主知识产权的新方法、新技术，实现高精度的囚禁离子光钟和光晶格原子光钟，获得高精度光学频率比值，实现可"搬运"光钟和光钟初步应用。

来源：科学网

National key R & D project on high-accuracy atomic optical clock launched

Recently a national key R & D project on high-accuracy atomic optical clock was launched.

According to reports, the high-accuracy atomic optical clock project aims to overcome several bottlenecks in high-accuracy time-frequency system hindering China's scientific development, and develop new methods, technology with independent intellectual property rights to produce high-accuracy trapped ion optical clock and optical-lattice clock, obtain high-precision optical frequency ratio and achieve the preliminary application of portable atomic clock as well as atomic clock.

Source: ScienceNet. cn

土星大气发现神秘粒子

美国宇航局(NASA)的"卡西尼"号探测器还在继续产生着令人惊讶的发现,而早在一个多月前,这架探测器已经在任务结束后于土星大气中烧毁。来自"卡西尼"号探测器的新数据表明,土星的宏伟光环正在将微小的尘埃颗粒注入行星的上层大气中,从而形成了一种复杂且意想不到的化学混合物。

来源:《中国科学报》

Mysterious particles found in the Saturnian atmosphere

NASA's Cassini spacecraft continued to produce surprising discoveries. A month ago, the spacecraft had been burnt down in the Saturnian atmosphere after completing its mission. New data from the Cassini spacecraft showed that Saturn's rings were putting tiny particles into the upper atmosphere of the planet, thus forming a complicated and unexpected chemical compound.

Source: *China Science Daily*

治癌神器，激光质子刀离应用又近一步

中科院上海光机所近日发布消息，该所强场激光物理国家重点实验室在徐至展院士、李儒新研究员的领导下，在激光质子刀研究中取得重要进展。研究人员利用圆偏振拍瓦级超强超短激光脉冲轰击纳米厚度薄膜靶，获得了大流强、准单能的高品质质子束，质子能谱峰能量达到 9 MeV，峰值流强高达 3×10^{12} protons/MeV/sr。这一结果代表着激光驱动的质子刀方案向前迈出了关键一步。10 月 17 日，相关研究成果已经发表于《物理评论快报》。

来源：看看新闻网

Laser proton knife, a most powerful weapon against cancer, is one step closer to practice

Shanghai Institute of Optics and Fine Mechanics (SIOM), Chinese Academy of Sciences, has recently announced that, under the leadership of academician Xu Zhizhan and researcher Li Ruxin, there has been an important development on the research of laser proton knife. Researchers applied circular polarizing petawatt-level ultra-intense, ultra-short laser pulse ablation of nano-thickness foil target and gained a mass-flux, quasi-monoenergetic high-quality proton beam with proton energy spectrum peak energy of up to 9 MeV and peak flux of up to 3×10^{12} protons/MeV/sr. The result represents a key step forward towards the laser-driven proton knife plan. Related studies have been published on Oct 17th on *Physical Review Letters*.

Source: kankanews.com

火星有条看不见的"尾巴"

据美国国家航空航天局(NASA)官网近日消息,NASA 的"火星大气与挥发演化探测器"(MAVEN)最新探测发现,火星拥有"隐形"的磁场尾巴(磁尾),且与太阳风相互作用而发生了扭曲。

来源:《科技日报》

An Invisible "Tail" of Mars

According to recent news released by nasa. gov, the latest discovery made by Mars Atmosphere and Volatile Evolution (MAVEN) reveals an "invisible" tail of magnetic field (magnetic tail), which is distorted by interacting with solar winds.

Source: *Science and Technology Daily*

月球地下存在巨大空洞

日本宇宙航空研究开发机构(JAXA)近日宣布,国际联合研究团队对绕月飞行的"月亮女神"雷达探测器获得的数据进行分析后,确认月球火山地区的地下数十米至数百米深处存在多个空洞,其中一个纵向空洞从东向西长达数十公里。

来源:《科技日报》

Giant holes found in the underground of the moon

Japan Aerospace Exploration Agency(JAXA) recently announced that, after analyzing the data collected by the lunar orbiter spacecraft and radar probe "SELENE(known in Japanese as Kaguya)", its Joint International Research Group identified several holes deep under tens, even hundreds of meters in the volcanic region of the moon, with one of which ranging longitudinally from east to west for tens of kilometers.

Source: *Science and Technology Daily*

中国科学家突破一维量子系统研究领域

中国科学技术大学潘建伟教授及同事苑震生等人与中科院武汉物理与数学研究所管习文研究组合作，近期通过对光晶格中的超冷原子进行量子调控和测量，在国际上首次获得了一维有限温多体系统在经典气体和量子液体之间转变的量子临界性质，并通过测量其相位关联观测到了拉亭杰液体的幂定律关联特性。国际权威学术期刊《物理评论快报》日前发表了该成果。

来源：人民网

Chinese scientists' breakthrough in the field of one-dimensional quantum system

Together with Guan Xiwen's Research Group from Wuhan Institute of Physics and Mathematics of Chinese Academy of Sciences, Professor Pan Jianwei from University of Science and Technology of China and his colleagues Yuan Zhensheng and etc., have recently first obtained the critical quantum properties of one-dimensional temperature-limited multi-body system while it transforms between ideal gases and quantum liquids by quantum controlling and measuring the ultracold atoms in optical lattice, and observed the colligative power law properties of Luttinger Liquid by measuring its phase correlation. The research findings have been published in the internationally authoritative academic journal *Physical Review Letters*.

Source: people. cn

中科院在国内首次突破下一代太阳自适应光学技术

近日,在中科院云南天文台的协助下,中科院光电技术研究所研究员饶长辉带领的太阳高分辨率光学成像研究小组,成功突破下一代自适应光学-多层共轭自适应光学(MCAO)关键技术。该试验的成功,标志着我国在下一代自适应光学技术领域取得重大突破,使我国成为继美国和德国之后,第三个掌握太阳MCAO技术的国家。

来源:科学网

Chinese Academy of Sciences made a first breakthrough in next generation solar adaptive optics technology

Recently, under the assistance of Yunnan Observatories of Chinese Academy of Sciences, a solar high resolution optical imaging research group headed by Rao Changhui, a researcher in Institute of Optics and Electronics, CAS, successfully developed a key technology for Multi-layer Conjugate Adaptive Optics (MCAO), the next generation of adaptive optics technology. The successful trial marks China's significant breakthrough in technology of next generation of adaptive optics, and builds China into the third country to boast solar MCAO technology after America and Germany.

Source: ScienceNet. cn

国家天文台测量出银河系旋转速度与质量

近日,国家天文台天体丰度与星系演化研究团组博士后依明阿吉与该台研究员赵刚合作,首次利用我国LAMOST望远镜释放的第四次巡天数据与美国斯隆数字巡天项目(SDSS)释放的第八次巡天数据中的天琴座RR变星,测量出银河系旋转速度与银河系质量。该研究结果已在国际期刊《天体物理学报》上发表。

来源：科学网

NAOC calculated rotation speed and mass of Milky Way

Recently, Dr. Yi Mingaji and researcher Zhao Gang from Stellar Abundances and Galactic Evolution Group (SAGE Group) of the National Astronomical Observatories (NAOC) has calculated the rotation speed and mass of the Milky Way using RR Lyrae-Variables in the 4th data release of Large Sky Area Multi-Object Fiber Spectroscopy Telescope (LAMOST) and 8th data release of Sloan Digital Sky Survey (SDSS). The study has been published on Journal *Chinese Journal of Astronomy and Astrophysics*.

Source: ScienceNet. cn

我国首次实现可扩展量子中继器的光学演示

日前，中国科技大学潘建伟教授及其同事在国际上首次利用参量下转换光源实现了基于线性光学的量子中继器中的嵌套纠缠纯化和二级纠缠交换过程。这两项成果论文日前分别发表于国际学术期刊《自然·光子学》和《物理评论快报》上。

受到通信链路衰减和噪声等因素的影响，直接进行量子通信的节点距离存在极限。为了突破这一极限，可以利用量子中继器连接多个通信节点，从而实现远距离的量子通信。

来源：人民网

China successfully conducted optical demonstration of scalable quantum repeater for the first time

Recently, Professor Pan Jianwei and his colleague from University of

Science and Technology of China have for the first time successfully demonstrated processes of nested purification and two-hierarchy entanglement swapping using spontaneous parametric downconversion sources for linear optical quantum repeaters. The study is published on *Nature Phontonics* and *Physical Review Letters*.

Due to factors like attenuation along communication line and noises, there is a limit to the distance between communication nodes. In order to break the limit, they use quantum repeaters to connect various communication nodes in order to achieve long distance quantum communication.

Source: people. cn

中国太阳观测技术获得新突破,空间天气预报将更准确

如何通过科技更清晰看到太阳活动区？中国科学家突破了下一代自适应光学-多层共轭自适应光学关键技术,这相当于给太阳望远镜带上校正"眼镜"。

近日,中国科学院光电技术研究所在中科院云南天文台1米新真空太阳望远镜上结合了该技术,获取太阳活动区大视场高分辨率实时图像。多层共轭自适应光学技术除了可校正地表层湍流波前像差外,还可对高层大气进行补偿,在更大视场范围提高观测清晰度。

来源:新华网

Breakthrough in solar observation will make space weather forecast more accurate

How can we observe more clearly the active region of the Sun? Chinese scientists recently discovered the key technologies of the next-generation adaptive optics - multi-conjugate adaptive optics, which will give the solar telescope "an extra pair of glasses".

Recently, scientists from the Institute of Optics and Electronics, Chinese Academy of Sciences applied the technology to the New Vacuum Solar Telescope at Yunnan Observatory, Chinese Academy of Sciences and managed to obtain wide-field-of-view, high-resolution and real-time images of solar active region. In addition to rectify the wave-front aberrations induced by atmospheric turbulence, the multi-conjugate adaptive optics technologies can compensate the upper atmosphere and improve observational clarity in larger field of view.

Source: xinhuanet.com

中国南极巡天望远镜首次实现越冬观测

日前,南极巡天望远镜 AST3-2 在 2017 观测年度首次成功克服极寒、暴风雪等恶劣条件,在南极首次实现了无人值守条件下的越冬观测。这表明,我国面向极端环境的望远镜研制、运行技术取得了突破性进展。

AST3-2 是中国于 2015 年 1 月架设在南极内陆冰穹 A 的第二台巡天望远镜。其入瞳直径 50 厘米,视场 8 平方度,是南极现有最大的光学望远镜,在极端环境下实现了无人值守全自动观测。

来源:科学网

China's Antarctic Survey Telescope for the first time succeeds in operation during harsh winter

Recently, the Antarctic Survey Telescope AST3-2 has for the first time succeeded in operation in harsh conditions, such as freezing coldness and snowstorms, without human attendance. This marks that China has made breakthroughs in the research and operation technology for telescopes used in extreme environment.

AST3-2 unit is the second survey telescope installed by China in January 2015 near Dome A in Antarctica. With 50 cm aperture and 8 square degree field of view, the unit is the largest optical telescope in Antarctica and supports automatic operation in extreme environment, without human attendance.

Source: ScienceNet. cn

上海光机所钙钛矿微腔的高品质制备及单模激光特性研究获进展

近日,中国科学院上海光学精密机械研究所强激光材料重点实验室研究员张龙、副研究员董红星领衔的微结构光物理研究小组,在光学谐振腔研究领域取得进展,相关研究成果发表在 ACS Nano 上。科研人员在单个微球三维结构谐振腔中首次实现了高品质、低阈值、窄带宽的单模激光输出,并且其激射范围可成功覆盖整个可见光区,研究成果将推动该研究领域的进一步发展。

来源:上海科协

Progress in high quality preparation of perovskite microcavity and single-mode laser property research by Shanghai Institute of Optics and Fine Mechanics

Recently, under the leadership of researcher Zhang Long and associate researcher Dong Hongxing from the Key Laboratory of Strong Laser Material of Shanghai Institute of Optics and Fine Mechanics, the Chinese Academy of Sciences, a microstructural optical physics research group made a progress in optical resonator and published related results on *ACS Nano*. For the first time, a single-mode laser with a very narrow line width was achieved successfully in the single submicron sphere three-dimensional cavity resonator at low threshold with a high cavity quality factor, and its wavelength covers the whole visible light range. This result will push the research into a wider arena.

Source: Shanghai Association for Science and Technology

新发现:距地球 11 光年系外行星或可供生命存在

日前,最新发现的一颗系外行星可能是迄今最有可能存在外星生命的星球之一,它距离太阳很近,仅相距 11 光年,就如同位于"地球的太空后花园"。

这颗行星质量与地球十分相似,环绕一颗小型光线昏暗恒星"罗斯 128"运行,目前科学家将这颗行星命名为"罗斯 128b",其表面温度可能适宜生命存活。这项最新研究报告发表在近期出版的《天文学&天体物理学》杂志上。

来源:新浪科技

Newfound exoplanet 11-light-year away from the earth may support existence of life

A newfound exoplanet may be one of the best bets to host alien life ever discovered—and it is right in Earth's backyard, cosmically speaking.

Astronomers have spotted a roughly Earth-mass world circling the small, dim star "Ross 128", which lies just 11 light-years from the sun. The planet, known as "Ross 128b", may have surface temperatures amenable to life as we know it. The researchers have announced their achievements in a new study published in the *Astronomy & Astrophysics* journal.

Source: tech. sina. com. cn

我国首次发现新奇拓扑量子态

近日,中国科学院合肥物质科学研究院稳态强磁场中心的郝宁宁研究员课题组，在拓扑新物态研究中取得最新进展，他们发现硫化铁化合物中存在一种交错二聚型反铁磁序，并且这种反铁磁序会调制体系进入一种新的拓扑物态：拓扑晶体反铁磁相。相关研究成果日前相继发表在欧洲物理学会《新物理学杂志》和美国物理学会杂志《物理评论》上。

来源：新浪科技

Novel topological quantum state first discovered in China

Recently, a research team led by Hao Ningning in the High Magnetic Field Laboratory of the Chinese Academy of Sciences has made new progress in the study of new topological state, discovering staggered-dimer-type anti-ferromagnetic order in iron sulfide compounds and that the antiferromagnetic order can modulate the system into a new topological state: topological crystal anti-ferromagnetic phase. The relevant research results have been published in *New Journal of Physics* edited by European Physical Society and *Physical Review* edited by American Physical Society.

Source: tech. sina. com. cn

美酝酿通过微波背景辐射验证宇宙"暴涨理论"

据《自然》杂志官网近日报道，美国研究人员近日草拟了一份新的实验计划，拟建造全新设施来研究宇宙大爆炸的微弱余光——宇宙微波背景辐射，从而验证早期宇宙在婴儿期是否经历过短时间的暴涨——也就是所谓的"暴涨理论"。

来源：《科技日报》

US researchers strive to confirm cosmic inflation through studying cosmic microwave background radiation

According to the official website of *Nature*, US researchers recently have drafted new plans to study the faint afterglow of the Big Bang—cosmic microwave background radiation—using a new facility. They hope it will confirm whether or not the infant Universe underwent a brief period of explosive expansion known as inflation.

Source: *Science and Technology Daily*

研究揭示宇宙射线和中微子可能来源

一项日前发表于预印本服务器 arxiv.org 的研究表明,被黑洞撕碎的白矮星或许能解释人们在地球上看到的高能宇宙射线和中微子雨。

宇宙射线和中微子是来自太空且每天都在轰击地球的亚原子粒子"降雨"的一部分。不过,是什么产生了这些难以探测的粒子?一个由来自德国电子同步加速器研究所的 Daniel Biehl 领导的团队发现,白矮星上的潮汐力瓦解事件或许要对此负责。

"当恒星离黑洞太近导致其被强引力撕裂时,潮汐力瓦解事件便会发生。"来自美国亚利桑那州立大学的 Cecilia Lunardini 介绍说,"被摧毁恒星的部分残骸降落到黑洞里,而这导致黑洞释放能量并且令粒子加速。"

来源:科学网

Research revealed the potential source of cosmic rays and neutrinos

According to a research on arxiv.org, white dwarf stars shredded by black holes could explain showers of high-energy cosmic rays and neutrinos we see on Earth.

Cosmic rays and neutrinos are part of the rain of subatomic particles from space that bombard Earth every day. But what produces these difficult-to-detect particles? A team led by Daniel Biehl at Deutsches Elektronen-Synchrotron in Germany suggest that tidal disruption events in white dwarfs could be responsible.

"A tidal disruption event is what happens when a star gets too close to a black hole and the strong gravity tears the star apart," says Cecilia Lunardini at Arizona State University. "Part of the debris of the destroyed star falls into the black hole, and this causes the black hole to emit energy and accelerate particles."

Source: ScienceNet. cn

研究称：失重会使宇航员出现空间感知错觉

载人航天科技的发展为长期驻留太空提供日臻完善的外部条件，但宇航员的部分生理机能尚未完全适应太空环境。俄罗斯一项新研究显示，人体对失重的反应会引发空间感知错觉，可能影响宇航员的工作能力。

来源：新华社

Exposure to zero-gravity causes spatial disorientation

The development of manned space flight technologies has made it possible for long stay in space. However, the physiological function of astronauts has not yet adapted to space environment. According to a recent study in Russia, exposure to weightlessness can elicit spatial disorientation, which could affect astronauts during their work.

Source: Xinhua News Agency

首个确认"星际访客"完成初步"体检"

欧洲南方天文台(ESO)科学家在 11 月 20 日出版的《自然》杂志发表论文称,10 月 19 日首个被发现的来自太阳系外的"星际访客",经过甚大望远镜精确测定,是一个暗红色长杆形多岩石小行星,其被国际天文学会命名为 1I/2017 U1。ESO 为它另取了一个夏威夷语名字 Oumuamua,意为"远方的信使"。

来源:《科技日报》

The first confirmed "interstellar visitor" completed preliminary "body check"

According to the article published by the European Southern Observatory (ESO) in the journal *Nature* on November 20, the first "interstellar visitor" from outside of the solar system discovered on October 19 was confirmed to be a rocky, dark red and cigar-shaped asteroid, based on the precise measurements by ESO's Very Large Telescope. The asteroid was first named by the International Astronomical Union as 1I/2017 U1, and later given a Hawaiian name by ESO as Oumuamua, which means "a messenger from afar".

Source: *Science and Technology Daily*

探索土卫二,俄富翁要抢 NASA "风头"

据《新科学家》杂志在线版近日消息称,在与著名科学家霍金联手启动 1 亿美元的"突破摄星"计划后,俄罗斯亿万富翁尤里·米尔纳现将目光投向了"几乎具备生命所需所有条件"的土卫二,他宣布将资助一个探索土卫二的项目,并在美国国家航空航天局(NASA)到达之前深入挖掘这颗星球的秘密。

来源:人民网

Russian billionaire wants to beat NASA in searching Enceladus

According to a report by the online version of the *New Scientist*, after jointly launching the $100 million "Breakthrough Starshot" project with renowned scientist Stephen Hawking, Russian billionaire Yuri Milner set his sights on Saturn's moon Enceladus, which scientists have designated one of the prime spots in the known universe where life could exist. He announced that he would fund a mission to Enceladus, and scour the secrets of the planet before NASA gets around to it.

Source: people. cn

闪电确是同位素产生的"自然通道"

近日,科学家通过辐射探测器首次发现了决定性证据:闪电能够引发大气核反应,并产生放射性同位素。该发现意味着闪电终于成为人们已知的可产生同位素的自然通道,同时也为深刻理解气象中物理学极端事件打开了一扇窗。

来源:《科技日报》

Lightning proves to be a natural channel to generate isotopes

Scientists have recently found for the first time the conclusive evidence with radiation detectors that lightning can trigger nuclear reactions in the atmosphere and produce radioactive isotopes. This means that lightning has become a known natural channel to generate isotopes, and it has also opened a window for fully understanding extreme weather events.

Source: *Science and Technology Daily*

上海微系统所等研制出微纳光纤耦合超导纳米线单光子探测器

上海微系统所/中国科学院超导电子学卓越创新中心尤立星研究员团队和浙江大学教授方伟、童利民团队合作，首次提出微纳光纤耦合的 SNSPD 器件结构。该结构将 SNSPD 器件置于微纳光纤的倏逝场内，实现纳米线对微纳光纤中传输的光子吸收。相关成果近日发表在《光学快讯》(*Optics Express*)上，该结果有望在新型 SNSPD 器件及微纳光纤领域开辟新的研究方向。

来源：上海科技

SIMIT develops micro-nano-fiber coupling SNSPD device structure

A research team led by Dr. You Lixing at Shanghai Institute of Microsystem and Information Technology (SIMIT) and Center for Excellence in Superconducting Electronics (CENSE) of Chinese Academy of Sciences cooperated with a team headed by Dr. Fang Wei and Dr. Tong Limin of Zhejiang University in developing the micro-nano-fiber coupling SNSPD device structure. In the structure, the SNSPD device is placed inside the evanescent field of micro-nano optical fibers, so that the nanowires can absorb the photons transmitted in the fibers. The research finding has recently been published on *Optics Express*, and it is expected to open up new possibilities for research on new-type SNSPD devices and micro-nano-optical fibers.

Source：stcsm.gov.cn

上海天文台科学家提出形成超大质量黑洞的新机制

中科院上海天文台研究员沈俊太课题组与美国罗格斯大学的 Jerry Sellwood 教授合作，提出了在宇宙早期不通过并合而形成超大质量黑洞的新机制。相关研究成果日前发表于天文学国际核心期刊《天体物理杂志》。专家表示，该机制既可以为星系并合中形成更大的超大质量黑洞提供原料种子黑洞，也可以在没有经历过并合的纯盘星系中形成较小的超大质量黑洞。

来源：科学网

Scientists of Shanghai Astronomical Observatory propose new mechanism for forming super-massive black hole

The Research Team of Shanghai Astronomical Observatory of the Chinese Academy of Sciences led by researcher Shen Juntai, together with Professor Jerry Sellwood of Rutgers University in the U.S., proposed a new mechanism for growing a super-massive black hole without galaxy mergers in the early universe. Relevant research results have been published in *Astrophysics Journal*, a key international astronomy journal. Experts say that this mechanism will provide seeds from which a super-massive black hole will sprout in bigger size through galaxy mergers, and super-massive black holes in smaller size might also form in a pure galactic disc without galaxy mergers.

Source：ScienceNet. cn

复旦大学研制出世界上首个全硅激光器

复旦大学信息科学与工程学院吴翔教授、陆明教授和张树宇副教授团队合作，研制出世界上首个全硅激光器。据悉，不同于以往的混合型硅基激光器，这次研究最终实现由硅自身作为增益介质产生激光。

来源：科学网

Fudan University develops the world's first all-silicon laser

Recently, a joint research team led by professor Wu Xiang, professor

Lu Ming and associate professor Zhang Shuyu at Fudan University developed what is claimed to be the first all-silicon laser. It is reported that, unlike the previous hybrid silicon-based laser, this study has used silicon nanocrystals with high optical gain to produce laser.

Source: ScienceNet. cn

中国科学院云南天文台国内首次实现月球激光测距

中国科学院云南天文台应用天文研究团组长期从事月球激光测距技术研究,经过对若干关键技术攻关后取得重大突破。1月22日晚,团组利用1.2m望远镜激光测距系统,多次成功探测到月面反射器Apollo15返回的激光脉冲信号,在国内首次成功实现月球激光测距。

来源:新浪科技

CAS Yunnan Observatories conducts China's first successful lunar laser ranging experiment

The Applied Astronomy Group of Yunnan Observatories, Chinese Academy of Sciences has long been devoted to lunar laser ranging experiments. After making several breakthroughs in key technologies, the group detected the laser pulse signals transmitted by the Lunar Roving Vehicle Apollo 15 by using a 1.2m telescope laser ranging system on the night of January 22. This is the first-ever successful lunar laser ranging experiment in China.

Source: tech. sina. com. cn

木卫二可能存在生命再添证据

据物理学家组织网26日报道,巴西科学家称,他们在地球上找到了与木卫二"欧罗巴"海底极其类似的环境,为木卫二可能存在生命再添证据。

木卫二是科学家寻找外星生命的主要目标,因为它可能为生命提供了宜居环境。在南非姆波内格金矿2.8千米深处,以圣保罗大学(USP)天体生物学研究中心研究员道格拉斯·加兰特为首的科研团队,不仅发现了与地球上生命历史有关的重大变化的痕迹,还发现了类似木卫二的环境。

来源:《科技日报》

New evidence of life probably on Europa discovered

According to phys. org on February 26, Brazilian scientists said that they had found an environment on earth similar to the seabed environment of Europa, which is new evidence that there may be life on Europa.

Europa is the main target for scientists to find extraterrestrial life because it may provide favorable environment for life. 2.8 km below Mponeng Gold Mine in South Africa, a research team led by Douglas Galant from the Astrobiology Research Center of Universidade de São Paulo (USP) found not only traces of the significant changes related to the life history on earth, but also an environment similar to that of Europa.

Source: *Science and Technology Daily*

便携传感器让大气中超细微粒无所遁形

大气中超细颗粒物的检测首次有了低成本便携式利器。近日,北京大学物理学院肖云峰研究员和龚旗煌院士带领的课题组,成功制备了基于纳米光纤阵列的全光传感器,新传感器的单颗粒粒径分辨率首次达到10纳米。

颗粒物的高灵敏传感检测在环境监控、国家安全和生化研究等方面具有重要意义。基于光学方法的传感技术具有非物理接触、易于操作且灵敏度高等优势,故而传统光纤传感器已在高灵敏检测领域"大显身手"。

来源:《科技日报》

Portable sensors capable of detecting ultra-fine particles created

A low-cost portable detector of atmospheric ultra-fine particles has been produced for the first time. Recently, a research team led by Researcher Xiao Yunfeng and Academician Gong Qihuang from School of Physics, Peking University has successfully produced an all-optical sensor based on nano-fiber array, and the new sensor has a single particle resolution of 10 nm, the highest resolution ever reached.

Sensitive sensing of particles is critical to environmental monitoring, national security and biochemical research. Optical sensing technology involves no physical contact and have easy accessibility and a high level of sensitivity, and thus the traditional optical fiber sensor is already widely used in the field of highly sensitive detection.

Source: *Science and Technology Daily*

投资近百亿，硬 X 射线自由电子激光装置在上海张江开工建设

4月27日，我国迄今为止投资最大、建设周期最长的国家重大科技基础设施项目——硬 X 射线自由电子激光装置在上海张江综合性国家科学中心开工建设。这一总投资近 100 亿元的"大国重器"计划于 2025 年竣工并投入使用，为科研用户提供高分辨成像、先进结构解析、超快过程探索等尖端研究手段。

来源：中新网

Construction of hard X-ray free electron laser devices starts in Zhangjiang Comprehensive National Science Center

On April 27, the construction of hard-X-ray free electron laser devices, a national major science and technology infrastructure project with the largest investment (nearly 10 billion yuan) and the longest construction period, was started at Shanghai Zhangjiang Comprehensive National Science Center. This pillar of China is scheduled to be completed and put into use in 2025, and will provide scientific researchers with such cutting-edge research methods as high-resolution imaging, advanced structural analysis, and ultra-fast process exploration.

Source: chinanews.com

清华团队刷新量子接口纠缠数量世界纪录

记者日前从清华大学获悉，该校交叉信息研究院段路明研究组在量子信息领域取得重要进展，首次实现25个量子接口之间的量子纠缠，刷新了量子接口纠缠数量的世界纪录。该成果相关论文近日发表在《科学进展》上。

来源：新华网

Researchers from Tsinghua University break the record in quantum interface entanglement quantity

Recently, the reporter learned from Tsinghua University that a team of researchers led by Duan Luming, a professor at the Institute for Interdisciplinary Information Sciences of the university has made important progress in the field of quantum information. They have achieved quantum entanglement among 25 quantum interfaces for the first time, which is an unprecedented record in the area. The research has been published in the journal *Science Advances*.

Source: xinhuanet.com

中科院物理所观测到锯齿形石墨烯纳米带边缘导电

近期,针对锯齿形边缘石墨烯纳米带,中国科学院物理研究所、北京凝聚态物理国家研究中心开展了磁输运测量研究。纳米物理与器件院重点实验室 N07 课题组研究员张广宇的博士生吴霜、沈成等人,利用课题组前期发展的氢等离子体各向异性刻蚀辅助的石墨烯纳米结构加工技术,在六方氮化硼绝缘衬底上加工了系列不同宽度的锯齿形边缘石墨烯纳米带。相关研究成果于 5 月 22 日发表在《物理评论快报》上。

来源:《中国科学报》

CAS' Institute of Physics finds that graphene nanoribbons with zigzag-edges could conduct electricity

The Institute of Physics and the Beijing National Laboratory for Condensed Matter Physics of CAS carried out a research on the magnetotransport properties of graphene nanoribbons with zigzag edges. Researcher Zhang Guangyu of the N07 Research Group and his doctoral students including Wu Shuang and Shen Cheng at the Beijing Key Laboratory for Nanomaterials and Nanodevices used hydrogen-plasma anisotropic etching-assisted graphene nanostructure fabrication technology developed before to fabricate zigzag-edged graphene nanoribbons on hexagonal boron nitride (h-BN) substrates. The research findings have been published in the journal *Physical Review Letters* on May 22.

Source: *China Science Daily*

寻找外星人没那么复杂 翻翻太空垃圾或许就有发现

据国外媒体报道,外星人爱好者们设计了多种搜寻外星生命迹象的复杂方法。但近日加那利天体物理学研究所的天文学家赫克托·索卡斯·纳瓦罗在《天体物理学期刊》上发表论文指出,我们也许想得过于复杂了。与其去找巨型建筑和太空船,不如找找更显而易见的东西,比如围绕遥远地外行星旋转的外星人卫星和太空垃圾。

来源:新浪网

Searching for aliens could be less complicated than we think-just look through the space junk

According to foreign media reports, alien enthusiasts have designed all sorts of complicated ways to search for signs of extraterrestrial life. However, as Hector Socas-Navarro, an astronomer at the Instituto de Astrofisica de Canarias, points out in his paper recently published in the *Astrophysical Journal*, people may be overthinking the process. Instead of looking for megastructures and spaceships, they should consider something a bit more obvious, such as alien satellites and space junk in orbit around distant exoplanets.

Source: Sina. com. cn

17

资本篇

特斯拉可能成为下一个苹果

特斯拉(Tesla)的首席执行官埃隆·马斯克大胆预言,他市值530亿美元的公司未来将会拥有堪比苹果(Apple)的估值。后者目前的市值为8 000亿美元,是全球最具价值的公司。他的理由是特斯拉将用"机器生产机器"的自动化技术颠覆制造业。尽管这看起来还只是空中楼阁,不过特斯拉的确有理由变成下一个苹果。

来源:财富中文网

Tesla may be the next Apple

Tesla CEO Elon Musk made a bold prediction that his company with the market value of ＄53 billion will have a valuation comparable to Apple's. At present, the latter's market value is ＄800 billion, being the most valuable company in the world. His reason is that Tesla will subvert the manufacturing sector with the automation technology "machine making machine". Though it looks like a castle in the air, Tesla does have the potential to be the next Apple.

Source: fortunechina. com

阿里集团将天猫保健食品注入阿里健康 持股增至45.8%

阿里健康5月19日宣布与阿里巴巴集团签署股份认购协议,阿里巴巴集团将天猫平台"蓝帽子"保健食品在线业务注入阿里健康,阿里巴巴持股比例将从约37.9%上升到约45.8%。

阿里健康认为,此次收购将给公司带来三大收益:进一步确保公司发展为阿里巴巴集团旗下医药保健旗舰平台;可以将更广泛之电商商家纳入到医药保健在线社群从而丰富生态,并与公司医药电商业务、智慧医疗服务、产品追溯平台服务这三大业务板块形成有机互补;获得更稳定的可持续收入增长。

来源:新浪科技

Alibaba Group integrates Tmall Healthcare Food into Ali Health with its shareholding increasing to 45.8%

Ali Health announced in May 19th that it will sign a shares subscription agreement with Alibaba Group which will integrate its Tmall online service of healthcare food approved by CFDA into Ali Health, with its shareholding proportion increasing from 37.9% to 45.8%.

Ali Health believes that this acquisition will bring three benefits to the company: further guarantee of its position as a medical & healthcare flagship platform under Alibaba; broader involvement of e-commerce companies into the healthcare online business community, which can improve the business environment, and complementing the company's medical E-commerce business, smart medical service and product tracking platform; making more stable and sustainable revenue growth.

Source: tech.sina.com.cn

阿里财报:各业务生态协同效应显现,全球化成亮点

日前,阿里巴巴集团公布 2017 财年第四财季财报及 2017 财年全年业绩。第四财季,阿里巴巴集团收入同比增长 60%,达到 385.79 亿元人民币;非美国通用会计准则下的净利为 104.4 亿元人民币,同比增长 38%。

在财报发布后的分析师会议上,阿里巴巴集团首席执行官张勇以"非常出色的一个季度和一个财年"进行总结。他将现在的阿里巴巴定义为"一个拥有 5.07 亿移动用户和 3.8 万亿元人民币 GMV 的经济体"。2017 财年,阿里巴巴的全球化战略正在加速布局。

有外媒评价:阿里目光早已经不再局限于中国,而是越来越多地转向国际市场;并进入支付、云计算、文娱等众多商业领域。"所有人都知道,马云要来了。"

来源:新浪科技

Alibaba's financial report highlights synergy of business ecologies and globalization

Recently, Alibaba Group announced its financial results for the quarter ended March 31, 2017 and the fiscal year 2017. It reported a revenue growth by 60%, reaching 38.579 billion yuan and a non-GAAP net income of 10.44 billion yuan, an increase of 38%.

At the subsequent analyst meeting, Zhang Yong, CEO of the Group, concluded that it was "another excellent quarter and fiscal year." He defined Alibaba as an economy with 507 million mobile users and a GMV of 3.8 trillion RMB. In the fiscal year 2017, Alibaba is accelerating its global strategy planning.

Some foreign media commented that the Alibaba was no longer contented with Chinese market and began to make foreign expansions in areas such as payment, cloud computing, culture, and recreation. "Everyone knows that Ma is coming."

Source: tech.sina.com.cn

共享办公品牌梦想加获浦发硅谷银行战略债权融资

近日,浦发硅谷银行宣布为梦想加提供战略债权融资。此轮战略债权融资所撬动的资本投入,将全部用于梦想加加速规模布局。梦想加是专注智能办公体验的共享办公品牌,3个月前,梦想加获得了由愉悦资本领投、闪银及险峰长青跟投的 2 000 万美金 B 轮融资,该笔融资也主要用来加速核心城市的空间布局。

——来源:36 氪

Co-working space company mydream+ obtains strategic debt financing from SPD Silicon Valley Bank

It was announced recently that SPD Silicon Valley Bank would provide strategic debt financing for mydream+. The capital input leveraged by the financing will be used for accelerating the expansion of business. Mydream+ is a co-working space company, specializing in smart office experience. Three months ago, mydream+ raised a series B financing of $20 million led by JOY Capital and joined by Wecash and K2VC. The fund was also used to accelerate its space distribution in core cities.

Source:36kr

张江人工智能团队 DeepBrain 获首轮融资

近日,张江人工智能团队 DeepBrain 获得金沙江创投、戈壁创投、钱世投资的 3 200 万元首轮融资。

资料显示,DeepBrain 主要为硬件厂商提供五大核心能力:语义技能商店、AI 人机对话引擎、机器人功能组件、大数据分析及家居互联服务。团队开发了全球第一个基于区块链的人工智能操作系统深脑链,用区块链技术来解决一些目前仅靠人工智能技术难以解决的痛点。

来源:人民网

Zhangjiang AI team DeepBrain completed its first round of funding

Recently, DeepBrain, an AI team based in Zhangjiang has raised in its first round of funding 32 million from GSR Ventures, Gobi, and Qianshi Investment.

Statistics have shown that DeepBrain mainly provide five core skills for hardware producers, namely: semantic skills store, AI human machine communication engine, robotic functional component, big data analysis, and home appliances interconnection. The team has developed the first block chain-based AI operating system called DeepBrain Chain, aiming to use block chain technology to solve the pain points that are not to be solved with AI alone.

Source: people. cn

推想科技完成 1.2 亿元 B 轮融资,加速 AI 在医疗行业商业化落地

9 月 21 日,推想科技宣布完成 1.2 亿元 B 轮融资,由启明创投领投,元生资本、红杉中国联合投资。据了解,这是目前国际医学影像人工智能行业内最大规模的单笔融资。

未来,推想科技的产品一方面将在广度上拓展——脑部 AI 临床解决方案、骨折 AI 辅助筛查、心脏 AI 辅助筛查、乳腺 AI 辅助筛查、腹部人工智能辅助筛查等都将陆续问世。另一方面,推想科技产品在深度上将不断向临床延伸,通过精确定位与描述病灶,辅助临床科室完成快速、个性化的干预决策。

来源:36 氪

Infervision raises RMB 120 million to accelerate commercial use of AI in medical industry

On September 21, Infervision announced that it has raised RMB 120 million in the B round financing. The investment was led by Qiming Venture Partners, with participation of Genesis Capital and Sequoia. It is said to be the biggest amount ever raised in a single round of funding in the international medial image AI industry.

Infervision will make efforts to expand its product category, including AI-based clinical solutions for brain, AI-assisted bone fracture screening, AI-assisted heart disease screening, AI-assisted mammary gland screening, AI-assisted abdomen screening, etc. Meanwhile, Infervision will move deeper into the clinical filed, by precisely positioning and describing the focus of disease to help clinical departments make rapid and personalized intervention decisions.

Source: 36kr

HTC400 万美元领投 VR 社交公司 VRChat

近日，VR 创业公司 VRChat 获得 400 万美元 A 轮融资，由 HTC 领投。在 2016 年，VRChat 就已经获得了 HTC 领投的 120 万美元天使轮融资。VRChat 是一款 UGC 型的社交 VR，通过与 Morph 3D 的合作，为用户提供了一系列的工具；用户可以轻松地设计自己的虚拟身份，创造独特的个性化身。

来源：36 氪

HTC led in the investment of four million dollars into VRChat

Recently, VRChat got A round of 4-million-dollar financing led by HTC. VRChat has already got angel round financing of 1.2 million dollars led by HTC in 2016. VRChat is a UGC-type social VR providing a series of tools for users through its cooperation with Morph 3D. Users can easily design their own virtual identities and create unique personalities.

Source: 36kr

联合国将推进谷歌资助的盲人音频引导项目 Wayfindr

英国非营利性组织 Wayfindr 创办一套供全球所有视觉障碍者使用的语音描述标准。谷歌慈善部门 Google.org 为这家非营利性公司投资了 100 万美元的资金,希望借此帮助 Wayfindr 打造一套可以利用智能手机为视觉障碍者提供标准的城市向导服务。Wayfindr 技术已经在伦敦地铁系统的尤斯顿站全球展开测试,而联合国最近宣布将推动该项目在全球范围内开展。

来源:36 氪

UN will advance the Google-funded blind audio and lead project Wayfindr

British non-profit organization Wayfindr has created a set of speech description standard for all visually impaired people around the world. Having invested $ 1 million in this nonprofit company, Google.org, the Google charity department, is in the hope of helping Wayfindr build a city guide service for all visually impaired people by virtue of smartphones. Wayfindr technology has been tested at the Euston Station in the London metro system, while the United Nations has recently announced that it will promote the development of the project around the world.

Source:36kr

以色列农业科技公司 Phytech 获 1 100 万美元 B 轮融资

农业公司 Phytech 日前宣布获得 1 100 万美元的 B 轮融资,由腾讯领投,Syngenta Ventures 跟投。截至目前,该公司已披露的融资总金额为 1 400 万美元。

来源:36 氪

Phytech, an Israeli agricultural technology company, received $11 million in round B financing

Recently Phytech, an agricultural company, announced to have received $11 million in round B financing, led by Tencent and followed by Syngenta Ventures. Up to now, the company has disclosed a total amount of $14 million in financing.

Source: 36kr

生物识别技术开发和应用公司眼神科技完成超亿元 A 轮融资

生物识别技术开发和应用公司眼神科技目前已完成 A 轮融资,领投方为先锋国盛(北京)股权投资基金管理有限公司,融资总额超过 1 亿元。眼神科技成立于 2016 年,是一家专注于生物识别技术开发和应用的公司。现已开发完毕并成熟使用的生物识别技术包括指纹、人脸和虹膜识别技术,正在研发中的有指静脉识别技术。

来源:36 氪

Eyecool Technology raised over ￥100 million in the A round financing

Eyecool Technology has finished its A round financing, with UCF Guosheng (Beijing) Equity Investment Fund Management Co,. Ltd as the lead investor and the total financing of over 100 million yuan. Eyecool Technology was established in 2016, with a focus on bioidentification technology development and application. The bioidentification technologies completely developed and widely used include fingerprint, face and iris identification and the finger vein recognition technology is under research and development.

Source: 36kr

人工智能公司旷视科技完成 4.6 亿美元 C 轮融资

国内人工智能公司旷视科技 Face＋＋已于近期完成 C 轮融资,本轮融资金额约为 4.6 亿美元,由中国国有资本风险投资基金、蚂蚁金服、富士康集团联合领投,中俄战略投资基金、阳光保险集团、SK 集团等参投。本轮融资很可能会被用于加快在城市综合大脑及手机智能领域的技术落地,打造智慧城市。

来源:36 氪

Face＋＋ completed its C round funding at a staggering US＄460 million

China's biggest facial recognition firm Megvii, more commonly known as Face＋＋, has raised ＄460 million in its C round funding. This round of financing was jointly led by Chinese state fund, Ant Financial and Foxconn Technology, with the participation of Russia-China Investment Fund, Sunshine Insurance Group, and SK Group. The funds can be used to accelerate the application of technologies in areas like comprehensive urban recognition and smart phones to build a smart city.

Source:36kr

利用雷达系统帮助无人车识别物体,Arbe Robotics 获 900 万美元 A 轮融资

日前,特拉维夫创企 Arbe Robotics 正在开发一款高分辨率的雷达系统,以帮助车辆检测和识别物体。近日公司获 900 万美元 A 轮融资,这轮融资会帮助它在未来 1 到 2 年内进行车内测试。

来源:36 氪

Arbe Robotics raises ＄9M to build high-resolution radars for autonomous cars

Arbe Robotics, a Tel Aviv startup that has been developing a high-resolution radar system to help self-driving vehicles to detect and identify objects, has raised ＄9 million in series A funding, which will help it conduct in-vehicle tests within the next one to two years.

Source: 36kr

美国网络安全公司 Tortuga Logic 获 200 万美元种子轮融资

日前,美国网络安全公司 Tortuga Logic 获 Eclipse 200 万美元种子轮融资。本轮融资将用于制造能检测出电脑硬件上"潜在漏洞"的产品。据悉,Tortuga Logic 的四位创始人有多年的系统安全科研经验,本项目也获得了美国国家科学基金会的资金支持。

来源:36 氪

US cybersecurity company Tortuga Logic raises ＄2 million in seed funding

US cybersecurity company Tortuga Logic has raised ＄2 million in seed funding from Eclipse Ventures. The company plans to use the cash to build products that will find "lurking vulnerabilities" on computer hardware. The four founders of Tortuga Logic have decades of experience in system security and received a grant from the US National Science Foundation.

Source: 36kr

创新工场出资 4 250 万元设人工智能研究子公司

11月17日,创新工场公告,公司拟与北京旷视科技有限公司、北京极科极客科技有限公司,共同出资设立控股子公司北京创新工场旷视国际人工智能技术研究院有限公司,注册地为北京,注册资本为 5 000 万元,其中公司出资 4 250 万元,占注册资本的 85.00%。此次对外投资构成关联交易。公司称,此次与旷世科技、极客科技共同出资设立公司,主要为聚焦人工智能基础研究,建立国际知名的人工智能生态圈,吸引国际人才落户北京,将技术成果应用到各产业,孵化企业推动市场化进程。

来源:36氪

Sinovation Ventures invests RMB 42.5 million in a AI research subsidiary company

On November 17, Sinovation Ventures announced that it planned to cooperate with Beijing Megvii Technology and Beijing Jike Jike Technology in setting up a holding subsidiary company Beijing Sinovation Ventures Megvii International Artificial Intelligence Institute. Registered in Beijing, the company will have a registered capital of RMB 50 million, of which RMB 42.5 million will be contributed by Sinovation Ventures, accounting for 85% of the total. This investment constitutes a connected transaction. Sinovation Ventures said that this new company would focus on conducting basic research of artificial intelligence, building an internationally renowned AI ecosystem, attracting international professionals to work in Beijing, applying technological achievements to various industries, and incubating companies to speed up the marketization process.

Source:36kr

AI 国家队"云从科技"今宣布完成 B 轮融资

近日,中国人工智能国家队云从科技正式完成 B 轮 5 亿元人民币融资,加上此前广州市政府对云从科技的 20 亿元政府资金支持,此次总计获得 25 亿元发展资金。本轮融资由顺为资本、元禾原点、普华资本联合领投,越秀产投、张江星河、前海兴旺跟投。同时,佳都科技、任煜男创办的杰翱资本等天使轮及 A 轮投资方均继续跟投此轮。华兴 Alpha 担任此次融资的独家财务顾问。

来源:36 氪

B round of financing of China's national AI team CloudWalk completed

China's national AI team CloudWalk recently raised 500 million yuan in its B round of financing. Coupled with the previous 2 billion yuan of financial support from Guangzhou Municipal Government, this round of financing added up to 2.5 billion yuan. This financing is jointly led by Shunwei Capital, Oriza Yuandian Venture Capital, and Puhua Capital, and followed by Yuexiu Industrial Investment Fund, Zhangjiang Galaxy Fund, and Qianhai Xingwang. In addition, investors participated in angel round and A round of financing, such as PCI and JR Capital (which is started by Ren Yu'nan), continued to invest. Huaxing Alpha served as the exclusive financial advisor for this round of financing.

Source:36kr

战略管理 SaaS 平台 Workboard 获 900 万美元 A 轮融资

战略管理 SaaS 平台 Workboard 获得 900 万美元 A 轮融资,由微软创投领投,成立 4 年,公司总融资额达到 1 210 万美元。Workboard 在云平台上提供分析和 AI 服务,帮助企业执行它们的战略。平台可以在 PC、iPad、移动 App

等多个设备运行。Workboard 使艰深晦涩的企业战略重点,变得更加透明,甚至具有了互动性。团队目标的可视化,让每个成员聚焦于最关键的工作。

来源:36 氪

SaaS platform Workboard raised ＄9 million in Series A round

Workboard, a SaaS platform that helps companies execute their strategies, announced a ＄9 million Series A round led by Microsoft Ventures. Since its founding four years ago, the total funding that the company receives adds up to ＄12.1 million. Workboard helps companies see through their strategic plans by using analytics and AI on a cloud-based platform that works on PC, iPad, and mobile apps. Workboard enables organizations to activate smarter strategies faster and make strategic priorities remarkably transparent and interactive. Team goals are visualized, so that each member can stay focused on the most critical work.

Source:36kr

创新生物药研发商三叶草生物获 6 280 万元人民币 A 轮融资

近日,成都创新生物药研发商三叶草生物制药宣布已获得 6 280 万元人民币的 A 轮融资,资方为四川天河生物医药产业创业投资基金。本轮融资将用于进一步推进其大分子生物药的开发,和扩大其团队规模。

来源:36 氪

Clover Biopharmaceuticals receives Series A funding of 62.8 million RMB

Recently, Clover Biopharmaceuticals, a Chengdu biotechnology company focused on developing novel and transformative biologic therapies, announced the completion of a RMB 62.8 million Series A financing from Tianhe Life Sciences Venture Fund. This round of funding will be used for facilitating macromolecular biomedicine and expanding its team size.

Source: 36kr

极奥科技获软银中国千万级元 Pre-A 轮融资

近日,智能出行领域的初创企业极奥科技宣布完成数千万元人民币 Pre-A 轮融资,投资方为软银中国资本(SBCVC)。极奥科技是一家利用众包车辆数据,生产高精度电子地图的企业,其产品和服务已经受到了多家车企、Tier 1 供应商以及多家国内地图商的认可,现已应用在安全辅助驾驶和无人驾驶等技术领域。这一轮资金主要用于布局交通场景重构。

来源:36 氪

GEO raised tens of millions of yuan in its Pre-Series A round of financing from SBCVC

Recently, the smart travel startup GEO announced that it has raised tens of millions of yuan in its Pre-Series A round of financing from SBCVC. GEO is a company specializing in producing high-precision electronic maps with crowdsourcing vehicle data. Its products and services have been recognized by many automobile companies, Tier 1 suppliers, and domestic map makers; and they have been applied to such technical areas as safety assistant driving and driverless driving. This round of financing will be mainly used to rebuild the layout of traffic scenes.

Source: 36kr

同心医联新一轮融资落定,中金康瑞医疗产业基金领投

2018年1月,同心医联宣布完成第四轮融资,本轮融资由中金康瑞医疗产业基金领投。CEO刘伟奇表示,本轮融资将主要用于在全国范围内布局第三方影像中心和影像医联体,以及搭建医疗健康服务联盟。同心医联创立初期,首先整合医疗资源,建立线上检查预约服务平台,后来同心医联开发出影像云平台,筹建多家影像中心,搭建影像医联体,促进分级诊疗。

来源:36氪

UNIMED completes its fourth round of financing led by Zhongjin Kangrui Medical Industry Fund

In January 2018, UNIMED announced the completion of the fourth round of financing led by the Zhongjin Kangrui Medical Industry Fund. Liu Weichi, CEO of UNIMED, said this round of financing will mainly be used for building national-wide third-party imaging centers and creating image-medical union, as well as establishing service alliance for health care. In its first several years, UNIMED mainly focused on integrating medical resources and setting up an online platform for checkup appointment. Later, it developed an imaging cloud platform, established a couple of imaging centers, and an medical imaging union, promoting the tiered medical service.

Source:36kr

安智汽车完成数千万元 A 轮融资

近日,安智汽车(苏州安智汽车零部件有限公司)宣布完成数千万元A轮融资,由上海物联网创业投资基金投资。成立于2015年1月的安智汽车,作为国内智能驾驶系统开发的领跑者,依托团队国际化开发经验与强大的工程设计能

力,自主开发完成了具有全面知识产权的 77GHz 毫米波雷达与多功能视觉系统,并搭建了更懂中国路况的 ADAS 驾驶辅助系统。安智汽车创始人郭健表示,本轮融资将用于产品研发、量产化落地及研发团队扩充等方面。

来源:36 氪

Anzhi Auto raises thousands of millions of yuan in the Series A round of financing

Recently, Suzhou Anzhi Automotive Parts Co., Ltd. announced that it had secured thousands of millions of yuan in its Series A round of financing. The investor was Shanghai IoT Venture Capital Fund. Established in January 2015, Anzhi Auto is a leader nationwide in intelligent driving system. Based on its international development experience and great engineering design capability, the company has independently developed the 77GHz millimeter-wave radar and multifunctional vision system and owns its intellectual property right. It has also built the ADAS driver assistance system which can better monitor the traffic situation in China. The founder of Anzhi Auto Guo Jian said that this round of financing would be used for the development and mass production of products as well as the R&D team expansion.

Source:36kr

张江该美科技完成天使轮融资

近日,位于张江的数字化齿科领域创新企业——该美科技宣布完成 1 000 万元天使轮融资,投资方为中科院体系专注于高科技成果转化的国科嘉和基金。本轮融资将用于种植软件和正畸软件、种植导板和矫治器的市场推广,并为扩大公司的业务范围和引入新的产品做准备。

来源:东方财富

Guide Mia Technologies in Zhangjiang completes angel round of financing

Guide Mia Technologies, a digital dental innovator based in Zhangjiang, recently announced that it has completed a 10 million RMB angel round of financing. The investor is Cash Capital Fund, a company under Chinese Academy of Sciences that specializes in commercialization of high-tech achievements.

This round of financing will be used to promote planting software, orthodontic software, planting guides and appliances, and to prepare for expansion of the company's business and introduction of new products.

Source: eastmoney.com

北京独角兽最多，互联网电商盛产

风投把估值超过10亿美元的公司称为独角兽，万得（wind）金融数据客户端指出，目前全球独角兽企业已经有276家。胡润百富董事长曾表示："基本上现在独角兽企业不是在美国，就是在中国。"那么，中国独角兽企业最爱的"栖息地"是哪里？

数据显示，总部驻扎在北京的最多，有54家；估值规模上，体量最大的区域还是北京，接近1.4万亿元，占近半数。涉及行业上，互联网服务、电子商务行业并列第一，各有22家企业上榜。位列第三的是互联网金融行业。

来源：新浪网

Beijing is home to most China's unicorns, especially internet and e-commerce companies

A unicorn is a startup company valued at over $1 billion. Wind's financial data shows that unicorn companies totaled 276 worldwide. Rupert Hoogewerf, president of Hurun Report Inc., said, "Today's unicorns have been concentrated in the U.S. and China." Then, where is the favorite "habitat" for unicorns in China?

Data shows that the largest number of unicorn enterprises, 54 in total, have their headquarters in Beijing. In terms of business valuation, the largest one is still Beijing, nearly RMB 1.4 trillion, accounting for almost half of the total. In terms of industry distribution, both the internet industry and the e-commerce industry rank first, with 22 companies on the list for each industry. The industry that follows is the internet finance industry.

Source: Sina.com.cn

金融街金融机构资产规模近百万亿，新兴金融业发展迅速

近5年来，北京金融街新入驻金融机构523家，一半以上为新兴金融业态；目前金融街的金融机构资产规模达到99.5万亿元，占全国金融机构资产规模近40%。被视为中国金融业"大脑"的金融街，正迈入高质量发展新时代。

来源：中新网

Assets of financial institutions in Beijing Financial Street reach nearly one hundred trillion yuan

In the past five years, 523 financial institutions newly settled down in Beijing Financial Street, more than half of which are of emerging financial industry. At present, the financial assets of financial institutions in the Financial Street total 99.5 trillion yuan, accounting for nearly 40% of the total assets of financial institutions across China. The Financial Street, known as the "brain" of China's financial industry, is entering a new era of quality development.

Source: chinanews.com

发射商用 SAR 卫星获取高分辨图像，芬兰 ICEYE 获 3 400 万美元 B 轮融资

日前，芬兰商业雷达卫星运营商 ICEYE 宣布，获得 3 400 万美元的 B 轮融资，由 True Ventures 领投。ICEYE 成立于 2012 年，制造商用微型卫星，搭载合成孔径雷达（SAR），可以在能见度极低的条件下得到高分辨雷达图像，不受天气及光照影响，能稳定地追踪拍摄对象的变化。

来源：36 氪

ICEYE garners USD 34 million Series B funding for the firm's SAR satellites

ICEYE, a Finnish commercial radar satellite operator, has announced USD 34 million Series B funding led by True Ventures. Established in 2012, ICEYE manufactures commercial microsatellites equipped with Synthetic Aperture Radar (SAR), which can obtain high-resolution radar images under conditions of extremely low visibility, unaffected by weather and lighting. Thus it can steadily track changes over time.

Source: 36kr

商汤科技完成 6.2 亿美元 C＋轮融资，将扩展国际化业务

商汤科技近日宣布获得 6.2 亿美元 C＋轮融资，联合领投方包括厚朴投资、银湖投资、老虎基金、富达国际等，此外本轮融资引入了战略投资方高通创投、保利资本和世茂集团。商汤科技称，本轮融资后公司估值超过 45 亿美元。

来源：36 氪

SenseTime closes USD 620 million C+ round of funding, eyeing international expansion

SenseTime recently announced that it had raised USD 620 million in the C+ round of funding, lifting its capitalization to over USD 4.5 billion. The round was led by Hopu Investment Management, Silver Lake, Tiger Fund, Fidelity International, etc., with introduction of strategic investors, including Qualcomm Ventures, Poly Capital and Shimao Group. SenseTime said that after this round of financing, the company's valuaion exceeds $4.5 billion.

Source: 36kr

法国创企 Klaxoon 获 5 000 万美元 B 轮融资

日前,法国创企 Klaxoon 宣布获 5 000 万美元 B 轮融资,它希望借此将过去两年里口碑相传的发展实现资本化。本轮融资由 Idinvest Partners 领投,参投方包括 BPI、Sofiouest、Arkea 和 White Star Capital Fund 等现有投资人。

来源: 猎云网

Klaxoon, a French start-up, raises $50 million in B funding round

A few days ago, French company Klaxoon, in the hope of capitalizing its good reputation build in past two years, announced a $50 million in B funding round. This round of financing was led by Idinvest Partners, with participation from existing investors including Stockholder BPI, Sofiouest, Arkea and White Star Capital Fund.

Source: lieyunwang.com

"宝宝树"获阿里巴巴战略投资,估值 140 亿元人民币

近日,传闻已久的"宝宝树"新一轮融资尘埃落定,最终与阿里巴巴集团达成资本战略合作,新一轮融资后宝宝树的估值达到 140 亿元人民币左右。"宝宝树"选择与阿里结盟,背后的逻辑是双方希望在电商和 C2M(包括定制产品等)等方面,做一些新事情。据悉,除资本注入外,双方将开展在电商、C2M(Customer to Maker)、广告营销、知识付费、新零售、线上线下母婴场景等多个层面的深层合作。

来源:36 氪

"Baby Tree" obtains strategic investment from Alibaba, with a valuation of RMB 14 billion

The rumor of Baby Tree's new round of funding has come to an end, as it has reached a strategic cooperation on capital with Alibaba. The new round of funding lifted Baby Tree's valuation to around RMB 14 billion. Baby Tree chose to partner with Alibaba, because the two sides hope that they do something in e-commerce and C2M (incl. product customization) areas. It was learned that they would, except for capital investment, carry out deep cooperation in spaces such as e-commerce, C2M (Customer to Maker), advertising and marketing, pay-for-knowledge, new retail and online and offline mother & children-focused scenarios.

Source: 36kr

18

教育篇

上海市科委与百联集团携手,将科普带进商场

9月27日,上海自然博物馆与百联股份联合举办的"百联·自然趣玩屋"公益活动正式亮相。首场"我为甲虫狂"主题活动在百联又一城购物中心举办,约20位6—12岁的小朋友在自然博物馆老师的带领下及家长的陪伴下,了解了甲虫的生活习性特点等相关知识,近距离观察甲虫标本,并亲手制作了甲虫模型,为甲虫涂上自己心仪的色彩。

据悉,这是上海市科委与百联集团携手开展科技创新与科普工作合作,让科普走进商场的创新举措。

来源:《上海科技报》

STCSM works with Bailian Group to popularize science in a shopping mall

"Bailian Natural Science House", a charitable activity co-hosted by Shanghai Natural History Museum and Bailian Group, was officially launched on September 27. The first thematic activity "Crazy for Beetles" was held in Bailian New Era Mall. Guided by teachers of the museum, about 20 children aged 6-12 years in company with their parents have participated in the activity to learn facts about beetles, such as their behaviors and habits, get a close look at beetle specimens, and make and color beetle specimens by themselves.

According to the report, it is the first cooperation between Science and Technology Commission of Shanghai Municipality (STCSM) and Bailian Group in technological innovation and science popularization, which leverages innovative methods to marry science popularization into shopping malls.

Source: *Shanghai Science and Technology*

我国高等教育在学总规模位居世界第一

9月28日,从教育部新闻发布会上获悉,我国高等教育在学总规模达到3 699万人,占世界高等教育总规模的五分之一,规模位居世界第一。

来源:新华社

China has the largest number of students receiving higher education

On September 28, the Ministry of Education announced that the total number of students receiving higher education in China had reached 36.99 million, accounting for one fifth of the world total and ranking the first place in the world.

Source: Xinhua News Agency

澳大利亚出台新规严防学生论文作弊

据澳洲新快网报道,由于学术作弊越来越普遍,近日,澳大利亚高等教育质量标准局出台了针对学生学术造假问题的处理办法,要求各大高校屏蔽售卖论文的网站,识别造假"热点",并考虑公开学术诚信违反行为数据。

南澳大学副教授布莱塔格近期调查发现,6%的澳大利亚学生曾涉嫌作弊,68%的学者曾被怀疑学术造假。

来源:中新网

Australia issued new rules to prevent students from cheating in essays

According to xkb.com.au, as academic cheating behavior become more common, the Tertiary Education Quality and Standards Agency (TEQSA) in Australia has recently taken new measures to deal with academic misconduct of students, which requires universities to block websites selling essays, and identifying "hot spots" of cheating. Moreover, the agency also considers publishing data on breeches of academic integrity.

A recent research by Associate Professor Bretag at the University of South Australia shows that, 6% of Australian students have been engaged in cheating, and up to 68% of scholars have been suspected of academic cheating.

Source: chinanews. com

"双一流"助推上海科创中心建设

日前,世界一流大学和一流学科建设高校及建设学科名单公布,已有高校陆续公布建设方案,"双一流"建设将进入具体实施阶段。作为最早对接落实国家"双一流"战略的上海高校,在科技创新、学科建设等方面提前布局,一些前沿基础科学研究取得原始创新成果,上海高校已开始主动服务于上海建设全球有影响力的科创中心。"双一流"的具体实施无疑将为上海高校带来新一轮跨越式发展,也将助推上海科创中心的建设与发展。

来源:中新网

Double First-rate assists the building of Shanghai Technology Innovation Center

Recently, the list of universities and disciplines of Double First-rate, aiming at building world-class universities and disciplines, has been released. Some universities have announced their building schemes, marking the start of implementation stage of Double First-rate building. Shanghai universities, as the earliest to understand and implement the national Double First-rate strategy, have made plans on scientific and technological innovation, disciplines building and other fields, which have won initial innovation achievements on frontier basic sciences. And the universities have proactively provided services for the building of Shanghai Technology Innovation Center with international impact. The implementation of Double First-rate will definitely provide a new round of leapfrog development for Shanghai universities, as well as assist the building and development of Shanghai Technology Innovation Center.

Source: chinanews.com

75所教育部直属高校公布预算,清华超200亿元

按照教育部的要求,75所教育部直属高校日前都在各自官网上公布了今年预算。清华大学仍是全国唯一一所预算超200亿元的高校,而且领先排名第二的高校100多亿元。令人意外的是北京大学今年预算大幅减少,导致"百亿高校"的排名发生变化。对很多"富裕"的高校来说,其收入中来自拨款的已是小部分,大部分则来自"事业收入"和"其他收入"。

来源:科学网

75 universities and colleges directly under the Ministry of Education announce their budget

According to the requirements of the Ministry of Education, 75 universities and colleges directly under the ministry announced their budget for 2018 on their respective official websites. Tsinghua University is still the only university in China that has a budget of more than 20 billion yuan, which is over 10 billion yuan more than the second-ranking university. What is surprising is that Beijing University's budget is significantly reduced this year, leading to a change in its ranking of ten-billion-yuan colleges and universities. For many "rich" colleges and universities, funding is only a small part of their income, with most of it coming from "businesses" and "other items".

Source: ScienceNet. cn

复旦大学生命科学学院与港城集团签订协议共建红树林湿地产学研基地

近日,由浦东新区区委宣传部牵头,钟扬同志先进事迹报告会在临港机关办公中心举行。同时,钟扬生前牵挂的红树林育苗基地也落户临港。会后,复旦大学生命科学学院与港城集团共同为临港红树林育苗基地签订了合作协议,为后续筛选并保存更加适应上海气候的红树植物进行引种试验和种苗培育提供了保障。

来源:上海科技

School of Life Sciences Fudan University and Shanghai Harbour City Development Group signs an agreement on jointly building the Industry-University Cooperative Research Center of Mangrove Wetland

Recently, with the lead of the Propaganda Department of Pudong New Area, the advanced deeds report meeting of Comrade Zhong Yang was held in the Work Center for Lingang Office. At the meeting, the center for mangrove seeds and seedlings, which Zhong Yang hoped to build during his lifetime, settled in Lingang. After the meeting, School of Life Sciences Fudan University and Shanghai Harbour City Development Group signed an agreement on jointly building the Industry-University Cooperative Research Center of Mangrove Wetland in Lingang. This agreement will facilitate the subsequent screening and preservation of mangrove plants which can better adapt to the climate of Shanghai for seed testing and seedling cultivation.

Source: stcsm. gov. cn

沪高校打造动物医学虚拟仿真实训中心

记者近日了解到,上海农林职业技术学院动物科学技术系副主任滑志民领衔打造了一个"动物医学虚拟仿真实训中心"。学校表示,这个实训中心是国内动物医学教育领域技术最先进、功能最全面的。原来的兽医临床教学需要动用相当数量的动物活体做实验,有了虚拟仿真实训中心,很多动物解剖、生理实验、手术通路讲解等,都可以通过虚拟实景完成。

来源:东方网

Shanghai-based vocational college sets up an animal medicine virtual simulation training center

Recently, a team of researchers led by Hua Zhimin, vice dean of the Department of Animal Science and Technology of Shanghai Vocational College of Agriculture and Forestry, has built an animal medicine virtual simulation training center.

According to the college, this training center is the most advanced and comprehensive center in the field of animal health education in China. In the past, veterinary clinical teaching required a considerable number of live animals for experiments. Now, with the virtual simulation training center, many animal anatomy experiments, physiological experiments, and surgical access courses can be performed through virtual reality.

Source: eastday. com

19

新能源篇

韩国科学家提高钙钛矿太阳能电池转化效率

通过改进钙钛矿太阳能电池金属卤化物吸光材料的制造方法,韩国科学家使这种类型太阳能电池的能量转化效率达到22.1%,而此前这类电池转化效率的最高纪录是20.1%。

钙钛矿太阳能电池的吸光材料通常采用铅或镍的卤化物,因其晶体结构与钙钛矿类似而得名。这类吸光材料光电性能优良、制造成本较低,是近年来太阳能发电领域的研究热点。

来源:科学网

South Korean scientists improve conversion efficiency of perovskite solar cells

By improving the production method of the light-absorbing material in perovskite solar cells, South Korean scientists have successfully improved the solar conversion efficiency to 22.1%, 2 point higher than the previous highest record.

Perovskite solar cell is named for its similar crystal structure with perovskite. Its light-absorbing material is usually made of lead or nickel halides which features low cost and excellent photoelectric performance and has become a hot spot of research on solar power generation.

Source:ScienceNet.cn

我国首次海域可燃冰试采成功

5月18日,由国土资源部中国地质调查局组织实施的我国海域天然气水合物试采在南海神狐海域实现连续8天稳定产气,试采取得圆满成功,实现了我国天然气水合物开发的历史性突破。这是我国首次也是世界首次成功实现资源量占全球 90% 以上、开发难度最大的泥质粉砂型天然气水合物安全可控开采。

来源：人民网

China Succeeds in Mining Combustible Ice in South China Sea

China Geological Survey (CGS) under the Ministry of Land and Resources has successfully extracted methane hydrate (NGH) in the Shenhu area of the South China Sea for eight consecutive days since May 10, marking that China has made a historic breakthrough in the exploitation of NGH. NGH consists of over 90% of the global total resource volume and is the most difficult resources to be tapped. This is China's, as well as the world's, first success in mining NGH safely and stably.

Source: people.com.cn

美太阳能研发转向聚光发电技术

美国能源部近日宣布投资 6 200 万美元，加大太阳能产业另一项重大技术——聚光太阳能发电的研发，以攻克太阳能电网稳定性、修复性以及电能储存等关键难题。目前太阳能发电厂主要基于两种技术将太阳能转换成电能：一种是光伏发电技术，需要配备昂贵的电池组或外部储能技术，只在艳阳高照时才能运转供电；第二种是聚光太阳能发电技术，通过透镜等将太阳光聚焦，利用获得的能量将水转化成蒸汽推动汽轮机运转，太阳能部分转化成热能储存在系统配备的熔盐罐中，可在夜晚或阴雨天持续供电。

来源：《科技日报》

US focuses new solar R&D on CSP

The U.S. Department of Energy (DOE) announced recently a USD 62 million investment into another important technology — the Contracting Solar Power (CSP), in order to address solar energy's critical challenges of grid reliability, resilience, and storage. The current solar power plants mainly use two types of technologies to covert solar energy into electricity. The first is the photovoltaic power generation, which only works when the sun is out, and coupled with expensive batteries or other forms of external storage; the other is CSP, which relies on mirrors to concentrate sunlight, and then converts liquid into turbine-driving steam. Some of that heat can also be stored using molten-salt tanks, allowing the plants to continue supplying electricity when the sun isn't shining

Source: *Science and Technology Daily*

来自水分蒸发的可再生能源前景可观

据英国《自然·通讯》杂志日前在线发表的最新能源研究报告称,天然水分蒸发代表了另一种前景可观的可再生能源来源。美国科学家对天然水分蒸发过程中可采集的能量进行评估,发现该过程可产生的功率密度是风电的三倍,这将为可再生能源面临的间歇性问题提供解决方案。

来源:《科技日报》

Water evaporation may bring considerable volume of renewable energy

A new energy research report published online by *Nature Communications* says that natural water evaporation represents another promising source of renewable energy. American scientists assessed the energy that could be collected in the evaporation of natural water and found that the power density of the collected energy is 3 times as much as that of wind power. This will provide a potential solution to the issue of intermittency of renewable energy.

Source: *Science and Technology Daily*

英开设首个太阳能农场,比亚迪和华为提供核心设备

日前,英国在贝德福德郡的 Clayhill 开设了首个无政府补贴的太阳能农场,这个 10 兆瓦(MW)的太阳能农场可以产生足够的电力为 2 500 个家庭提供动力。英国可再生能源开发商 Anesco 公司发起、资助和建造了 Clayhill 项目,其太阳能光板和电池存储单元由制造商比亚迪提供;而华为则提供了在欧洲首次使用、具有"突破性"的 1 500 伏的转换器,据说能最大限度地提高转换功率。

来源:环球网

First solar farm in Britain, and BYD & Huawei: core equipment providers

Britain has recently built the first subsidy-free solar farm in Clayhill, Bedfordshire. The solar farm, with capacity of 10 MW, is capable of generating sufficient electricity to power 2 500 homes. Anesco, a renewable energy developer in the UK, initiated, funded and built the Clayhill project. BYD provided the solar panels and battery storage units, while Huawei offered 1 500v solar converters, a breakthrough which was said to maximize the conversion power, firstly used in Europe.

Source: huanqiu.com

我国兆瓦级风力发电机首次批量打入欧盟市场

近日,中车株洲电机有限公司与德国风电巨头森维安公司签署框架供货合同,未来三年将向后者出口至少 100 台 3.7MW-144 机型风力发电机。这是我国兆瓦级风力发电机首次批量打入欧盟,也是中国风电装备在全球高端风电市场的新突破。

来源:《经济参考报》

China's megawatt wind turbines to enter into the EU market in large numbers for the first time

According to a framework supply contract signed recently, CRRC Zhuzhou Electric Locomotive Co., Ltd. will export at least 100 3.7MW-144 type wind turbines to the German wind power leader Senvion in the next three years. This will be the first time for China's megawatt wind turbines to enter into the EU market in large numbers, as well as a new breakthrough for China's wind power equipment exploring the global high-end wind power market.

Source: *Economic Information Daily*

首个氢能工程技术研发中心在京成立

近日,我国首个军民融合氢能工程技术研发中心在中国航天科技集团组建成立,这也是我国首个综合使用氢能源促进相关产业发展的平台。新成立的氢能工程技术研发中心将加深对氢能的利用,完成氢能利用产业链的军民用共性关键技术攻关,形成完全自主知识产权,建立氢能产业链技术体系和标准体系,实现氢能利用技术在国防和民用领域广泛应用。

来源:央视网

China launches first hydrogen energy engineering R&D center in Beijing

China's first civil-military Hydrogen Energy Engineering Research and Development Center was inaugurated at China Aerospace Science and Technology Corporation (CASTC). It is China's first platform that uses comprehensively the hydrogen energy to drive the development of related industries. The new center will further explore the ways of hydrogen energy utilization, complete the development of key technologies for industry chain of civil-military hydrogen energy utilization and obtain independent intellectual property rights of them. Meanwhile, the center will work to build a technological system and a system of standards for the industry chain, and realize universal application of hydrogen energy utilization technologies in national defense and civil spaces.

Source: cctv. com

20

计算机篇

迄今最精准数字人脸模型建成

近日,英国伦敦帝国理工学院(ICL)计算机科学家詹姆斯·布斯的团队开发出一种新方法,可以自动构建能处理面部特征的3D变形模型(3DMM),并将之应用于不同的人种。该方法中的面部扫描系统还可以用于识别如威廉姆斯综合征等遗传疾病,提高通过面孔特征判断患病可能性的准确率。

来源:中国科技网

The most accurate digital model of a human face was created

Recently, James Booth, a computer scientist at Imperial College London (ICL), and colleagues have developed a new method that automates the construction of 3D morphable model (3DMM) and enables them to incorporate a wider spectrum of humanity. Facial scans using this technology can also be employed to identify possible genetic diseases such as Williams syndrome to improve the accuracy of disease diagnosis through facial features.

Source: stdaily. com

美国研究人员实现以生物手段让电脑感染病毒

美国华盛顿大学研究人员日前成功运用生物学手段使计算机感染恶意代码。在实验中,研究人员将恶意软件存入合成DNA中,并演示了植入的代码如何损害连接着基因测序仪并对这段DNA进行分析的电脑。研究人员表示,距离此类攻击成真可能还需数年时间,目前还未发现有黑客发动此类攻击的迹象。但该实验让人们意识到,如果不及时采取预防措施,技术高明的黑客很可能会利用这种新技术夺取计算机系统的控制权。

来源:36氪

American researchers infect computers with virus by biological means

Researchers at the University of Washington have successfully used biological techniques to infect computers with malicious code. In the experiment, the researchers deposited the malware into synthetic DNA and demonstrated how the embedded code damaged the computer that was connected to the gene sequencer and analyzed the DNA. Researchers said it could be years before such attacks come true and that there is no sign of any such attack. But the experiment has led to the realization that, if preventive measures are not taken in time, skilled hackers would probably use this new technology to seize control of computer systems.

Source：36kr

微软测试"眼控技术"，动动眼睛就能控制电脑

日前，微软公司正在测试一项革命性的技术：允许用户用眼睛操作屏幕和鼠标，甚至使用键盘打字以及将文本转化为语音。微软公司鼓励员工开发新项目、新技术来满足用户需求。

Windows10用户只要给计算机配上兼容的视觉跟踪设备即可尝试该功能。该功能的目的不仅仅是创造一种使用电脑的高科技方式，而是旨在提升残疾人的生活品质。

来源：环球网

Microsoft is testing 'eye control' that lets users control their PC just by looking at the screen

Microsoft is testing a revolutionary feature that will makes it possible to operate an on-screen mouse, keyboard, and text-to-speech using just users' eyes. Microsoft encourages its employees to develop new projects and new technologies to meet users' needs.

Windows 10 users with the compatible eye-tracking device already on their computer can try out the feature. It aims not only to create a high-tech way of using PC but also to improve the life quality of the disabled.

Source: huanqiu. com

量子计算机研究取得新突破：用现有技术生产量子芯片

澳大利亚研究人员日前宣布，他们发现一种构建量子计算机的新方法，能以更简单、更廉价的方式批量生产量子计算机。这种新型芯片设计能让硅量子处理器克服当前所存在的两个局限：必须精准放置原子；原子必须分开放置，但又要相互连接。当前，谷歌和 IBM 等科技公司都在利用各种方法来开发量子计算机。

来源：新浪科技

Quantum computer research achieves new breakthroughs: using existing technologies to produce quantum chips

Researchers in Australia recently announced that they discovered a new, simpler and cheaper way to mass-produce quantum computers. The new chip design enables silicon quantum processors to overcome two existing limitations: to place atoms accurately; atoms must be placed separately but also connected. Currently, technology companies like Google and IBM are using various methods to develop quantum computers.

Source: tech. sina. com. cn

上海大学自主研发三值光学计算机

传统电子计算机通常用"1"和"0"代表电位高与低两种物理状态,以二进制运算。但如果"二"变成"三",有3个物理状态值参与运算,将会给计算机世界带来怎样的颠覆?据悉,上海大学研究团队日前研制成功完全自主创新的一台三值光学计算机原型机,以光的力量突破传统计算机运算能力提升瓶颈。

来源:上海观察

A ternary optical computer successfully developed by Shanghai University

Conventionally, computers based on the binary system use "1" and "0" to represent the physical states of high and low respectively. How would the world of computer be disrupted if we replace "binary" with "ternary" to allow three physical states to be involved in computation? According to reports, a research team from Shanghai University has successfully developed a prototype of a ternary optical computer which is totally based on its independent innovation, breaking the limit of traditional computers with the power of light.

Source: Shanghai Observer

中国超算获戈登贝尔奖:高分辨率模拟唐山大地震

11月17日,在美国丹佛举行的全球超级计算大会上,由清华大学地球系统科学系副教授付昊桓等共同领导的团队所完成的"非线性地震模拟"获得国际高性能计算应用领域最高奖"戈登贝尔"奖。

据清华大学地球系统科学系介绍,此项成果基于"神威 太湖之光"超级计算机的强大计算能力完成。项目团队成功地设计实现了高可扩展性的非线性地震模拟工具。

来源：新华社

Chinese researchers win Gordon Bell Prize of supercomputing application

On November 17, a Chinese team headed by Fu Haohuan, associate professor from the Department of Earth System Science, Tsinghua University won the 2017 ACM Gordon Bell Prize at the Supercomputing Conference in Denver in the U.S. State of Colorado for their successful Nonlinear Earthquake Simulation on Sunway TaihuLight.

The research relied on the powerful computing capability of the supercomputer Sunway TaihuLight, according to the team from the Department of Earth System Science, Tsinghua University. The team developed a piece of software with high expansibility that was able to conduct nonlinear earthquake simulation.

Source: Xinhua News Agency

平板成"昨日鸡肋"，谷歌安卓官网删除平板类别

和个人电脑一样，全球平板电脑已经成为"夕阳惨业"，销量下滑多年。据外媒消息，日前谷歌安卓官方网站中正式删除了平板电脑品类，表明谷歌也对平板这种产品失去了关注的兴趣。谷歌这样的举动，表明科技行业正在逐步失去对平板电脑的兴趣和关注度。在过去多年中，平板电脑大幅下跌，已经有大量的厂商退出了平板电脑市场。

来源：腾讯科技

Google removes the 'Tablets' section from the official Android site

Like personal computers, tablet PCs has become a "sunset industry" globally, with the sales declining for years. According to foreign media reports, Google has removed the 'Tablets' section from its official Android site, showing that Google has also lost its interest in tablet products. This indicates that the technology industry is paying less and less attention to tablets. Over the years, the sales of tablet PCs has been declining sharply and a large number of manufacturers have gotten out of the market.

Source: tech. qq. com

美宣布造出"世界最强大"超级计算机

美国能源部下属橡树岭国家实验室近日宣布，造出一台名为"顶点"的超级计算机，称其运算能力是目前"世界最强大的"。

橡树岭国家实验室说，"顶点"的浮点运算速度峰值可达每秒 20 亿亿次。其中使用了 4 608 个计算服务器，每个计算服务器中又含有两个国际商用机器公司生产的 22 核 Power 9 处理器和 6 个英伟达公司生产的 Tesla V100 图形处理单元加速器。

来源：新华网

US announces the world's most powerful supercomputer

The U. S. Department of Energy's Oak Ridge National Laboratory recently unveiled Summit, the department's newest supercomputer, claiming that Summit is currently the world's "most powerful and smartest scientific supercomputer".

According to the lab, Summit has a peak performance of 200 000 trillion calculations per second. It consists of 4 608 compute servers, each containing two 22-core IBM Power9 processors and six NVIDIA Tesla V100 graphics processing unit accelerators.

Source: xinhuanet. com

21

共享经济篇

戴姆勒与美国 Via 合作在欧洲开展拼车服务

9月4日,德国戴姆勒宣布进军汽车拼车领域,将与在纽约等地开展拼车业务的 Via 组建合资公司,在欧洲启动服务。在欧洲市场,首先将于年内在伦敦提供服务,然后扩大至各国的主要城市。未来,将与公共交通工具合作,提供合资公司的拼车系统,开发包括自动驾驶功能等在内适合拼车的车辆。

来源:36氪

Daimler works with Via to provide ride-sharing services in Europe

On September 4, Germany's Daimler announced its move into the ride-sharing industry by setting up a joint venture company with Via, which has ride-sharing business in New York and many other areas, so as to provide the services in Europe. In the European market, the services will first available in London this year and then in major cities of other countries. In the future, the JV company will cooperate with players doing business in public transportation vehicles to provide its own ride-sharing system and develop vehicles suitable for ride-sharing, which may be equipped with functions like autonomous driving.

Source:36kr

首钢集团自主研发和制造的三款单车立体车库亮相

近日,首钢集团自主研发和制造的三款单车立体车库在首钢园区亮相,提供了共享单车停放新模式,计划明年在京启动试点。一座树状外观的车库占地不大,大概只有粗树干的面积,16辆共享单车停在了有编码的"树杈"上。

来源:《北京日报》

Shougang Group unveils its independently developed three-dimensional garage for three types of bicycles

A self-developed and constructed three-dimensional garage for bikes of three styles by the Shougang Group made its debut at one of its industrial parks, providing a new model for bike-sharing parking. The company plans to embark on a pilot project starting in Beijing next year. A tree-shaped garage doesn't take up much space, roughly the size of a big trunk. Each trunk has 16 coded forks that can park 16 shared bikes.

Source: *Beijing Daily*

摩拜进军共享汽车领域，或命名为"摩卡"

11月3日，该公司与贵州新特电动汽车签约，将在共享汽车领域展开合作。摩拜单车和贵州新特电动汽车，就定制摩拜出行共享汽车、助力电动车、建设智能化电动汽车共享平台，发起成立共享汽车投资基金等方面达成合作协议。根据介绍，贵州新特电动汽车将生产定制MOCAR摩卡品牌专版产品。这意味着某种程度上摩拜单车未来的汽车共享平台，可能被命名为"MOCAR摩卡"。

来源：腾讯财经

Mobike to enter the car-sharing industry and its products probably to be named "MOCAR"

On November 3rd, Beijing Mobike Technology and Guizhou Xinte Electric Automobile signed a contract to cooperate on car-sharing. The two companies reached a cooperation agreement on customizing shared cars, electric vehicles, building a shared platform for intelligent electric vehicles, and setting up an investment fund for car-sharing. It is learnt that Guizhou Xinte Electric Automobile will customize shared cars with the brand of MOCAR, indicating that Mobike's car-sharing platform will probably be named "MOCAR".

Source: finance. qq. com

一些众创空间的共享工位为啥成鸡肋

早期创业者往往缺资金、缺知识交流、缺平台,但大多数众创空间管理者,实际上并不关心这些早期创业者的内在需求,这直接导致众创空间中的"共享工位"成为"鸡肋"。少了一大群小型、微型的早期创业项目,众创空间被寄予厚望的"对新兴产业促进作用"这一功能也就可能无法实现。

来源:《中国青年报》

Why shared offices of many maker spaces left vacant

Entrepreneurs often lack funds, expertise and platforms, but most maker space managers actually fail to cater to the inherent needs of entrepreneurs, leaving shared offices of many maker spaces vacant. Without small and micro start-up projects, the original function of maker space-boosting the development of emerging industries-may not be realized.

Source: *China Youth Daily*

美团打车"飓风行动"再升级,增设线下验车、人脸识别和临检三大机制

美团打车整治"套牌车"专项"飓风行动"近日再升级。上海地区所有新注册车辆和驾驶员,均需前往线下验车点进行核验;自5月30日起上线人脸识别比对系统,确保驾驶员和注册人一致;此外,美团打车将于6月中旬形成"线下

验车、人脸识别、临时抽检"三大审核机制,对在网运营的车辆随机进行审核。

来源:36氪

Meituan Dache upgrades "Storm Action" to add offline vehicle verification, facial recognition, and occasional inspection

Meituan Dache recently upgraded its "Storm Action" for cracking down on "fake plate vehicles". According to the action, all vehicles newly registered on the platform and their drivers are required to go to offline checkpoints for verification. And a new facial-recognition-based identity matching system would be launched on May 30 to ensure that the actual driver and the registrant are the same person. In addition, Metuan Dache would form three reviewing mechanisms by mid-June, including "offline verification, facial recognition and occasional inspection", to randomly check vehicles running under the platform.

Source:36kr

中国共享经济未来5年有望保持年均30%以上高速增长

近年来,共享经济发展迅速并已成为中国经济社会发展的生力军。相关数据显示,2017年中国共享经济市场交易额约4.9万亿元,比上年增长47.2%。国家信息中心分享经济研究中心预计,未来5年中国共享经济仍有望保持年均30%以上的高速增长,农业、教育、医疗、养老等领域均有可能成为共享经济的新"风口"。

来源:《人民日报》海外版

China's sharing economy will continue to grow at an average annual rate of over 30%

In recent years, the fast-growing sharing economy gas become a new engine for China's economy and society. According to statistics, China's sharing economy market had a turnover of about RMB 4.9 trillion in 2017, a year-on-year increase of 47.2%. The Sharing Economy Research Center of the State Information Center predicts that China's sharing economy will continue to grow at an average annual rate of over 30% in the next five years, and it may extend to such areas as agriculture, education, healthcare and senior care.

Source: *People's Daily* Overseas Edition

百度 AI 携手 PonyCar 落地共享出行行业

最近,百度 AI 的应用场景扩展到了共享经济领域,将"人脸核身解决方案"应用到电动汽车分时租赁平台 PonyCar 上,代表着百度人脸识别技术首次落地交通服务领域的身份验证场景中。首批搭载百度人脸核身解决方案的共享汽车,将在深圳和广州两个城市进行试点,用户可在"PonyCar"App 中体验尝鲜,感受真正的智能、共享出行。

来源:36 氪

Baidu AI marches into car sharing industry with PonyCar

Recently, Baidu AI expanded its application scenario to cover the sharing economy, by providing its "facial recognition-based identity verification solution" to PonyCar, an electric car rental platform. This marks the first application of Baidu's facial recognition technology in the identity verification scenario of transportation service. The first batch of shared cars equipped with facial recognition technology will be launched in two pilot cities, Shenzhen and Guangzhou. Users can download "PonyCar" app to start their first ride to enjoy a truly smart experience of shared mobility

Source: 36kr

22

人工智能篇

谷歌推出职位搜索引擎：把找工作这事儿也人工智能化

5月18日，谷歌宣布在美国推出一款名为 Google for Jobs 的职位搜索引擎，该服务将瞄准所有类型的职位——从入门的服务业岗位到高端专业职位。

这项服务还将使用谷歌的机器学习和人工智能技术，以便更好地了解职位的分类方法和相关性。该公司 CEO 桑达尔·皮猜（Sundar Pichai）在 I/O 开发者大会上简短演示了这项服务。

来源：新浪科技

Google Is Launching a Job Search Engine: AI Will Help Job Hunting

On May 18, Google announced that it is launching a job search engine called "Google for Jobs" in the U.S. The service will focus on all types of jobs -from entry-level and service industry positions to high-end professional jobs.

It will also leverage Google technologies like machine learning and AI to better understand how jobs are classified and related. Google CEO Sundar Pichai gave a brief preview of the job search engine at Google's developer conference I/O.

Source: tech.sina.com.cn

机器人很快可以相互培训新技能

如果人们能够不用编程教机器人执行新任务，那么很快，机器人助手将会成为人们日常生活的一部分。现在，一个叫 C-LEARN 的新系统能够让机器人彼此共享技能。这带来了方便，但也让人担忧：担心机器人统治整个社会。

来源：科学网

Robots will soon be able to train each other new skills

If robots can learn to perform new tasks without human's algorithms, then they will soon become part of human's daily life. Now, a new system called C-LEARN could help robots to learn from each other. The system is designed to make robots more efficient, but there is also a concern about robots taking over the world.

Source: ScienceNet. cn

科学家研发无需电池和电线可折叠机器人

据国外媒体报道,可折叠机器人能够进入传统机器人无法到达的环境、完成传统机器人无法实现的任务。但这些设备存在一个巨大的缺陷:它们必须配备电池或电线。如今,哈佛大学的研究人员找到了该问题的解决方法。他们设计出的可折叠机器人能够利用无线磁场进行控制,可折叠机器人是一种时髦的、可按需生产的机器人。使用者可将其折叠起来,送入其他形状无法进入的环境,然后再让机器人恢复形状、执行任务。

来源:新浪科技

Scientists develop battery-less and wireless foldable robots

Foreign media reported that foldable robots can work in the conditions where traditional robots find hard to reach and complete missions that their traditional counterparts are not able to. However, their functions are still hugely limited since they require onboard batteries or a wired connection to a power source. A team of researchers at Harvard University has found a solution to the problem. They have created fashionable folding robots that are controlled through a wireless magnetic field and manufactured on demand.

Users can fold the robot and send it to the environment that is hard to get into, and then the robot will recover to the normal size and do its job.

Source: tech. sina. com. cn

人工智能大幅提高引力透镜分析能力

据物理学家组织网近日文章称,美国斯坦福直线加速器中心(SLAC)国家实验室和斯坦福大学的最新研究首次表明,人工智能神经网络可以准确地分析引力透镜,且比传统的方法快1 000万倍,报告发表于英国《自然》杂志上。

来源:《科技日报》

AI improves the analytical ability of gravitational lenses

It was reported in the phy. org that researchers from the Department of Energy's SLAC National Accelerator Laboratory and Stanford University have for the first time shown that neural networks—a form of artificial intelligence—can accurately analyze the gravitational lenses 10 million times faster than traditional methods. And this study was published in *Nature*.

Source: *Science and Technology Daily*

模拟大脑:基于老鼠神经元的 AI 设备能识别爆炸物

近日,在坦桑尼亚举办的全球 TED 大会上,尼日利亚科学家艾加比展示了一款由小鼠神经元制成的人工智能计算设备模型,其拥有"嗅觉",能识别出爆炸物以及疾病标记物的气味,可用于机场安检和疾病检测等领域。研究人员表示,这款名为"Koniku Kore"的设备有望成为未来机器人的大脑,而将生物细胞与电子电路整合,有望成为开发模拟大脑的主流手段。

来源:《科技日报》

Simulated brain: AI devices based on neurons from mice can detect explosives

Recently, on TEDGlobal 2017 Conference held in Tanzania, Nigerian scientist Agabi unveiled an AI computing device model made by neurons from mice which has the sense of "smell", making it detect explosives, sniff out disease markers, so it can be used in areas such as airpark check and disease detection. Researchers showed that this device named "Koniku Kore" is expected to become the brain of future robot. And the integration between biological cells and electronic circuits is hopeful to become the major method of developing simulated brain.

Source: *Science and Technology Daily*

人工智能可根据照片推测性取向

日前，斯坦福大学研究人员开发的一个算法能够根据面部照片推测出该人士的性别取向。通过对约会网站上公开的面部照片进行测试，其准确率达到91%，但同时也为社会带来了伦理方面的思考。根据新的研究，人工智能能够基于面部照片准确地推测出照片的主人是同性恋还是异性恋，这似乎表明机器对于人类性取向有更准确的辨识度。

来源：网易科技

AI can speculate sexual preference according to photos

Lately, researchers from Stanford University developed an algorithm that can speculate a person's sexual preference according to his/her mug shot. The algorithm was tested by analyzing mug shots posted on dating websites and the accuracy rate can be 91%. However, it also brings reflections on ethics in the society. According to a new research, AI can guess the owner of the mug shot is homosexual or heterosexual, which shows that robots may have more accurate identification about human sexual preference.

Source: tech. 163. com

IBM 将斥资 2.4 亿美元 与 MIT 合作建立 AI 实验室

近日,IBM 公司宣布,将斥资 2.4 亿美元(约合人民币 15.6 亿元)与其长期合作伙伴麻省理工学院(MIT)共同建立一个沃森品牌旗下的人工智能(AI)研究实验室。这次 IBM 在 AI 领域的投资仍备受关注。MIT 是人工智能领域的先驱,全球最早建立的 AI 实验室之一便建立于此。业界也始终将 MIT 视为 AI 圣地。MIT 与 IBM 的合作由来已久。在 20 世纪 50 年代,"蓝色巨人"就与 MIT 的林肯实验室合作建立了一个防空系统。在 20 世纪 80 年代,IBM 研究院和 MIT 都是超导联盟的一部分。

来源:环球网

IBM will invest 240 million dollars to establish AI laboratory with MIT

Recently, IBM announced that it will invest 240 million dollars (about 1.56 billion yuan) to jointly establish an AI research laboratory of Watson system with MIT. This investment in AI made by IBM still catches many eyes. MIT is the pioneer in AI and established one of the earliest AI laboratories in the world. The industry always regards MIT as the holy land of AI. The cooperation between MIT and IBM started a long time ago. In 1950s, "Big Blue" built an air defense system by working with Lincoln Laboratory of MIT. In 1980s, both the IBM Research and MIT are parts of Consortium for Superconducting Electronics (CSE).

Source: huanqiu. com

浙大海生物清洗机器人首试成功

浙江大学哈姆（HOME）海生物清洗机器人日前在我国东海平湖油气田海试成功，这是国内首次使用专用机器人对钻井平台导管架海生物进行清洗作业。该款机器人采用空化射流、导管自适应、视觉导航控制等技术。

来源：人民网

First trial success of marine life cleaning robot by Zhejiang University

HOME, a marine life cleaning robot developed by Zhejiang University, succeeded in its first trial operation in the Pinghu oil and gas field in the East China Sea. It is the first time that a specialized robot has been used to clean marine life on the jacket system of oil drills. The robot adopts a series of technologies, such as cavitation jetting, pipe self-adaptation and visual navigation control.

Source: people. cn

可识别与分拣分子的 DNA 纳米机器人诞生

近日，著名杂志《科学》发表一项新的研究，来自加利福尼亚理工学院的华裔科学家钱璐璐及其团队研发的 DNA 机器人诞生了。这项由 DNA 制成的微型机器人，具备分拣、搬运分子货物的能力。钱璐璐团队研究人员表示，这样的 DNA 机器人不仅可以对不同荧光分子进行识别、分拣，还可以将目标分子转运到特殊地点"卸货"，当多机器人协同工作时，准确率更是接近 100%。

来源：环球网

Scientists build DNA nanorobot to identify and sort molecules

Recently, in a study published in the journal Science, Chinese-American scientist Qian Lulu and her team at the California Institute of Technology designed a group of DNA robots. The robots, made entirely out of DNA, could sort and transport molecules. Researchers of Qian's team said that the DNA robots not only can recognize and sort fluorescent molecules, but also can deliver these molecules to designated places. When these robots work together, the amount of the accuracy of cargo delivery to the desired locations could reach close to 100 percent.

Source: huanqiu. com

世界首台自主种牙手术机器人亮相,精准度惊人

近日,世界首台自主式种植牙手术机器人在西安空军军医大学口腔医院亮相。手术中,医生轻点鼠标操作电脑程序,这台自主式种植牙机器人按照预先设定的运动路径进入患者口腔;在确定牙齿缺失位置后,机器人移动机械"手臂"将种植体拧入牙齿缺失的窝洞内。不到一个小时,两颗种植体被成功植入患者口腔。

来源:央视网

World's first autonomous dental implant robot conducted an operation with amazing accuracy

Recently, the world's first autonomous dental implant robot made its public debut in an operation at the Stomatological Hospital of the Air Force Medical University. During the operation, with a click of mouse to start the program, the robot moved along the predefined route to the mouth of the patient. After identifying the location of the missing teeth, the robotic arm installed two implants into the patient's cavities. The whole process took the robot less than an hour.

Source: cctv. com

刷脸技术走进银行，ATM 机刷脸取款业务现已实行

近期，刷脸技术成功走进银行。9月18日，建设银行陕西省分行营业部的银行 ATM 机上新增一项服务业务——刷脸取款。据建设银行陕西省分行营业部营业室大堂经理介绍，客户只要在 ATM 上通过输入手机号验证身份开通后，即可享受真正的"刷脸取款"，最快仅需几十秒。开通后，首先在 ATM 机上点击"刷脸取款"，输入银行预留手机号码，注视屏幕上方的摄像头，输入取款金额就会吐出钞票。

来源：36 氪

Banks introduce facial recognition technology to ATMs

Recently, face-scanning technology has been introduced to banks. On September 18, a new service of drawing money through face scanning was added to an ATM of China Construction Bank Shaanxi Branch Banking Department. According to a lobby manager of the Banking Department, after verifying their identity by inputting their mobile phone numbers into an ATM, clients will be able to draw money through face scanning in at least tens of seconds. After opening this service, they need to click "draw money by scanning face" on an ATM, enter the phone numbers they have put in, look at the camera at the top of the screen, enter the amount they want to withdraw, then the money will get outside of the ATM.

Source: 36kr

智能勺能跟踪狗狗进食时间

近日，一家总部位于加利福尼亚州圣克鲁斯的创业公司推出了一款智能宠物食品勺，可以跟踪狗狗进食的时间。另外，当狗粮库存不足时，会自动订购更

多的狗粮。这种智能勺旨在更加合理地喂养宠物狗,通过使用 LED 来指示是否是喂养狗狗的合理时间。

来源:环球网

Smart spoon knows when to feed dogs

Recently, a startup based in Santa Cruz, California released a smart pet spoon that can keep track of dogs' mealtime. When the dog food storage runs short, it will automatically purchase more. The spoon is designed to feed dogs in a more proper way. With the LED lights, one can know the best time to give food.

Source:huanqiu.com

中科院"步态识别"技术:不看脸 50 米内在人群中认出你

人脸识别技术已经被广泛应用,步态识别技术也来了。只看走路姿势,就可以识别出个人身份。自动化所副研究员黄永祯介绍,虹膜识别通常需要目标在 30 厘米以内,人脸识别需在 5 米以内;而步态识别在超高清摄像头下,识别距离可达 50 米,识别速度在 200 毫秒以内。

此外,步态识别无需识别对象主动配合,即便一个人在几十米外带面具背对普通监控摄像头随意走动,步态识别算法也可对其进行身份判断。

来源:央广网

"Gait recognition" technology from Chinese Academy of Sciences: recognize you within 50 meters in the crowd without face-scanning

Face recognition technology has been widely used, and gait recognition technology has emerged as the next big thing. Personal identity could be identified just with walking posture. Huang Yongzhen, a deputy researcher at the Automation Institute of Chinese Academy of Sciences, said that iris recognition needed to be carried out within 30cm of the targets, and face recognition 5 meters. However, with the ultra-high-definition camera, gait recognition can make identification from a distance as far as 50 meters in less than 200 milliseconds.

In addition, gait recognition does not need the active cooperation from the object of identification. Gait recognition algorithm can determine the personal identity even if a person wears a mask, turns his back and moves around under an ordinary surveillance camera dozens of meters away.

Source: cnr. cn

沃尔玛引入货架扫描机器人,强调并非为取代人类

沃尔玛在美国50多家店铺引入货架扫描机器人,能够自动对货架进行扫描。当货架上的产品不够时,它会通知管理人员。它还可以自动扫描货架上的产品是否缺货,识别价签是否标注正确,货物摆放位置是否正确,对缺失价签进行补贴。这款机器人是全自动的,能够根据3D成像进行自动避障。沃尔玛负责美国地区和电子商务的CTO Jeremy King 表示,这一机器人在检查货架时,比起人类效率,要高出50%;比人类的速度快3倍,准确率也更高。但同时沃尔玛强调,该款机器人是用于协助人类的,而非取代人类,在抓取物品时,这款机器人的表现还不完美,人类员工还是远远优于机器人的。

来源:36氪

Walmart denied the introduction of shelf-scanning robots to replace humans

Over 50 locations in US of Walmart deployed shelf-scanning robots to audit its stores automatically. When there aren't enough products on shelves, the robots will inform managing staff. They can also scan the products on shelves to check if they are in stockout, with right price tags and in the right positions and retag the missing price tags. The robots are full-automatic and can avoid obstacles automatically based on 3D imaging technology. Jeremy King, CTO of Walmart US and eCommerce, said that these robots are 50% more efficient and 3 times faster than human employees in shelf-scanning, with higher accuracy. But meanwhile, Walmart emphasized that these robots are used to assist human employees, not to replace them because they still remain to be improved in grabbing things that human employees are far ahead of them.

Source: 36kr

科大讯飞:"智医助理"机器人顺利通过临床执业医师综合笔试

11月6日,"2017年临床执业医师综合笔试"合格线公布,科大讯飞"智医助理"机器人取得了456分的成绩,超过临床执业医师合格线(360分),属于全国53万名考生中的中高级水平,进一步验证了科大讯飞在认知智能技术研发方面取得的显著进展。下一步,讯飞"智医助理"机器人将致力于辅助医生进行临床诊疗,成为医生临床工作中的助手。

来源:36氪

iFLYTECK's "Smart Medical Assistant" robot passes the Comprehensive Written Examination of Clinical Practicing Physician

On November 6, the pass mark of the "2017 Comprehensive Written Examination of Clinical Practicing Physician" was published. iFLYTECK's "Smart Medical Assistant" robot achieved 456, a score higher than the required score of 360 for passing the test, ranking middle-high level among the 530 000 examinees. This achievement further demonstrates iFLYTECK's breakthrough in R&D of cognitive intelligence. In the next stage, the efforts regarding the robot will be focused on assisting doctors making clinical diagnosis, developing it into the true assistant of doctors in their work.

Source: 36kr

人工智能可从嘈杂声中分辨特定声音

近日,美国剑桥三菱电机研究实验室的研究人员开发出的声音识别 AI 设备,能实时分离多个声源,大大提升了自动语言识别能力。

这项技术首次在日本东京先进技术综合展览会上公开展示,被团队称为"深度聚类"机器学习,可识别多个声源"声纹"中的独特功能。智能技术使用多名人士讲的英语进行了培训和学习,即便说话人是日本人,也能轻松地分辨出来。

来源:《科技日报》

Artificial intelligence device enables recognition of specific sounds from noises

Recently, researchers at the Mitsubishi Electric Research Laboratories (MERL), located in Cambridge, the USA, have succeeded in developing an artificial intelligence device for sound recognition, which enables real-time recognition of multiple sound sources and dramatically improves the ability of automatic speech recognition.

The technology makes its debut at Combined Exhibition of Advanced Technologies held in Tokyo, Japan. Built with machine learning technology named as "deep clustering" by the research team, the intelligent device is functioned with the capability to recognize the voiceprints of multiple sound sources. Through the intelligent technology, it is trained and educated with the speeches of various English speakers and is now able to easily recognize what a Japanese people is speaking in English.

Source: *Science and Technology Daily*

德国研究人员提出新人工智能算法,可以提升模糊照片分辨率

德国马克斯·普朗克智能系统研究所的研究中,研究人员提出了一种利用人工智能制作高分辨率照片的新方法。EnhanceNet-PAT 是德国研究人员新的人工驱动的替代方案,通过机器学习,他们的软件追求的是忠实的纹理合成。该算法给出了数以百万计的低分辨率图像,并将其放大。在跟高分辨率的原始照片进行比较之后,该算法能感知差异并从错误中学习。尽管结果并不符合原版,但 EnhanceNet-PAT 想象出了一个高分辨率的图像,并相应地为低分辨率图像添加像素。熟能生巧,一旦软件被训练出来,它就不再需要原始照片了。

来源:快科技

German researchers work out a new AI method to upscale low-resolution images to high-resolution

Scientists at the Max Planck Institute for Intelligent Systems in Germany utilize the artificial intelligence of a software to create a high definition version of a low-resolution image. EnhanceNet-PAT is their new manually-driven alternative method. Through machine learning, their software aims for faithful texture synthesis. The algorithm is given the task of upscaling millions of low-resolution images to a high-resolution version. Then, the new one is compared with the original, and the algorithm can notice the difference and learn from the mistake. Although the result does not match the original exactly, EnhanceNet-PAT imagines a high-resolution image, and adds extra pixels to the original low-resolution images. Once EnhanceNet-PAT is trained, it no longer needs the original photos.

Source: mydrivers.com

日本研发智能宠物装可推测救助犬干劲,促使犬类高效救援

近日,日本东北大学研究小组宣布,成功为灾害救助犬研发出一种智能宠物装,能够对救助犬的活动进行远程操作,从心跳变化来推测活动中的灾害救助犬"干劲"如何,并促使救援行动高效完成。研究团队发现,救助犬高水平的注意力能够使救援搜查活动更加高效地进行。

来源:环球网

Japan developed smart pet clothing to tell rescue dogs' vigour and facilitate them to be efficient

A research team from Tohoku University in Japan lately announced that they have successfully developed a smart pet clothing which can conduct remote manipulation on activities of rescue dogs, evaluate their vigour during disaster assistant activities by their heart rate change and facilitate rescues to be efficient. The research team found that a high-level of attention of rescue dogs enables their productive work in rescue and search.

Source: huanqiu.com

新型深度学习 AI 软件问世:不受限于互联网

近日,加拿大研究人员研发出一种新技术——深度学习人工智能软件。小到智能手机,大到工业机器人,都能应用这款软件。同时,这款软件的开发也为

人工智能不再受限于互联网和云计算铺平了道路。

来源：环球网

New deep-learning AI software emerges: not limited by the internet

Researchers in Canada have developed a novel technology to produce a deep-learning AI software that is fit to use in everything from smartphones to industrial robots and could pave the way for artificial intelligence to break free of the internet and cloud computing.

Source: huanqiu.com

中国航天科工二院研发"空间萝卜"多功能机器人

日前，中国航天科工二院二部研发出了一款集聚攀爬翻越等多种武艺于一体的"空间萝卜"多功能机器人。该机器人采用仿生设计，重5千克，长度小于1米，可实现0.5毫米的末端重复定位精度。相比其他产品的平面爬行，该机器人可实现大角度交叉面的跨越，同时因串联足式的样式使得整机结构紧凑，将手足设计成一体，达到了操作便捷、智能灵活的特点。

来源：科学网

CASIC Second Institute developed a multi-purpose robot Space Radish

Recently, the Second Department under the Second Institute of China Aerospace Science and Industry Corporation has developed a multi-purpose robot Space Radish that can climb and cross. The robot uses bionic design, weighs five kilograms, measures less than one meter, and can achieve 0.5

mm terminal repeat positioning accuracy. Different from other robots that move on a flat surface, this robot can cross intersecting surfaces at large angles. In addition, due to the in-line foot type, it has a compact structure of hands and feet, making it easy to operate, smart, and flexible.

Source: ScienceNet. cn

人脸识别厕纸机：取纸得刷脸，再取要等 9 分钟

曾有媒体报道静安区某公厕前些年开始免费提供厕纸后，由于如厕者不文明使用，人均扯下 1.6 米厕纸的现象。而在日前开幕的 2017 中国厕所革命创新博览会上，一种通过人脸和虹膜识别技术来取厕纸的机器可以有效遏制免费厕纸的浪费现象：如厕者若要取纸，必须站在取纸机前，取纸机会"吐"出一定长度的厕纸；若同一人要再次取纸，必须等待 9 分钟。

来源：上海科技

Facial-recognition toilet-paper dispenser provides toilet paper only after scanning face of users, who must wait nine minutes for another piece of paper

Overuse of toilet paper in a public restroom of Jing'an District was reported after the restroom began to provide free toilet paper and the length of paper tore by every toilet-goer reached 1.6 meters. On the 2017 Chinese Toilet Revolution Innovation Expo which kicked off recently, a toilet-paper dispenser with facial and iris recognition technologies will effectively curb the overuse of free toilet paper as the machine will provide a piece of toilet paper of a certain length only after scanning the face of the user. Users must wait nine minutes for another piece of paper.

Source: stcsm. gov. cn

英伟达与小松携手瞄准建筑机械无人化

12月13日,英伟达宣布与日本机械制造商小松展开合作,将向小松提供人工智能半导体,未来建筑机械的自动驾驶将被提上议事日程。在日本,英伟达还与丰田和发那科等企业展开合作,在广泛领域增加合作伙伴,试图构建人工智能时代的基础。

来源:环球网

Nvidia joins Komatsu's automate construction machinery

On December 13, U.S. chipmaker Nvidia announced that it is teaming with Japan's machinery manufacturer Komatsu to provide it with AI semiconductors. The integration of AI and construction machinery will be put on the agenda. In Japan, Nvidia is also partnering with other manufacturers, including Toyota Motor and robotics maker Fanuc, so as to build partnerships in a variety of industries to establish a foundation for the AI era.

Source: huanqiu.com

我国首款嵌入式人工智能视觉芯片发布

12月20日,中关村前沿技术企业地平线机器人技术团队发布中国首款嵌入式人工智能视觉芯片。在人工智能视觉识别领域,该类芯片每帧中可同时对200个视觉目标进行检测,为我国智能驾驶、智能城市发展提供基础支撑。

据介绍,此次地平线团队发布的芯片包括面向智能驾驶的"征程1.0"处理器和面向智能摄像头的"旭日1.0"处理器。该类芯片完全由中国企业自主研发,具有高性能、低功耗、低延时等特点,可直接嵌入至终端设备。

来源:上海科技

China's first plug-in AI vision chip launched

On December 20, Horizon Robotics, an AI startup in Zhongguancun, launched China's first plug-in AI vision chip. In the area of AI visual recognition, the chip can detect 200 visual targets in every frame at the same time, providing basic support for the development of intelligent driving and smart city in China.

It is learnt that the chips launched by Horizon Robotics include the "Journey 1.0" processor for intelligent driving and the "Sunrise 1.0" processor for smart camera. The chips, independently developed by Chinese companies, have features of high performance, low power consumption and low latency, and can be directly plugged in terminal equipment.

Source: stcsm. gov. cn

百度AI与南方电网广东公司跨界合作,将共建人工智能应用创新工作室

12月20日,百度与南方电网广东公司在广州签署战略合作框架协议,就践行国家"互联网+"智慧能源行动计划达成深度战略共识。双方宣布将全面在创新研究及人工智能多样化应用层面深度合作,携手推动电力产业的智能化升级。

来源:搜狐新闻

Baidu and China Southern Power Grid to cooperate in building an AI application innovation studio

On December 20, Baidu and China Southern Power Grid in Guangzhou signed a strategic cooperation framework agreement and reached a deep strategic consensus on implementing the national "Internet +" smart energy action plan. The two sides announced that they would seek full and close cooperation in innovation research and diversified application of AI, so as to jointly promote the intelligent upgrading of the electric power industry.

Source: news. sohu. com

AI 新算法测寿命,或能助人类更长寿

一项新的研究表明,利用 AI 技术可以检测人的细胞年龄,并依此制定出个性化医疗方案,从而帮助人们实现长寿的愿望。

据悉,科学家开发的这种 AI 算法被称为"Aging. AI",根据人们的血液样本可以计算出生理年龄,并验证某些生活方式的改变和药物是否能提高人们长寿和健康的几率。目前,该项目已经为 13 万人提供了准确的结果。研究人员表示,"Aging. AI"算法还可以用来评估药物和其他医疗方法对患者身体健康的影响,即在治疗前后测量患者生理年龄。

来源:《科技日报》

A new AI formula may help people live longer by predicting life expectancy

Artificial Intelligence (AI) could help people live longer by detecting your cellular age and designed a tailor-made medical regime, according to new research.

Scientists developed a computer algorithm called "Aging. AI" that can calculate people's biological age based on people's blood samples, and reveal whether certain lifestyle changes and medical products could increase the chance of living a long and healthy life. The formula has provided accurate results for 130 000 individuals. Researchers say the formula can also be used to assess the effect of drugs and other procedures on general physical health by measuring biological age before and after medical treatment.

Source: *Science and Technology Daily*

"模拟医生"随访 仁济手术人工智能随访助手上线

近日,仁济医院东院日间手术病房正式上线人工智能 AI 随访助手。该人工智能 AI 随访助手是个机器人,可以根据规定问题模板模拟"医生"打电话给病人,随访问题主要包括患者出院后是否有呕吐、疼痛、发热、伤口渗血感染等情况。AI 的上线不仅大大提高了随访效率,还确保了随访信息采集的全覆盖及准确性。

来源:看看新闻

AI-powered follow-up assistant put to use in day-care surgery wards of Renji Hospital East Branch

Recently, AI-powered follow-up assistant has been put to use in day-care surgery wards of Renji Hospital East Branch. The assistant is a robot that can make phone calls to patients to ask them some specific questions, such as whether patients feel sick or pain, have a fever, or the wound oozes blood and is infected. The use of AI has not only greatly improved the follow-up efficiency, but also ensured the full coverage and accuracy of follow-up information collection.

Source: kankanews.com

人工智能诊断皮肤癌,打败 17 国 58 名专业医生

近日,来自德国、美国和法国的一个研究小组用超过 10 万张图片对一个人

工智能系统进行训练,使它能够区分出危险的皮肤病变和良性的皮肤损伤。这台机器——一个深度学习卷积神经网络(CNN)在区分恶性黑色素瘤和良性痣照片的测试中,打败了来自17个国家的58名皮肤科医生。其中超过一半的皮肤科医生是"专家"级别,有5年以上的经验,19%的人有2到5年的工作经验,29%的人是初学者。这项研究的第一作者、海德堡大学的 Holger Haenssle 在一份声明中说:"CNN检测出了更多的黑色素瘤,这意味着它比皮肤科医生的敏感度更高,但它还是误诊了少部分恶性黑色素瘤。"因此,机器不可能完全取代人类医生,而只能作为一种辅助手段。

来源:网易科技

Artificial intelligence better at finding skin cancer than doctors

Recently, A team of researchers from Germany, the United States and France taught an artificial intelligence system to distinguish dangerous skin lesions from benign ones, showing it more than 100 000 images. The machine a deep learning convolutional neural network or CNN was then tested against 58 dermatologists from 17 countries, shown photos of malignant melanomas and benign moles. Just over half the dermatologists were at "expert" level with more than five years of experience, 19 percent had between two and five years' experience, and 29 percent were beginners. "The CNN missed fewer melanomas, meaning it had a higher sensitivity than the dermatologists, and it misdiagnosed fewer benign moles as malignant melanoma," the study's first author Holger Haenssle of the University of Heidelberg said in a statement. Therefore, it is unlikely that a machine will take over from human doctors entirely, rather functioning as an aid.

Source:tech.163.com

亚马逊要用人工智能算法设计新服装

近日,在线零售巨头亚马逊开发了一种人工智能算法,这种算法可以通过分析一堆图片来设计服装,以复制该风格,然后将其应用于从头生成的新项目上。亚马逊的一系列机器学习项目将有助于公众和时尚设计师寻找下一个大的服装趋势。

来源:新浪科技

Amazon uses AI algorithm to design new clothes

Recently, the online retailer giant Amazon has developed an artificial intelligence algorithm, which can design clothes by analyzing a pile of pictures, copy the style, and then apply the style to the new project from scratch. Amazon's series of machine learning programs will help the public and fashion designers look for the next big fashion trend.

Source: tech. sina. com. cn